ENGELS, ARMIES, AND REVOLUTION

The Revolutionary Tactics of Classical Marxism

Engels, Armies, and Revolution

THE REVOLUTIONARY TACTICS OF CLASSICAL MARXISM

by

MARTIN BERGER

ARCHON BOOKS

1977

Library of Congress Cataloging in Publication Data

Berger, Martin, 1942-
    Engels, armies, and revolution.

    Based on the author's thesis, Pittsburgh.
    Bibliography: p.
    Includes index.
    1. War and socialism. 2. Engels, Friedrich, 1820-1895. I.
Title.
HX545.B4   1977   335.43'8'35502184   77-24300
ISBN 0-208-01650-3

For Louisa

Contents

Acknowledgments

The late Paul Noyes, then at Columbia, first encouraged my interest in military history, and Richard N. Hunt of the University of Pittsburgh was responsible for my introduction to Marxist studies. Dr. Hunt allowed me to pursue the crucial intersection between military thought and Marxism, and supervised the dissertation upon which this book is based.

During the research for my dissertation, I was supported for two years by the Mellon Foundation as I worked in the Columbia University and New York Public Libraries. The Youngstown Educational Foundation bore part of the typing costs for one draft of the book, and Hildegard Schnüttgen of the Youngstown State University Library was helpful in obtaining materials through interlibrary loan. Special thanks are due to Professor W. O. Henderson of the University of Manchester, who very kindly sent me a portion of his biography of Engels in advance of its publication.

Parts of the manuscript have been read and weeded of some infelicities by Joseph Geneve of New York City and by James Ronda, Lowell Satre, and Agnes Smith of Youngstown State University. The Ohio Academy of History and the Bloomsburg State College Annual History Conference have also enabled me, by presenting papers, to test portions of my argument against scholarly criticism.

My thanks to all these helpful individuals and institutions, and to my family, who have made this work possible by giving me time.

M. B.

Introduction

> "The philosophers have only *interpreted* the world differently; the point is to *change* it."[1]

Marxism is at least two things: a prism for analyzing the world, and a device for changing it. Despite the founders' clearly expressed preference for changing over analyzing, most of the enormous literature of Marxist studies now deals with Marxism as a system of ideas. Some scholars discuss the ideas of Marxism because they believe them to be accurate, while others consider them an interesting collective delusion. Nearly all, however, discuss Marxism as a system for analyzing society and not as a tool for changing it. Almost invariably, if a book promises to deal with Marxist revolutionary tactics, it turns out to be a book about Leninism or Maoism, or some other variant of Marxism that is not the classical species developed by Marx and Engels themselves.

Why this preference for theory over practice, maintained in the face of Engels' assertion at Marx's graveside that Marx—and by implication Engels as well—had been first and foremost a revolutionary? No doubt the location of the classical Marxist texts on revolutionary tactics has contributed to the neglect of the subject; the relevant material is scattered through the voluminous works of the founders, and occurs chiefly in the relatively obscure military writings of Engels. But sources on such matters as the concept of alienation have been extracted from obscure and diverse corners of the Marxist corpus with the utmost diligence. Is the concept of revolution, and how one should go about it, so much less important? Why the persistent willingness to assume that Marxism in its original form was a revolutionary theory without a theory of revolution?

One reason for the general tendency to disregard the tactical program of classical Marxism is the predominant role of Friedrich Engels in developing it. Engels was by his own admission the junior member of the partnership, and is therefore customarily relegated to a position as the hind end of the compound personality Marxandengels. This shorthand is convenient, and in most areas appropriate. But in military studies it was Marx who deferred to his colleague; in the vital matter of tactics Engels was the originator, and not simply a vulgarizer of Marx's ideas. In Engels' *militaria* are to be found such conceptions of revolutionary tactics as were developed by the original brand of Marxism.

Perhaps even more significant in explaining the neglect of classical Marxist tactics is the inescapable fact that the solutions Engels and Marx devised lacked continuity, intellectual symmetry, and success. The problem of how to make the revolution was often discussed, but never solved. This area of Marxist thought therefore lacks the attractive coherence of some other areas; scholars with a fondness for order may have been repelled by the sense of tentative, unsuccessful tinkering that hangs over Engels' and Marx's discussions of tactics.

But despite their imperfections, the efforts of Engels and Marx to find a route to revolution are important. Even though the final fruit of Engels' studies, which I have labelled the Theory of the Vanishing Army, failed to convince later socialists, the founders' inconsistencies and hesitations shaped their whole attitude toward revolution. And even more—the failure of Engels and Marx to provide a convincing formula for making a revolution left the socialist movement with a tactical vacuum. Perhaps it is not too much to claim, then, that Engels' *militaria* made it necessary for Engels' successors either to scrap the idea of revolution (as in Bernstein's revisionism) or to devise novel schemes to make revolution happen (as in Sorel's Myth of the General Strike and Lenin's innovations in party organization). No system of ideas can remain pure as it passes through new generations of disciples, but classical Marxism's unsatisfactory legacy in the crucial area of revolutionary tactics created an inescapable need for immediate and radical changes.

Engels devoted much of his life to the study of war and armies. Although his military criticism is nowhere organized into a coherent, comprehensive treatise, his works and letters are so full of his martial preoccupations that Robert Michels has called him an "essentially military" writer. Engels' intimates called him "General," and he went so far as to cultivate a military bearing, causing a reporter to remark in 1893 that he could be "mistaken for a high-ranking officer off duty."[2]

Engels took his military studies seriously, and excelled at them. He attained considerable public and professional success with his writings on military affairs (see Chapter Two), but he did not shape the course of nineteenth-century military thought; during Engels' lifetime, military science had more impact on Marxism than Marxism had on military science. Jehuda L. Wallach points out that Engels' 1859 pamphlet *Po und Rhein* might have been read with profit by the German General Staff (Engels had discussed with remarkable prescience the basic outline of the Schlieffen Plan, down to describing Belgian neutrality as a scrap of paper that either side would violate if necessary, and had pointed out some of the Plan's difficulties); but he also points out that it was unlikely that the Staff would have studied the work of a civilian.[3] Engels did have a correspondent on the Staff in the 1890s (see Chapter Two), but that is hardly the same as providing the Staff as a whole with texts for study.

August Happich's dissertation on Engels' brief active military career was obviously written because Engels was Engels, not because Engels determined the course of the 1849 campaigns in which he took part. Some of the most thorough discussions of Engels' military writings are developed in the standard biographies, where they remain secondary themes, and most of the discussions of Engels' military concerns would surely not have been written had Engels not been a major figure in the history of socialism.[4]

If Engels' military writings had little direct impact on the conventional bourgeois military science of his day, they also failed to influence the efforts of professedly Marxist warriors. Trotsky, the Red Army's principal organizer, may have read some of Engels, but he was not given to citing the Marxist classics to justify his actions. The most convincing effort to link Engels' military writings with Lenin's revolutionary practice rests on the vague rules for revolution that Engels laid down in 1851 and 1852, rather early in his military studies, as well as on the strong possibility that reading Engels' correspondence led Lenin to Clausewitz. In 1923 Karl Radek could claim that prewar Marxism had produced little military literature, "with the exception of a few little-known works of Engels"—of which Radek cited only the *Anti-Dühring*(!)[5] References to Engels in Soviet military works[6] and the publication of Engels' *Ausgewählte militärische Schriften* by the Defense Ministry of the German Democratic Republic seem motivated more by piety than by practical relevance.

One quite perceptive study from the German Democratic Republic concludes that although Engels' works were admired by Lenin and Frunze and do provide revolutionary inspiration, they can do no more than sketch out a few broad principles; modern socialist military science must be based upon socioeconomic and technical relations which Engels could not foresee. Some useful work on Engels' military thought has come from military writers, but it contributes to the study of Engels' life and work, rather than to the development of European military thought.[7] Perhaps the principal direct result of Engels' military studies has been to add a bit of glamor to the study of military science in Communist states.

So much for the importance of Engels' military writings, considered in terms of their purely military significance. Only in the context of Marxist revolutionary theory are Engels' studies of war and armies genuinely important, but in that context they are very significant indeed. Engels studied the odds facing efforts at insurrection, the effects of war upon the prospects for revolution, and the role of the army in revolutionary tactics. As this book will demonstrate, his conclusions on these matters helped to shape the whole classical Marxist approach to revolutionary timing and tactics.

Since Engels was so much more important as a theorist of revolution than as a military writer, his *militaria* will be discussed in terms of their effect on his and Marx's revolutionary thought, ignoring Ernst Drahn's assertion that no one should presume to discuss Engels' military thought without assessing all the military literature that Engels read and judging Engels' pronouncements in the light of contemporary military theory.[8] The sources of Engels' military knowledge are treated as a secondary theme, and no claim to exhaustiveness is made. A critical study from a technical military viewpoint might indeed be interesting, but the revolutionary significance of Engels' military thinking is much more important.

Engels' military writings center around two great problems: the relationship between war and revolution, and the relationship between armies and revolution. Parts II and III of the present study consider these two themes. But before discussing the development of Engels' ideas on these two major problems, we must investigate the origins of his interest in military science.

The career into which the military writings fit may be sketched briefly in order to put the military studies into perspective. Engels was born into a Rhenish textile-manufacturing family in 1820, and left grammar school in 1837 to begin his long, intermittent, and uncomfortable association with the family business. In 1838 he went to Bremen, where he served a sort of businessman's apprenticeship with a friend of his father's and amused himself by writing articles and poems for minor papers. During this period he read and argued himself out of his inherited Pietism into a position of radical Hegelianism; when he left Bremen to do his year of army service in 1841-42, he attended and criticized the philosopher Schelling's Berlin lectures against Hegel. After his military service, Engels went to England to work for the family firm's Manchester branch.

On his return to Germany in 1844 he met and impressed Marx, who was two years older than he and already prominent in radical journalism (a meeting in 1842 had made no great impression on either). Engels' firsthand acquaintance with English industrial conditions, the subject of his important book on the English working class, had made him knowledgeable in areas where Marx was not, and his essay on political economy helped to turn Marx's attention toward economics. The two cooperated in literary projects and in the organization of the Communist League, and on the outbreak of revolution in 1848 they collaborated in editing the *Neue Rheinische Zeitung*, the most important German radical paper of the revolutionary period. After the paper was shut down,

Engels fought in the Baden campaign of 1849 and returned to Manchester, where he worked for the family firm in positions of increasing importance, using his income to support the Marxes. In 1870 he retired as a partner in the firm and moved from Manchester to join Marx in London. After the death of Marx in 1883, Engels worked on the completion of *Capital* and dispensed fatherly advice to the world's socialists.[9]

Having established the broad outlines of Engels' career, we turn to the circumstances which led this remarkable businessman-revolutionary to educate himself in military science.

PART I

A Revolutionary's Military Education

CHAPTER 1

Engels' Early Encounters with the Military: Juvenilia, the Prussian Army, and the Revolutions of 1848-49

Let us consider the possibility that Engels was all along a militarist in revolutionary clothing. Perhaps, as Grace Carlton's popular biography suggests, he was a normal enough lad ("like most boys, he would 'play at soldiers'") who fell in with evil companions in his adolescence. Carlton uses Engels' fascination with military affairs throughout his life to show that he was really much too sensible to be a communist at heart.[1] Perhaps her thesis ought not to be dismissed out of hand, and we should inspect the young Engels to see if he was indeed obsessed with *militaria* before he became a Marxist. While we cannot hope to weigh the embryonic Marxist against the embryonic military critic with decisive result,[2] the tone of Engels' early comments on military affairs may at least suggest whether he turned to military science because the subject amused him, or because he wished to serve the cause of the revolution.

We may dismiss as irrelevant to the contemporaneous military scene the book of knightly adventures that Friedrich Engels Senior found in his fifteen-year-old son's desk, and turn at once to the pirate story that Engels wrote at the more mature age of sixteen. This tale of Greek corsairs butchering Turks does demonstrate not merely a joy in combat, but a fascination with the hardware of war. "Look at our guns, our ammunition, our arsenal," invites one of the pirates; and the hero, a boy orphaned by the Turks, is given his pick of a huge inventory of edged weapons and small arms, all described at length, which must have weighed the pirate vessel down considerably.[3] More than any other of Engels' early writings, the pirate story shows a zest for martial adventure; but it is not sufficient in itself to prove Engels a confirmed militarist.

Friedrich Engels' first recorded comments on contemporaneous armies were made in letters and articles written three
years later, while he was learning the ways of the business world in
Bremen. In August, 1839, he wrote to his sister Marie describing a
parade of Hanseatic troops. The force consisted of forty soldiers,
twenty-five musicians, and six or eight officers. Engels was not
impressed. The mustaches of the whole lot were scarcely equal to
that of a single Prussian hussar, and the parade lasted only "two
whole minutes—the soldiers came, drew up, presented arms, and
departed." Engels praised the music, mocked the inhabitants of
Bremen for overpraising it, and went on to discuss the fate of a
deserter, who had asked Engels' landlord (an Evangelical pastor)
to intercede for him, but who would probably get sixty lashes.

Thus in Engels' initial comment on military life the prevalence
of severe corporal punishment was only reported, not deplored,
and Engels was obviously interested enough to write down his
impressions. But the nearest thing to an expression of enthusiasm
for the military was an implied admiration for the mustaches of a
Prussian hussar.

A year later, Engels again reported to his sister on the activities
of the local armed forces. He had ridden three hours to see the
combined maneuvers of the Bremen, Hamburg, Lübeck, and
Oldenburg armies, altogether a regiment strong. He described
how the soldiers carried their bayonets so as to avoid sticking one
another while marching, and estimated that the mustaches of any
three soldiers combined added up to less than his own growth of
three days. (Engels was devoting a good deal of attention during
this period to the cultivation of mustaches.)[4] Three weeks later he
again visited a camp, but his account deals almost exclusively with
the antics of a drunken Frenchman whose connection with the
army is not clear. An abbreviated account of the maneuvers—
Engels' first published military criticism—appeared in the *Morgenblatt für gebildete Leser,* to which Engels contributed local
color articles. In mock battle, he reported, "our soldiers stood their
ground so staunchly that the noise of their firing broke several
window-panes."

And a year later Engels included a bit of military commentary in
a travel piece for the *Morgenblatt,* describing a Bremerhaven fort
"whose brick walls show only too plainly that it is there purely *pro*

forma." No doubt, he declared, the fort's flimsiness was the reason why visitors were not allowed to go in, as they could in all Prussian forts.[5]

Thus Engels, in his Bremen period, was in some degree a connoisseur of fortresses, and would ride three hours to look at an encampment. But his comments on military exercises and the like seem inspired less by a fixation on soldiering than by boredom and a lack of other subjects to discuss. The August 1841 letter describing the exercises also contains several sketches, one of which depicts Engels stretched out in a hammock, smoking a cigar. When, toward the end of his stay in Bremen, he contempl-ated a vacation, he thanked God for his imminent escape from that tiresome city, "where there is nothing to do but fence, eat, drink, sleep, and study [*ochsen*], *voilà tout.*"[6] Watching the soldiers was not worth including in his inventory of minor pleasures.

If Engels' troop-watching in and around Bremen inspired him, it inspired him to compose a mock-military account of a quarrel between two Elberfeld preachers. Two full pages of the Marx-Engels *Werke* are taken up by such lines as "Paniel, who had 4267¾ infantry and 1689¼ cavalry, attacked." This translation of theologi-cal argument into military terms might be construed to show a fascination with things military, but the martial images are used to *ridicule,* as if Engels considered armies and their activities inherently silly and amusing. (Similarly, in 1847, he depicted the true-socialist Püttmann as a uniformed bear, addressing his troops with sword in paw and pointing to the sun of Austerlitz as he growled commands.)[7]

The closest that Engels came to studying military literature during his residence in Bremen was his reading of Jakob Vene-dey's *Preussen und das Preussenthum,*[8] which he praised highly, sending five forbidden copies to friends in Prussia. While Vene-dey's work is not exclusively or primarily concerned with military systems, it does contain an articulate statement of contemporary German liberalism's condemnation of standing armies as degrad-ing, unnecessary, and expensive. Such as Engels' military reading was, then, it was antimilitarist. And in his two poems on Napoleon, he ignored the military genius to praise the great man, in keeping with the Rhineland liberals' admiration for the Emperor as the source of their relatively enlightened legal code and an alternative to the Prussian despotism that had succeeded Napoleon's rule.[9]

Nor should Engels' riding and fencing be seen as anything more than recreation. Only later, in the 1850s, would he feel it necessary to justify his riding as "the real school" for cavalry operations.[10] Engels' youthful encounters with military affairs, taken as a whole, demonstrate no special abhorrence of war and its arts, so there is no reason to suppose that his later military studies compelled him to overcome an ingrained distaste. But neither did Engels display any passionate, or indeed any serious, interest in the profession of arms. His attention to military matters in this early period was that of an observer, interested in his surroundings in general, and alert to novelties that could be depicted in his letters and articles.

Before the Revolutions of 1848 sharpened his interest in military questions, Engels endured his only formal military training, courtesy of the Prussian artillery. He entered the service without conspicuous enthusiasm. "In a week or two," he wrote to Marie, "I shall go off to Berlin, there to fulfill my duty as a citizen—that is, if possible, to free myself from the military." How it would turn out, he said, remained to be seen; and, as it turned out, he failed to fail the physical, and joined the army as a one-year volunteer.[11]

His enlistment may have had a voluntary element, since he later wrote that medical exemptions were easily obtainable by brib-ery,[12] but the one-year enlistment was the easiest legal way to fulfill his military obligation. Young men of the educated classes, who could pay for their own equipment, could take this option and serve for one year instead of the three required of ordinary subjects. After service they became eligible for positions as *Landwehr* (National Guard) officers. The great reformer Boyen had instituted this system with the intention of training *Landwehr* officers free from the narrow caste spirit of the officer corps, thus bridging the gap between army and society; but according to Friedrich Meinecke, Boyen's idealism led him to neglect the details of the one-year volunteers' training. Boyen's less idealistic successors did not share his enthusiasm for the *Landwehr* and imitated his inattention to the training of the volunteers, so the regular army units with which the volunteers served did not take them very seriously.[13] If we can judge by the letters that he wrote during his year in the Army, Engels did not take his service very seriously either.

As a volunteer, he was allowed to live in his own rooms, and his military duties did not prevent him from enjoying Berlin. Indeed, if he had any zeal for entering the service, the attractions of Berlin's intellectual life probably outweighed those of the army. Bruno Bauer had been forced out of the university, and Marx had left, months before Engels arrived; but Berlin was nevertheless and improvement over Bremen.

The surviving letters from Engels' military year are unenlightening as to his intellectual development, not so much because they deal with such trivialities as his military duties[14] as because they were addressed to his sister Marie, toward whom he customarily adopted a frivolous, somewhat patronizing tone. Insofar as they concern his duties, they concentrate on the ludicrous side of army life. "I think you would laugh youself sick," he told his sister, "if you could see me in my jacket, the big fat sponge in my hand, standing beside the six-pounder and leaping to the wheel."

That was the only sentence that Engels devoted to his duties. The remainder of the letter discussed "artillery-medicine," which relied on various alcoholic remedies; he discussed a comrade's disciplinary problems; he described the view from his window, the weather, food, and the theater, and he sketched himself:

> Here you see me in uniform, with my overcoat draped in a manner most romantic and picturesque, but terribly non-regulation. If I went out on the street this way, I should be in constant danger of arrest, which is not at all pleasant. Because if I go out with so much as a button unbuttoned or my collar crooked, any officer or noncom can have me arrested. You see, it's dangerous to be a soldier, even in peacetime.

The real bane of his existence was compulsory chapel, which he had so far succeeded in avoiding.

He wrote again three months later, cataloguing his sorrows. He had been subjected to parade drill all morning, and had seen the unpleasant side of his lieutenant colonel; he had parade duty at church the following Sunday; and the local beer was wretched. He speculated that some malign combination of electrical charges caused his company to precipitate rain or snow whenever it approached the sandy exercise field. On the other hand, there were compensations; he had been promoted to Bombardier (equivalent to Private First Class) and could wear "the braid and the cords and the blue collar with red facings." These details of uniform, he said, were doubtless beyond Marie's comprehension, "but so long as you know I'm a Bombardier it is sufficient." In addition, he had enjoyed a concert by Liszt, whom he sketched.

Engels' attitude toward the army was summarized in his last letter from Berlin:

> I let my captain grunt and bellow at me, and think to myself that it makes no difference, and thumb my nose at him; if he is too hard on me—as he was last Wednesday, when everyone else was excused and I alone, just because my boy didn't inform me of the change, had to march out to the firing-range at noon to see an inexecutable business not being executed— then I report sick, this time with a toothache, which has spared me a night march and two hours of drill. Unfortunately I have to report myself well again today. When I'm on the sick list, I go sightseeing if I please; Berlin is a big place, and only three officers from our company know me—they're not likely to run into me, and I'll get into trouble only if they send the company medic here to see me; but that is no problem, and at worst, if he doesn't find me at home, I'll get to see someone's bad side. It makes no difference anyway!

Engels followed this exposition of his relations with the Army with a poem on Marie's existence in her girls' school in Ostend, a description of the dog which accompanied him to the taverns and growled at anyone designated as an aristocrat, and a discussion of a corrosive local wine.[15]

So ended Engels' correspondence concerning his military service. His comments on the army formed a very minute part of his literary output; during his year in Berlin he wrote some ten articles and two poems for the *Rheinische Zeitung*, a book review for the *Deutsche Jahrbücher*, and a long, satirical antireligious poem, *Der Triumph des Glaubens*. He also covered Schelling's anti-Hegel lectures at the University of Berlin for the *Telegraph für Deutschland* and composed two anti-Schelling pamphlets.[16] It seems unlikely that even so quick and facile a writer as Engels could have turned out such a volume and variety of work had he been devoting himself single-mindedly to military studies. What is remarkable is that the army, in which he was nominally on active service, occupied so little of his attention.

When Engels' tour of duty ended, his captain provided a generalized letter of recommendation, but he had not been promoted to corporal. On at least one occasion, his military service—though performed without zeal or distinction—led him to identify himself as a soldier: "I am not a Doctor, and never will be," he wrote to Arnold Ruge; "I am only a merchant and Royal Prussian artillerist."[17] This was surely more an admission than a boast; but later, when he was called upon to discuss military affairs, his unspectacular experience in the Prussian Army helped him to consider himself a qualified commentator.

During the period between the end of his military service in 1842 and the outbreak of revolution in 1848, Engels had little to say on military topics. Occasionally he touched on ideas that he subsequently developed, but his treatment was sketchy and superficial.

In February, 1845, he made his first tentative start at analyzing the relationship between social systems and their military organizations. The occasion was a series of public meetings that Engels and Moses Hess addressed in Engels' home town. "Miracles are happening here in Elberfeld," Engels reported to Marx; the audiences ranged "from plutocracy to greengrocers, lacking only the proletariat."[18] Three meetings drew crowds of 40, 130, and 400 before the police terminated the thriving series.

Engels explained that one of the differences between bourgeois and communist societies was the waste of money and manpower required by capitalism's standing armies. Since a communist society would not require armies to keep the downtrodden in their place, it could defend itself against external attack, if necessary, by rallying its people. The achievements of the French in 1792, defending a bourgeois sham-fatherland, demonstrated that a people defending a society that was really their own would be unconquerable. Engels' condemnation of standing armies and his faith in the power of national risings (both ideas that he later repudiated) were standard ingredients in Rhineland liberalism; he differed from Venedey and Karl Rotteck only in adding the novel twist that made communism a necessary prerequisite to the abolition of standing armies.[19]

Soon afterward an article in the Chartist *Northern Star* foreshadowed—again in a sketchy fashion—Engels' concern with the army as a factor in revolution. Explaining the continental situation to the English workers, Engels praised the "half-and-half reformers" Hardenberg, Stein, Schön, and Scharnhorst for giving Prussia "above all, the military organization, which gives the people a tremendous power, and which some time or other will be used against the Government." Another *Northern Star* article was less prophetic, showing more than a trace of the barricade romanticism that Engels spent much of his later career denouncing. The Paris workers, he said,

> talk not much of a revolution, this being a thing admitting of no doubt, a subject upon which they one and all agree; and when the moment will have arrived, at which a collision between the people and the government will be inevitable, down they will be in the streets and squares at a moment's notice, tearing up the pavements, laying omnibuses, carts and coaches, across the streets, barricading every alley, making every narrow lane a fortress, and advancing, in spite of all resistance, from the Bastille to the Tuileries.[20]

Both Engels' facility in English and his sophistication in military affairs improved in later years.

In general, Engels' military comments before 1848 are remarkable only for their insignificance and superficiality, which tend to indicate that at this time he was not seriously occupied with military questions. The omission of these early observations from Engels' *Militärische Schriften* is understandable. If he was a militarist or a military buff, he concealed it very well; it seems more plausible to suppose that it was the events of 1848 and 1849 which first compelled him to recognize the importance of war and armies. Together with the circumstances of his postrevolutionary exile, the revolutionary campaigns led Engels to devote much of his life to examining military issues and their relationship to the problems of revolution.

The principal contribution of Marx and Engels to the revolutions of 1848 and 1849 was the *Neue Rheinische Zeitung,* "Organ of

Democracy," which urged the formation of a unitary German republic as a necessary prerequisite to communism. Engels' contributions, which he later described proudly as "bursting like shells," outnumber those of Marx, despite Engels' occasional absences from the paper's offices in Cologne. While Engels wrote on a variety of subjects, including some long series of reports on the sessions of the revolutionary assemblies in Frankfurt and Berlin, his special province was the military and diplomatic side of the European revolutionary scene. Though he had not yet studied military science, he was willing enough to comment on the martial developments that helped to shape the revolution's prospects. We shall examine the *Neue Rheinische Zeitung* articles more closely in discussing the development of Engels' ideas on war's relationship to revolution (especially in Chapter Four), but now we must consider that paper as a stage in Engels' military education.

Even before the foundation of the *Neue Rheinische Zeitung*, Engels had begun his comments on the revolution by greeting the Paris February revolution with a discussion of its tactical implications. The authorities had blundered by parcelling out troops among "strategic points," rendering them unavailable for active use against the insurgents. "One more demonstration," Engels concluded, "how fruitless are all defensive plans against a mass uprising in a great city!"[21] He later modified his view of the irresistibility of urban risings, but the article set the pattern for much of his revolutionary journalism: military pronouncements were used to lend weight to revolutionary exhortation, and to encourage revolutionary action.

In his *Neue Rheinische Zeitung* articles Engels discussed the June uprising in Paris, the Prussian military action in Posen, the campaigns in Italy and Hungary, and various lesser episodes. His reports sometimes held out false hopes to the revolutionaries, but this undue optimism was seldom based on an overestimation of the purely military elements involved. Thus in discussing street fighting in Frankfurt, Engels praised the rioters and suggested several places that he considered ripe for demonstrations in sympathy with them; but he concluded that "nevertheless, as we see it, there is little hope for the victory of the brave insurgents."[22] Though the *Neue Rheinische Zeitung* praised the Hungarian revolutionary leader Kossuth more highly than Engels' later

assessment, and the Austrian general Radetzky was accorded little
respect, the expected salvation of the revolutionaries was, in every
case, to depend on some external event: the Russians would not
enter Hungary in force after all, or there would be a radical
revolution in Paris, changing the political face of Europe.

Engels' most elaborate and ambitious military studies in the
Neue Rheinische Zeitung were his analyses of Charles Albert's
Italian campaign of 1849 and the fighting in Hungary. In the Italian
articles, Engels attributed the success of the "foolhardy" Radetzky
to Charles Albert's treason and the inherent flaws of monarchy.
The first of the two principal Hungarian articles was largely taken
up with praise of the Magyars, allegedly a progressive folk
surrounded by hopelessly reactionary Slavic masses, and of
Kossuth—"for the first time in many years we find a genuinely
revolutionary character . . . who for his nation is Danton and
Carnot in one." The second article, which appeared in the *Neue
Rheinische Zeitung*'s last issue, went into great detail on the raising
of the Hungarian army and the operations of Bem and Görgey.
Only the Russians' approach, according to Engels, had saved
Vienna from the Hungarians, and the Russians could not intervene
in real force because they were compelled to keep troops in
Poland. Eventually France and Germany would be drawn in on
the Hungarians' side.[23]

Apart from the forecast, the article was a capable analysis, and
its comprehensiveness illustrates the seriousness with which
Engels took his role as the military critic of the *NRZ*.[24] Marx was so
impressed with Engels' articles that two years later he assumed
that Engels would be able to turn out a full-dress history of the
Hungarian revolution almost overnight, and Gustav Mayer reasonably concludes that the Hungarian war "first awoke in him
that deep involvement in the concerns of the General Staff, which,
germinating in the soil of his natural gifts," eventually made
Engels a military expert.[25]

Engels' military expertise, such as it was, served the *Neue
Rheinische Zeitung* against the conservative *Kölnische Zeitung*,
which Engels derided for saying that Cavaignac intended to blow
up the whole Faubourg St. Antoine in Paris; the district was as
large as all Cologne, so demolition was hardly practicable. When
the same journal hailed the fall of Budapest, Engels contended

that since the city lacked fortifications, and its protecting river was frozen over, presenting no military obstacle, the *Kölnische Zeitung*'s exultation amounted to a confession of ignorance.[26]

But Engels' journalistic sallies against the ideological foe were a minor contribution to the revolution's progress, and even his analyses of the Italian and Hungarian campaigns did little to advance the cause. They are interesting in that they show Engels working as a military critic, but they are less important than his contributions to the revolutionary grand strategy of the *Neue Rheinische Zeitung*. War, especially against Russia, seemed intimately bound up with the revolution's chances in Germany and Western Europe. The purposes of Engels's persistent and energetic war cries are examined below (chapter four); for the moment it is sufficient to note that his role as a preacher of war was, at this time, perhaps more significant than his role as a military reporter and critic.

Until the *Neue Rheinische Zeitung* was closed down by the resurgent forces of reaction, Engels' military activity remained almost exclusively journalistic. There is no evidence that he had any connection or sympathy with the German Legion that Bornstedt and Herwegh formed in Paris to carry revolution into Germany; both at the time and afterward he disavowed any connection with "the great crusade going forth . . . to conquer a German Republic."[27] In general, Engels' pen was more useful than his sword, and he indulged his taste for personal heroics only when the revolution broke out in his home town of Barmen-Elberfeld.[28]

Engels had no part in instigating the Elberfeld disorder, which arose when local *Landwehr* units refused to march against Baden and the Bavarian Palatinate, for having accepted the Frankfurt Assembly's constitution. On May 3, 1849, Elberfeld's *Landwehr* troops pledged their lives and honor to the defense of that constitution.[29] On May 9, two companies of Prussian infantry, plus a few lancers and two guns, arrived to test the *Landwehr's* resolution. The *Landwehr* men were dragged from the tavern where they had been deliberating; they refused to surrender their arms; the regular troops refused to fire on them; a mob freed sixty-nine workers imprisoned for demolishing a factory in March, 1848. Barricades went up all around the square with a speed that convinced some observers that professional revolutionaries were at work.[30]

An assault against the barricades produced only the death of the captain leading it, and the troops spent the night in the square, departing at dawn through the only open street.[31] Elberfeld found that it had made a revolution, and was beset by swarms of would-be helpers from out of town, including "the Cologne writer Engels, from Barmen,"[32] who arrived on May 11. Engels attached himself to Dr. Höchster, one of the leaders of the Elberfeld Committee of Public Safety, and in Höchster's name wrote to Otto von Mirbach, a former Prussian officer who had served in the Polish uprising of 1846. Mirbach received the letter on May 12 and went immediately to Elberfeld, where he assumed command of the city's defenses.[33]

In addition to recruiting Elberfeld's military chief, Engels himself served as a military specialist. As the *Neue Rheinische Zeitung* later summarized his service, Engels announced on his arrival that:

> he had come, first, because he had been commissioned in Cologne to do so; second, because he thought he might be usefully employed in a military capacity; and third, because as a son of this region, he held it a matter of honor to be present at the first armed uprising of the Bergish people.

He wished, he said,

> to occupy himself purely with military matters, and to remain entirely separate from the political character of the movement at hand, since at this time only a black-red-gold movement [i. e., a bourgeois nationalist movement, as opposed to a red one] was possible, and any step against the constitution must be avoided.

The local authorities, according to the *NRZ*, were fully satisfied with Engels' statement; but Engels found it hard to keep military and political actions separate.

He did find some military employment. He led expeditions to arsenals at Grafrath and Kronenberg, carrying off shoes, socks, and muskets—at Grafrath he refused to give a receipt for the goods removed, though a member of his party wrote one out. He was appointed Inspector of Barricades, and commissioned to dispose the available artillery to his satisfaction. While arranging guns on the Haspeler Bridge, between Elberfeld and Barmen, he is said to have met his father returning from church, whereupon a lively discussion took place in the middle of the bridge.[34]

However conscientiously Engels tried to "occupy himself with purely military matters," and remain aloof from the political side of the revolution, he found that even in Elberfeld's revolutionary microcosm it was impossible to conduct military operations in a political vacuum. For one thing, Elberfeld possessed a remarkable variety of military organizations. They varied in their attitudes toward the revolution, though socially all were bourgeois in composition, since members could afford to purchase their own arms. The *Landwehr* which had precipitated the rising showed no appetite for revolution or counterrevolution; more conspicuous was a volunteer *Bürgerwehr*, organized in March, 1848. It had become an agency for the protection of property, and the Committee of Public Safety was hard put to prevent the election of an outright reactionary as its leader. The *Bürgerwehr* declined to turn over its arms to the revolutionaries, and so did a *Schützengilde* organized by the local delegate to the Frankfurt Assembly in the Spring of 1848.[35]

Engels insisted that the *Bürgerwehr* be disarmed. Such a step seems only reasonable, since the revolutionaries needed arms, and did not need a potentially hostile armed force within Elberfeld; but while Engels thought the disarmament could be carried out in an instant, his commander, Mirbach, evidently thought the measure impolitic.

Engels made Elberfeld nervous, and his insistence on disarming the *Bürgerwehr* increased the suspicion in which he was held. One of the members of the Committee of Public Safety—himself rumored to be conspiring against the property owners—described Engels as subject to fantasies, and "one of those who are ruining everything."[36] Engels' "fantasies" included efforts to spread the revolution beyond Elberfeld, which could hardly hope to stand alone against the Prussian army; like the seizure of the *Bürgerwehr's* arms, this was a sensible policy, and like the seizure of the arms, it was not carried out. Demonstrations of sympathy in the surrounding areas remained scattered and ineffectual. Elberfeld was embarrassed at having made a revolution at all; the revolution was bad for business, and Engels' radical reputation and advocacy of vigorous measures made him a scapegoat, whose expulsion might calm the moderate citizens.[37]

His public image in Elberfeld is perhaps best illustrated by the affair of the red flags. Someone removed all the black-red-gold (liberal-nationalist) flags from the barricades and replaced them with red ones made from the curtains of the mayor's house and skeins of Turkey-red yarn (a specialty of the Elberfeld dyeing industry). One account has it that Engels put up the red flags and had to be got out of town for his own safety; Engels said afterward that the red flags appeared spontaneously, along with the black-red-gold tricolors.[38] The story that Engels was responsible for the red flags had some currency at the time, since the resolution expelling him from Elberfeld included a specific statement that the tricolor was the sole flag of the Elberfeld revolution, which was dedicated exclusively to the defense of the Frankfurt constitution.

Whether or not Engels had put up the flags, he was a symbol of radicalism that the revolutionaries in Elberfeld wished to do without, and according to the *NRZ*, he was told that:

> although there was no complaint against his conduct, nevertheless, the Elberfeld bourgeoisie were alarmed by his presence, fearing that he would proclaim a red republic at any moment, and in general wished that he would go away.

Finally, after Engels insisted that only a written request from the whole Committee of Public Safety would get him to leave, the Committee duly ordered that "Citizen Friedrich Engels of Barmen, lately resident in Cologne" should "leave the territory of this community, *since his presence might give rise to misunderstandings as to the character of the movement.*" Thus ordered out, *"in full recognition of his efforts,"* Engels insisted that Mirbach also sign the order for his expulsion, and Mirbach did.[39]

His first active experience of revolution a failure, Engels returned to Cologne, to participate in the last four days of the *Neue Rheinische Zeitung's* publication. His departure was not enough to save the Elberfeld revolution; on the day that Engels left, Elberfeld's Frankfurt delegate, C. H. A. Pagenstecher, returned from Berlin, where he had gone to ask amnesty for the *Landwehr* men whose stubborness had touched off the uprising. Pagenstecher lent travel money to some apprehensive mutineers, promised that the king would accept a German crown from the princes, and told the people to tear down the barricades and deserve their sovereign's love and mercy. The barricades came down.[40]

In Cologne, the *Neue Rheinische Zeitung* was banned by the authorities, and its last, red-printed issue appeared on May 19. Engels and Marx went to Baden, where a revolution more substantial than Elberfeld's was in progress.

Baden's government, perhaps the most liberal in Germany, had recognized the Frankfurt constitution. But radical elements demanded that Baden also pardon those jailed after the abortive revolutionary crusades led by Hecker and Struve in 1848, and actively assist the Bavarian Palatinate's revolt against the King of Bavaria, who had refused to accept the constitution.[41] (The Palatinate was not contiguous with Bavaria, and many of its inhabitants disliked Bavarian rule, much as Engels' Rhenish neighbors disliked the Prussians.) On May 11, 1849, a mutiny in Rastatt fortress and popular demonstrations led to the establishment of a revolutionary republic in Baden, headed by the leader of the parliamentary opposition.[42]

This was the revolutionary movement that had attracted support among the Elberfeld *Landwehr;* but although Engels had done his best to help, and the *Neue Rheinische Zeitung* had supported the revolt, Marx and Engels were not welcomed as advisers by the revolutionary government. After being rebuffed, they were arrested in Hesse and transported to Frankfurt, where they separated. Marx went to Paris, and Engels returned to Kaiserslautern in the Palatinate, where he wrote two articles for the official paper of the Palatine revolution. One piece was judged too radical for publication; the other recapitulated the *NRZ's* revolutionary grand strategy, calling for war against Russia. Soon the republican West and despotic East would "fight out their great struggle on German soil," all nationality questions would cease to apply, and only one question would remain: "Will you be *free*, or Russian?"[43]

Without further outlet for his revolutionary journalistic efforts, and perhaps somewhat chastened by his experiences in Elberfeld, Engels contented himself with watching the futile preparations that others were making to ward off the expected Bavarian and Prussian attack. He may have been overwhelmed by the sheer futility of the revolutionaries' efforts. Despite a surplus of swords, which gave their bearers a martial appearance as they clattered through the streets, the rebels were ill armed. *Bürgerwehr* units were not disarmed, and on at least one occasion, troops armed with pikes faced Prussian needle-guns.

Leadership was little better than armament. (Engels considered that part of the problem was that all the competent Polish revolutionary émigrés had already gone to Hungary, so that the Palatinate and Baden got only the leftovers.) It was left to Engels, in the absence of an intelligence service, to discover in a days-old copy of the *Kölnische Zeitung* information as to the numbers and disposition of the Prussian forces.[44]

Though the revolution's prospects were discouraging, Engels had some ideas as to what should be done. To be sure, the fate of the Palatinate and Baden depended ultimately on events in Paris and Hungary, but Engels opposed inaction, relying on Parisian or Hungarian developments "or even on real miracles—mutiny in the Prussian army, etc." Since the Baden revolution, which had begun in Rastatt fortress, had at its disposal a well-equipped regular army, it should immediately throw ten thousand troops into Frankfurt. This stroke would encourage revolutions that smoldered elsewhere in Germany, and terrify existing governments everywhere.[45]

Engels considered his plan superior to that of Franz Sigel, which overlooked both the moral importance of Frankfurt and the strategic importance of the Main. In view of the state of Baden's army, much of which had dispersed on the morrow of the revolution, Engels' plan was probably too ambitious to be practical. Sigel's more modest offensive dissolved in panic when the revolutionary force crossed into Hesse and found that the Hessians were not to be vanquished by revolutionary proclamations. But there was little chance that Engels' plan would be spoiled by being put into execution. He could not direct the preparations for the fight, so *ganz gemütlich* he laughed at them.[46]

There was much to laugh at. While August Willich kept the garrisons of Landau and Germersheim bottled up in their forts, Engels tried without success to persuade the Palatine government to let someone use two seven-pounder howitzers that sat idle in Kaiserslautern. Engels thought that Willich could have taken Landau if he had had the guns; instead, a self-appointed Colonel Blenker undertook an assault typical of the whole Palatine campaign. Armed with three small signalling guns and a cannon-ball that fit none of them, all loaded in a hay wagon, Blenker attacked the fort with a motley force that fled when a gun was fired. This imbecilic effort enabled the officers in the fort to retain control over the wavering garrison.[47]

Amateur strategists pored over maps in the taverns, seeking some military Philosopher's Stone, said Engels;

> it was a matter of nothing less than the possibility of holding a small province like the Palatinate, subject to attack from several sides, with an almost entirely imaginary force, against an altogether real army of 30,000 men and 60 guns.

The most popular solution of the tavern strategists was to imitate Kossuth, whatever that might mean. When Engels asked one enthusiast if he really expected to beat the Prussians with 30,000 sabres and a few rusty muskets, he was arrested as a spy and jailed for twenty-four hours, until friends secured his release. Perhaps the very hopelessness of the situation allowed Engels to be detached and amused; his account of the revolutionary scene in the Palatinate has none of the ferocity which he and Marx ordinarily turned upon revolutionary incompetents.

As soon as he got out of prison, Engels went to Offenbach and took a position as adjutant to August Willich, thus enlisting in the service of a revolution that he considered foredoomed and rather silly. As he wrote afterward, the Prussians were coming,

> and since with this the business took an interesting turn, since I didn't want to pass up the chance for a bit of military education, and mainly because the *Neue Rheinische Zeitung*

had to be represented, *honoris causa,* in the army of Baden and the Palatinate, I girded on a sword and reported to Willich.[49]

There is more than a hint of embarrassment in Engels' explanations of his motives for enlisting. He insisted that he had no part in the revolution's political side, and joined up only when the Prussians appeared. He had held himself aloof from the "so-called revolution" but could not resist the urge to fight the Prussians.[49]He seems to have regarded his participation in the campaign as frivolous and not quite proper.

Nevertheless, he enjoyed it. He appears to have been quite proud of his unit; the mocking tone of his memoir vanished after he joins Willich, and ludicrous and contemptible elements in the revolutionary forces are described only by way of contrast with Engels' own corps. Even when Engels describes the defection of students from Willich's *Freischaar* his description only serves to praise by contrast the steadfast workers who remained.[50]

Engels was kept busy. "His energy and courage were accorded uncommonly high praise by his comrades," said one observer of the campaign; "as, for example, he had carried out his duties as adjutant on foot, lacking a horse." His first mission was to go to Kaiserslautern to get ammunition to replace that expended in a clash with Bavarian forces. Kaiserslautern, it turned out, was already in enemy hands, but Engels obtained cartridges from troops that were in disorderly flight and in no shape to make effective use of their ammunition. He was sent off again for provisions, and on returning to Willich he came under fire for the first time at Rinnthal, where he attempted to deploy some sharpshooters and was outflanked and nearly captured by the Prussians. After delivering a message to another unit, he rejoined the Willich corps as the remnants of the Palatinate's forces crossed into Baden.[51]

When Willich (with characteristic optimism) attempted to surprise some 4000 Prussians in a dawn attack with 700 men, Engels was in the patrol that encountered Prussian pickets and drew fire, leading to the rout of the undertaking as the Baden dragoons (in characteristic panic) fled through the ranks of their own infantry.[52] Willich's corps missed the fight at Waghäusel on

July 21, and after Willich had persuaded other leaders to make a stand at Ubstadt, missed that battle as well. On the morning of the 24th they were nearly overtaken by Bavarian forces, and were so far behind the revolutionary rear guard that in some towns they were mistaken for their Prussian pursuers.

The revolutionary army was reassembled at Rastatt, and Engels took part in the string of battles along the Murg river. Here, he said, Willich was ordered to give up a position that could have held the entire valley, and the military fortunes of the revolution were finally and irretrievably lost.[53] Mieroslawski resigned as commander-in-chief and the remaining forces moved on south toward the Swiss border and asylum. At several places Willich argued for making a stand, and in the last war council of the German revolution, held at the edge of Swiss territory, his was the only voice for offering battle. (Swiss authorities had said that such a fight would compromise Swiss neutrality and would result in the refusal of asylum.)[54] In every case his adjutant Engels, who had considered the revolution's position hopeless before the first defeat, supported Willich's desire to fight on.

Despite the revolution's collapse, Engels was pleased with his own role. He had been in the thick of it; he wrote to Jenny Marx that "the much-praised quality of courage in battle is the most ordinary characteristic that one can possess." The whistling of bullets was a trivial thing; and in addition to proving his own valor, he had aided the communist cause.

> *Enfin*, I've come through it all right, and *au bout de compte* it's a good thing that someone from the NRZ was there, because the whole motley pack of democrats were in Baden and the Palatinate, and now congratulate themselves on their imaginary exploits.

Had he not been there, "it would have been said that the men of the *NRZ* were too cowardly to fight."[55] But Engels had been there, and had demonstrated his courage, to his enemies and to himself.

Engels' experience in Willich's *Freischaar*, together with his term in the Prussian army, comprised the whole of his practical acquaintance with military affairs. In 1860, when Engels first submitted an article to the *Allgemeine Militär-Zeitung*, he listed his service in the armies of Prussia and Baden as credentials. All his experience thus preceded his serious study of military theory, so that he never had an opportunity to apply it.

He included his "glorious adventure in Baden" among the factors that led him to take up the study of military science—perhaps because he had so enjoyed his baptism of fire that he wished to learn more about war, perhaps because he hoped to prevent such chaos in future revolutionary campaigns. His participation in the disasters of the Palatinate and Baden certainly helps to explain the persistent distrust of amateurism, spontaneity, and disorder that marks his subsequent military writings. The *Reichsverfassungskampagne* had been fun, but it was no model for the conduct of a successful military operation. After writing his "cheerful account of the nonsense in Baden and the Palatinate,"[56] Engels set about attempting to improve the revolution's prospects in the next round. He sailed to England, where circumstances led him to begin studying military science.

CHAPTER 2

Engels' Military Studies and Their Revolutionary Purposes

Since Engels' early career reveals no sign of an obsession with war and armies, how are we to explain the diligent study of military science which he began in the 1850s? The answer lies in Engels' willingness to do whatever he could to help the revolutionary cause. Military studies surely required less self-sacrifice than working as a capitalist exploiter in the offices of Ermen and Engels, but they were undertaken in the same spirit of service to the revolution that sent Engels to his hated desk each day for twenty years, in order that Marx might eat and work.

The most immediate and compelling reasons for Engels' military studies were generated by the relations between Marx and Engels and their fellow émigrés. Twenty years afterward, Engels distilled his recollections of the 1850s into a law of émigré relations: "after every unsuccessful revolution or counterrevolution," he wrote,

> there develops a feverish activity among the fugitives abroad. The various factions assemble, charge one another with having wrecked the cause, and accuse one another of treason and all other possible deadly sins. Meanwhile they remain in fevered communication with the homeland, organize, conspire, print leaflets and papers, and swear that in twenty-four hours it will break out again, that victory is certain; and in expectation thereof they divide up the offices. Naturally disappointment follows on disappointment, and since they attribute these not to inevitable historical conditions, which they do not wish to understand, but to particular errors of individuals, mutual accusations accumulate, and the whole

> thing culminates in a general brawl. That is the story of all
> exile groups from the royalists of 1792 down to the present
> day; and whoever among the refugees has good sense and
> judgment withdraws from the useless wrangling as soon as
> propriety will permit, and finds something better to do.[1]

This was a fair description of the activities of the revolutionary
refugees of the 1850s, though it was only after considerable
expenditure of time and energy that Marx and Engels withdrew
from the émigré brawls.

Refugee politics were fairly congenial at first, as Marx and
Engels cooperated with other exiles of various political shades in
raising money for their neediest comrades. But in September,
1850, the Communist League was destroyed by a split between the
factions surrounding Marx on the one hand, and Engels' former
commander August Willich on the other. After the split, one of
Marx's partisans was wounded in a duel with Willich, and in
February, 1851, two supporters of Marx were expelled bodily
from a Willich meeting, amid shouts of "Spy! Spy!" and "Haynau!
Haynau!"[2] (Haynau's name was synonymous with brutality as a
result of his role in suppressing the revolutions in Italy and
Hungary.)

The verbal combat was even fiercer than the physical clashes,
and Marx's and Engels' assaults on their rivals show them at their
most petty and disagreeable;[3] but personal qualities of Marx and
Engels, such as a propensity to invective and a will to dominate,
were not the cause of the dispute. The Marx and Willich factions
disagreed on the nature of revolution and the way to bring it
about.

Unlike the Marxist "party of the *Neue Rheinische Zeitung*," the
"Willich-Schapper faction" remained an action party, believing
that the imposition of the Seventeen Demands would effect the
transition to Communism immediately in the next revolution.
Though neither faction defined its version of Communism very
explicitly, Marx's conception was clearly more sweeping and less
subject to prompt realization. The immediate cause of the
disagreement, however, centered more on the *means* of revolution than the ends. Marx believed that the revolution would be
brought about by the force of circumstances, Willich by force of
arms.[4]

Willich, who lived with his fellow soldiers in an improvised barracks in London, hoped to assemble a company of heroes whose valor and military skill would revive the German revolution.[5] Marx and Engels considered such an enterprise frivolous and foolish, and they opposed it as injurious to the revolutionary cause. In their view, revolution was not purely or even primarily a military phenomenon; the avoidance of military blunders might be useful to the survival of a revolution once begun, but courage and training alone could not create a revolution.

Thus, although Marx's disgust at the successful money-raising tours of Willich's ally, the poet Gottfried Kinkel, doubtless contained a note of pecuniary envy, he and Engels were offended by the basic premise of Kinkel's "revolutionary loan"—the idea that a revolution could be *made* by "a small, well-armed band, *amply* supplied with money." Such a view demonstrated the military clique's arrogant refusal to let matters develop without their intervention; they had, Marx wrote at one point, "*decided* to suspend world history till Kossuth's return." Already in 1850 Marx and Engels announced: "*A new revolution is possible only as a consequence of a new crisis. It is, however, just as inevitable as this.*" A revolutionary attempt before the crisis would be foolish, and would succeed only in getting people shot.[6]

In the Marxist view, the timing of the revolution would depend on objective economic conditions, not on the revolutionaries' will power. The contrary view that revolution could be brought about by the resolution and conspiratorial organization of the revolutionaries is usually identified with the name of its most illustrious exponent, Auguste Blanqui; therefore the relations among the revolutionary émigrés in 1850, when Marx and Engels first cooperated with putschist elements in the Communist League and then split away from them, are generally discussed in terms of a brief Blanquist period in the development of Marxism.

Marx, it is said, was misled as to the imminence of a revolutionary resurgence, so until his studies in the British Museum persuaded him to revise his timetable of expectations, he and Engels associated themselves with the Blanquist conspirators.[7] Thus in the discussion of the disagreements between Marx and Engels and their conspiracy-oriented comrades, Willich and his military revolutionist group appear as a minor subspecies of Blanquist. The general emphasis on Blanqui is understandable, for he was undeniably a more important figure than Willich. But although Marx and Engels repudiated an approach to revolution which Blanqui and Willich shared, they attacked Willich fiercely and frequently, and Blanqui hardly at all.

Despite their tactical differences with him, Marx and Engels repeatedly expressed respect for Blanqui. In 1869 Marx was delighted to learn that Blanqui admired him and liked his *Poverty of Philosophy*, and he defended Blanqui against Professor Beesly's vague suspicion that the great conspirator was not an "honorable man." One of the several things wrong with the revolutionary outlook in Paris in 1870, according to Marx, was that "Blanqui appear[ed] entirely forgotten." And even when Engels dismissed Blanqui as a "revolutionary of a bygone generation" in his reliance on the well-organized minority, he concentrated on attacking Blanqui's disciples as lacking their master's forcefulness, thus implicitly praising Blanqui's revolutionary spirit.[8]

Why this double standard? Why attack Willich and not Blanqui? Nicolaievsky and Maenchen-Helfen suggest that Marx and Engels tolerated the Blanquists because in France "conspiracy had become an essential part of the revolutionary movement and had to be reckoned with."[9] Perhaps, then, Germany's less hallowed revolutionary traditions permitted more forthright attacks on conspiratorial projects proposed by a German Blanquist like Willich. Perhaps more important, the different revolutionary traditions of France and Germany meant that Marx had little immediate chance of challenging Blanqui's leadership of the French movement, while Willich threatened Marx where his influence was greatest. The fact that Willich was conspicuously present in London while Blanqui was shut up in the prison at Belle Isle must also help to explain Marx's and Engels' concentration on the lesser figure.

Besides, Blanqui seemed a more thoroughgoing revolutionary than Willich, and Marx and Engels preferred Blanqui's vehement putschism to Willich's relatively tepid putschism. When Blanqui damned the revolutionary leaders of 1848 for hesitation and undue moderation, Marx and Engels were wholeheartedly on his side.[10] Blanqui was an ally of sorts against the "democratic lieutenants" who surrounded Willich.

Something in the military emphasis of Willich and his associates was inherently offensive to Marx and Engels. Marx had condemned the civilian "professional revolutionary" of the French conspiratorial type as useless except to the police, but Willich and company were attacked more often, and attacked not just as putschists and fools, but as soldiers. According to Gustav Adolf Techow, Marx declared while drunk that officers were "always the most dangerous in a revolution," seeking constantly to take over. *"One must keep dagger and poison ready for them,"* Marx allegedly declared.[11]

Despite his years in the Prussian Army, Willich was anything but an orthodox martinet; he had distinguished himself in Baden leading a *Freikorps,* not a regular army unit, and later, after service in the American Civil War, he delivered himself of the remarkable opinion that the Union's war effort had suffered mainly from an excess of military professionalism. He recommended an extreme form of militia system with no peacetime army at all, and amateur officers.[12] Nonetheless, to Marx and Engels he represented an approach to revolution that concentrated on the narrowly tactical aspects of insurrection, overlooking the great economic and social tides that would be necessary to create revolutionary conditions.

Willich's side of the controversy is not fairly represented in the surviving documents, but there is some evidence that the image of him as a contriver of far-fetched revolutionary plots is not entirely inaccurate. Engels' contemptuous reference to a Willich scheme to "revolutionize the world with the Prussian *Landwehr*" bears a certain resemblance to the project described by someone who was persuaded to talk to the Prussian police, and who had no particular reason to malign Willich. Line and *Landwehr* companies were to be assembled and revolutionary committees elected in them, whereupon Willich would appear in person, chase Napoleon III from France, and march with the triumphant French revolutionary forces into Germany, proclaiming a republic.[13]

One of Willich's proposals included a generous promise to summon Marx to Cologne within forty-eight hours of the takeover; Marx was to be in charge of finances and social reform, furnished with a bodyguard, and empowered to issue orders enforceable on pain of death. But Willich's generosity was beside the point. Marx and Engels objected to the whole idea of conspiracies, not to being left out of them. In trying to conjure up a revolution through his own efforts, instead of working to predict and prepare for the inevitable crucial moment, "friend Willich" mistook "pure laziness for pure act."[14] The activist, do-it-yourself approach to revolution left no middle ground between Willich's ambition to be Moses and Joshua in one and "conquer the communist Canaan with 5000 picked men" and total inaction. Impatience made Willich a "pure dreamer"; as Marx summed up the putschist outlook, unless the Willich group could come immediately to power, they might as well go to sleep. Marx, in contrast, insisted that the workers would have to endure "fifteen, twenty, fifty years of civil war" before conditions and the workers themselves would be ready.[15]

A revolutionary military dictatorship, as proposed by Techow, could not exercise the iron discipline necessary; "only the terror, the civil power" could manage it, in Engels' view; certainly Willich, "the perfect *capitaine d'armes* and *Feldwebel*," was not the man to run the revolution.[16] The purely tactical side of a revolution was a secondary consideration. When in 1853 Kossuth and Mazzini inspired an abortive uprising in Milan, Engels assessed the situation: the city's narrow streets, thick walls, and barred windows were ideal for street fighting, but the attempt was hopeless from the start for political and social reasons. There was no prospect of mutiny in the Austrian garrisons, and the peasants were at best neutral toward the high-born revolutionaries. The only advantage to a revolt launched in such inauspicious circumstances was that its failure created dissension among the revolution-makers, and might put an end to such futile adventures.[17]

After the split with Willich, Marx and Engels had consoled themselves with the fact that they were no longer bound up with useless organizations, and could pursue their work without the hindrance of imbecile associates. What need had they of a party—"that is, a bunch of asses who pledge themselves to us because they think we are like them?" Once the conditions were right, they promised, the soldiers would "find themselves." But the soldiers had found themselves too soon, and as the military leaders of the revolution gathered around Willich, Marx and Engels ceased to revel in their freedom from party entanglement. Willich threatened to capture the leadership of the German revolutionary movement; his victory would mean the triumph of the narrow, impatient military-putschist concept of revolution. Willich was not only wrong, but dangerous; it was necessary to oppose him by all available means.[18]

Engels made light of his earlier praise for Willich's conduct in the Palatinate and Baden:

> To say that Mr. Willich could lead 700 men more capably than the first student, subaltern, schoolmaster, or shoemaker to come along is indeed "high recognition" of a Prussian lieutenant who has had twenty years' preparation! Dans le royaume des aveugles le borgne est roi![19]

He wrote to Weydemeyer that he had never heard Willich speak an honest word, and joined Marx in gloating over Willich's involvement in a scandal.[20] He also supplied Marx with information for use in the anti-Willich pamphlet *Der Ritter vom edelmüthigen Bewusstsein (The Knight of the High-Souled Conscience)*.[21] Another scurrilous booklet, this one attacking others in addition to Willich, was prepared for the police spy Bangya.[22]

But simply maligning Willich and the other supporters of the military-revolutionist view was not enough to eliminate their influence. The officers might plausibly claim that their military training qualified them to direct revolutions; even if one did not agree that revolution was merely a subspecies of war, violence was commonly involved in revolutions, and the officers were trained in the manipulation of violence. Their professional credentials gave their opinions an air of authority, not easily challenged by journalists. It appeared that the intellectual battle between the Marxist and military concepts of revolution would have to be fought, in part, on the officers' own ground, and Engels vowed to equip himself with the necessary theoretical weapons.

> We shall show these gentlemen what "*das* Zivil" means. All this business convinces me that I can do nothing more worthwhile than to advance my military studies, so that at

least one "civilian" will be able to compete in matters of
theory. At any rate I'll get far enough that such asses will not
be able to look down on me.

Marx replied that all the officers were terrified at the prospect
of Engels' competition, and that Engels would surely soon justify
their apprehensions. In the summer of 1852, Engels predicted that
when he had studied *militaria* for another year the "democratic
lieutenants" would be thunderstruck. He would soon be "far
enough along to venture before the public with independent
military judgment."[23]

To acquire the military expertise that he needed to defend the
revolutionary cause against Marxism's rivals, Engels began a
reading program guided by Joseph Weydemeyer, an experienced
officer untainted by association with Willich. Self-instruction,
Engels declared, was nonsense, and could produce no coherent
grasp of a subject.[24] (In 1842 he had written apologetically to
Arnold Ruge that he was "merely autodidact in philosophy";
presumably Weydemeyer's tutelage would make his studies in this
new field systematic and respectable.) Engels reminded
Weydemeyer that he had never advanced past the rank of
Bombardier, and asked for basic, lieutenant's-examination books.
He had forgotten much, even in his own service, the artillery, and
there was much more that he had never known; he needed maps;
he inquired whether Clausewitz was worth the trouble, and
whether Jomini was any good.[25]

At this point Engels had already read Carl von Decker's popular
text on secondary operations, which he had used while writing his
memoir of the Baden campaign,[26] and he had read Napier's
History of the War in the Peninsula, which he praised as "by far the
best piece of military history I have yet seen."[27] This praise of
Napier was the only expression of opinion in Engels' initial, very
humble, letter to Weydemeyer. Engels had already sent Marx an
assessment of Wellington's generalship, based on Napier,[28] but
Weydemeyer must have seemed a more exacting audience.
Engels maintained the modest tone of a seeker of wisdom.

Again in August, 1851, Engels asked Weydemeyer to recommend the "dullest and most ordinary" elementary works,[29] but by
January, 1852, he ventured to send Weydemeyer a four-part article

on the prospects of a French invasion of England. (Louis Napoleon had recently seized power, and was widely expected to attack his neighbors.) Discounting the significance of his study, Engels presented it "as a military problem, which one attempts to understand and solve just as one does a problem in geometry." He demonstrated his new skills in estimating the forces that the French would need, and assessing the strength of England's defenses.[30] He went into greater detail in a letter, presenting his conclusions—"much too technical for the paper"—to Weydemeyer "as a professional man."[31]

Engels' mentor must have approved of the article. The paper for which it had been written collapsed, but in November, 1852, Weydemeyer published the surviving installments in another paper, over Engels' protests that the piece had become dated and irrelevant.[32]

Engels' military studies continued through 1852. Books arrived from Germany; a man who wanted Engels to get him a position with the family firm bought a Prussian artillery officer's library in Cologne and sent it to Engels in Manchester.[33] A work on fortifications drew praise as "more historical and materialistic" than any military work Engels had seen; and a large theoretical work by Willisen, who had commanded the Schleswig-Holstein forces in 1848, provided the encouragement that a student draws from bad books, to which he can feel superior. "What can one say," Engels asked,

> of a work on military science that begins with the concept of Art in general, says that cooking is likewise an art, expands on the relationship between Art and Science, and finally resolves all the rules, relationships, possibilities, etc., of the Art of War into the single absolute formula that the stronger must inevitably defeat the weaker!

By April, 1853, Engels was sufficiently fortified by his studies to write to Weydemeyer as an equal. He had "significantly improved" his understanding of military affairs over the winter, and he laid down some conclusions: virtually all German military literature written since 1822 was pretentious rubbish; Sir Charles Napier was the greatest living general; Jomini's account of

Napoleon's campaigns was on the whole sounder than Clausewitz's. One of the most remarkable aspects of the 1848-49 campaigns, he observed, was the widespread reverence for lines and positions hallowed by Napoleon: "Charles Albert believed no more deeply in the virginity of Mary, than in the magical power of the plateau of Rivoli." Engels asked no questions, humble or otherwise.[34]

Engels hoped to supplement his reading program by writing a military history of the Hungarian campaigns of 1848-49. The project would allow him to practice his skills, and might help to finance his military education. The writing would take ten to twelve weeks, even if Engels had the Austrian and Hungarian sources at hand; Engels insisted that he could not dash it off for the *Neue Rheinische Zeitung's* reincarnation as a journal.

> There is nothing like military history for blundering, when one speculates without having available all the data on strengths, provisioning, munitions, etc. All that is fine for a newspaper, when all the papers are equally in the dark and it is a matter of drawing the right conclusion from the couple of facts that one has. But to be able to say, *post festum*, in all the decisive instances, here this should have been done, and this was done right although the outcome seems to argue against it—for this, I think, the material on the Hungarian war is not yet sufficiently available.

Perhaps, though, some publisher could be persuaded to pay for the necessary books and maps, debiting their cost against expected royalties.[35] Engels considered the project again in 1852, a year later, when the Hungarian leader Görgey's memoirs appeared. He congratulated himself on having guessed the course of events rather well from the fragmentary sources available for his *Neue Rheinische Zeitung* articles in 1848-49, but he never got round to the book.[36] Probably the troubles in the Crimea provided too much immediate occupation for his talents.

By September, 1853, as Russo-Turkish relations moved toward open war, Engels had spent two years reading military science. The Crimean War gave him his first real chance to practice military journalism, and the way in which Engels and Marx approached the war illuminates the relationship between the partners. Much of Marx's scanty livelihood came from the articles which he wrote, often with Engels' assistance, for the New York *Tribune*. If military movements occurred in Turkey, said Marx, he would "rely on immediate instructions from the war-ministry in Manchester."[37] Soon Engels received an urgent request for "at least a couple of pages" on the Turks' alleged crossing of the Danube, which Marx could not ignore in his *Tribune* correspondence, and which he feared to interpret on the basis of mere layman's common sense.

Marx had previously dismissed the Eastern Question as "primarily military and geographical, and thus not in my department," and though he discovered a positive enthusiasm for international relations, he continued to leave the military side to Engels.[38] Military dispatches were a trump card to be played against Marx's rival A.P.C., who also sent European correspondence to the *Tribune;* Marx demanded military commentary immediately, lest A.P.C. gain on him by plagiarizing an article from the London *Times* and sending it to New York.[39] Marx asked Charles Dana of the *Tribune* to cease annexing the military pieces as unsigned leading articles, or to leave Marx's byline off *all* articles, "since I do not wish my name to appear only under indifferent stuff." Now was the time "to show [Dana] through the *militaria* that he can't do without me."[40]

Marx did succeed in extracting a higher rate of pay from Dana, and General J. Watson Webb's *New York Courier and Enquirer* praised Engels' "well-written article upon the Russian plan of operations," though Webb doubted "whether either belligerent— *Omar Pascha* or *Gortschakoff* will conduct operations on anything like the plan our Phalanstrian neighbor [the *Tribune*] suggests." The *Tribune* bragged that one of Engels' articles had been lifted by the London *Daily News*, then stolen from the *Daily News* by a New York German paper. "While we protest at its dishonesty," said the *Tribune*, "we record the compliment thus paid to American journalism." Dana reported the rumor that Winfield Scott was writing the *Tribune*'s war commentaries, and although during the Civil War Engels and Marx denounced Scott as a senile fool, in 1854 the general was only sixty-eight, and Marx considered the attribution a compliment to Engels' skill.[41]

Marx encouraged Engels' military studies and praised his accomplishments—"mes remerciements pour le beautiful article," he wrote on receipt of one of Engels' *Tribune* pieces—and he generally refrained from trespassing on Engels' specialty. Marx used military imagery in discussing class warfare, the reserve army of the unemployed, and the like, and he sometimes drew upon military analogies for facetious effect (comparing the Russians' problems at Sevastopol with his own financial conflict with his landlord, for instance),[42] but he had little interest in war. When Engels went off to see the fighting in 1849, Marx did not accompany him.

In a history of the nineteenth century compiled by a truly single-minded military buff, Marx would figure only as Engels' research assistant. He sent Engels a list of military works he had come across in the British Museum, and Engels asked him to check that library's holding of military journals. He provided information on the Spanish artillery and the Neapolitan army for Engels' series, "The Armies of Europe," in *Putnam's Magazine*,[43] and he furnished Engels with many curiosities that he thought Engels should find interesting: the organization of the Grand Mogul's army, a mythical contraption for projecting fire under the sea (said to have demolished the Turkish fleet at Sinope), Carthaginian mercenaries, Machiavelli's account of *condottieri* tactics,[44] and the like. Marx also endeavored to supply Engels with information in the form of refugee Hungarians, such as the Baroness von Beck, who as "Kossuth's spy" was privy to inside information on the Hungarian campaigns of 1848-49, and was "too dumb to conceal the truth."[45]

In addition to encouraging and assisting Engels' military researches, Marx did some independent reading in the field. He had borrowed Engels' copy of the Decker text on secondary operations in 1851, probably to use while composing anti-Willich pamphlets, and he borrowed it again in 1855.[46] He may have read Clausewitz on Napoleon's Italian campaigns, unless two articles that the *Werke* attributes to him were written by Engels; he took careful notes on Spanish guerrilla activity during the Peninsular War, and used his observations in his studies of the revolution in Spain in the 1850s.[47]

He also read the Napier work on the Peninsular War. When

Dana sent Marx (who, he assumed, had written the military articles published under his name) a review copy of a book on the Mexican-American War, Marx read it instead of forwarding it to Engels. "Ripley seems to me—thus *purely a layman's opinion*—to have modeled himself as a military historian *plus ou moins* on Napier," Marx concluded. He reiterated his opinions in two more letters, but Engels does not appear to have commented on Marx's comments.[48]

Marx occasionally ventured a suggestion—surely it was clear that the inconclusive slaughter around Sevastopol indicated leadership of less than Napoleonic caliber; or was it perhaps that great fortifications were the antidote to decisive, Napoleonic warfare? (Engels thought not.)[49] But in general, Marx approached military subjects in a spirit of reluctance and trepidation.[50] His handling of an analysis of British troop movements in the Crimea that Ferdinand Lassalle produced in 1854 was typical. Engels told Marx what was wrong with Lassalle's effort, and Marx wrote to Lassalle using Engels' letter almost verbatim, only deleting the uncomplimentary references to Lassalle.[51]

Marx was not the only admirer of Engels' military writings. Engels' career as a military journalist was distinguished; he was respected in bourgeois and aristocratic military circles. Indeed, in 1854 he considered becoming a full-time military writer. With Marx's encouragement, he applied to the London *Daily News*, promising to omit politics from his articles. Military science, he said, was like mathematics and geography in its freedom from political coloration. Marx's hopes were high; he parodied Lord John Russell's oratory—"I hope, Sir, you will leave Manchester, Sir, for ever, Sir";[52] but the *Daily News* declined Engels' first article, allegedly after it had already been set in type. Someone must have told the editor that Engels had been only a one-year volunteer (he had described himself as educated in the Prussian artillery) and was a communist. Marx suspected Russian agents.[53]

Engels' hopes died hard,[54] but he found no position as a full-time military correspondent to deliver him from his detested desk at the Manchester mill.[55] His next approach to the military establishment was conducted much more skillfully than his overture to the

Daily News. His 1859 strategic pamphlet *Po und Rhein* was
published anonymously, so that it could be acclaimed in circles
that might have been put off by Engels' political orientation, and
Savoyen, Nizza und der Rhein was signed "by the author of *Po
und Rhein*" in order to establish that writer in a solid position
"before he appears to the Lieutenants officially (i.e., on the title-
page) as a civilian."

The stategy worked nicely; when Marx visited Germany in the
spring of 1861, he reported that *Po und Rhein* was much discussed
in both Prussian and Austrian military circles, and widely attributed to some Prussian general.[56] *Po und Rhein* and the 1865
pamphlet *Die preussische Militärfrage und die deutsche Arbeiter-
partei* were favorably reviewed in the *Allgemeine Militär-
Zeitung.*[57]

Engels used the pamphlets to establish a connection with the
Allgemeine Militär-Zeitung. When he submitted an article on the
English Volunteer Riflemen, he identified himself as the author of
Po und Rhein and *Savoyen, Nizza und der Rhein,* using the
pamphlets to offset the admitted slightness of his formal military
training. As he wrote to Marx (whom he informed of the project
only after the *Militär-Zeitung* had printed his article), "I don't dare
sail under false colors among these official military people."

Once the *Militär-Zeitung* had used the article, Engels translated
it into English and placed it in the *Volunteer Journal for
Lancashire and Cheshire.*[58] Thus he had approached the German
journal as a source of information on an English topic, and then, on
the strength of his German publication, approached the English
journal as a foreign observer with publications in the field—all
without misrepresenting his credentials. This first *Volunteer
Journal* piece was widely discussed in London and Manchester
papers, to Marx's astonished delight; Engels had sent copies to the
papers, describing the article in an anonymous covering letter as
"the first professional opinion of a foreign military paper on the
voluntary movement." The *Volunteer Journal* connection, which
Engels considered "worth a lot to me in military affairs,"[59]
produced several more articles in the next two years. Some of
them were collected in a pamphlet, *Essays Addressed to Volunteers,* in 1861, and the *United Services Gazette* gave the collection a
good review.[60]

Engels published many more military commentaries, in such periodicals as the *Manchester Guardian,* the *Pall Mall Gazette,* and the *Tribune,* as well as German socialist papers. His *Pall Mall Gazette* series on the Franco-Prussian War was a major triumph, and "the General," as Marx's daughter Jenny named him, achieved considerable acceptance in military circles. On the eve of his first visit to England in 1894, Hellmut von Gerlach discussed travel plans with his circle of reactionary notables, and was astonished to hear Major Otto Wachs of the German Great General Staff, "then the strategic authority for the whole right-wing press," declare that Gerlach must "look up my friend Friedrich Engels." Wachs considered Engels unexcelled among contemporary military writers in knowledge, objectivity [*Sachlichkeit*] and clearness of judgment.[61]

As a military writer, Engels had made it. But was success as a military publicist what he wanted—or did he entertain more active ambitions, which he did not fulfill?

Engels' initial approach to his military tutor Weydemeyer, in 1851, presented his interest in military science as a theoretical matter. Poor eyesight made him unfit for active service, he said; he wished to go "into detail only insofar as it is necessary in order to understand and correctly assess historical events of a military nature." He sought polemical weapons for use against the Willich group:

> The great importance of the *partie militaire* in the next outbreak, an old inclination, my Hungarian war-articles in the paper, and finally my glorious adventure in Baden—all these have driven me to it, and I want to bring myself at least to the point where I shall be able to enter into theoretical discussions to some extent, without making a fool of myself.[62]

But these indications that Engels envisioned himself as a military publicist do not rule out the possibility of more active ambitions. He was surely somewhat diffident in approaching Weydemeyer, and may therefore have concealed the full extent of his intentions.

The Marxists would, after all, have to replace Willich and the rest of the military-putschist faction, as well as discredit them. Those revolutionary officers who had not shown themselves thoroughly incompetent in 1848-49 now appeared politically irresponsible, besides being hopelessly alienated from Marx and Engels by their ferocious disputes. The military side of the next revolution was too important to be left to the generals on hand, but generals would nevertheless be required.

At times Engels seemed to envision himself in very active service. When an outbreak seemed imminent in November, 1857, he wrote to Marx that his studies would immediately take a more practical turn. He would throw himself into the organization and basic tactics of the Prussian, Austrian, and Bavarian armies—and in addition practice "riding, i.e., fox-hunting, which is the real school."

He reported enthusiastically on his cavalry studies. After seven enjoyable hours in the saddle, he had seen only two in the whole field who rode better than he, "but they had better horses." Twenty people had fallen, two horses had been ruined and one fox killed; Engels was at the death. Again in February, 1859, he spent seven hours on horseback, jumping five-foot hedges. He was learning to surmount the problems of rough terrain, and would give the Prussian cavalry a real contest.[63] Marx did not share Engels' enthusiasm:

I congratulate you on your equestrian performances. But don't break your neck jumping, for soon you will have more important opportunities to risk your neck. You seem to ride this hobby rather hard. In any case, I doubt that the cavalry is the specialty in which you are most necessary to Germany.[64]

"Anyway, sois tranquille," Engels replied; "my neck will be broken in some other way than falling off a horse." Hunting was "au fond the material basis of all [his] war-studies," and "Louse-Bonaparte" had risen to his undeserved eminence mainly because he sat a horse well. (In fact Engels did have a fall, but he did not complain of its results till 1892, almost a quarter of a century later.)[65] He ceased reporting his equestrian exploits to Marx—who arrived in Manchester for a visit in 1865 to find his host absent on a hunt—but he kept up his riding.

When revolution appeared imminent in 1859, Engels expressed his hopes thus: "Who knows what sort of foxes I'll hunt next season!" As his prospects of active service declined with age, riding remained an aid to physical fitness, and at the age of sixty-four, he discussed his health in terms of readiness for duty on horseback.[66]

Mounted or not, Engels had some sort of practical role in mind for himself in 1853, when he considered it highly important that he work through at least the Hungarian and Italian campaigns of 1848-49 before the next revolutionary outbreak. He asked Weydemeyer for sketches of the Prussian forts, and discussed the relevance of Napoleon's Russian campaign to the problems that any revolution would inevitably face in defeating Russia. Perhaps he hoped to be one of those supreme commanders, directing field commanders by telegraph, that he expected modern warfare to produce;[67] in any case, whatever ambitions he had toward personal command went unrealized, and his self-denial (he was leading a "very sober life" in 1856, anticipating approaching campaigns) went unrewarded.[68]

Engels passed up an invitation from Paul Lafargue to go to Paris and assist the Commune,[69] and his closest approach to military policy-making was the suggestions for the defense of Paris that he had already sent to the Government of National Defense. Despite the weighty opinion of Hans Delbrück that Engels had the makings of a great *Feldherr*,[70] it may have been just as well for Engels that he did not have the chance to serve as a general of the revolution.

As Engels observed repeatedly, revolutions tend to disorganize armies, and Engels had a low tolerance for disorder. He was almost compulsively neat in his person and his working area, and his polemics against anarchist antiauthoritarian rhetoric ring with the conviction that no one can run a railroad, a cotton mill, or anything of much complexity, without some sort of order.[71] Engels could not control people by sheer force of personality; when the *Neue Rheinische Zeitung* was left under Engels' command for a time, Marx returned to find the staff on the verge of duels. Entrusted with an army that would inevitably have been disorderly and prone to talk back, Engels would probably have suffered the frustrations of the Commune's third military chief, the excellent soldier Rossel.[72]

Engels' aspiration to participate personally in the revolution's military struggles and his aspiration to perfect himself as a military publicist are not necessarily in conflict. Both efforts grew out of the conflict between the Marxist and military-putschist schools of revolution in the 1850s. That conflict receded into insignificance as the military approach, failing to produce the immediate success that it demanded, declined into "pure laziness." By 1860 Marx, while assailing a new foe, could say kind things about Willich's character; in 1864 Engels could remark that Willich had made a better showing in the American Civil War than had any of his fellow Forty-Eighters; and in 1875 Marx attributed the *Flüchtlingszeit* squabbles to the frustrations of exile, which could lead astray even so sound a man as Willich, who had proved himself "more than a phantast" by his exploits in the American Civil War.[73]

Even the military-revolutionist approach that Willich had personified lost its menacing aspect. Engels praised Garibaldi's successes in 1860 and 1861 with wholehearted enthusiasm; it did not occur to him to worry over Garibaldi's demonstration that in some circumstances a revolutionary legion of five thousand men might invade a country to great effect.[74] And in 1863, Marx eagerly advocated the formation of a German legion to aid the Polish insurrection.[75] With the Willich faction only a fading memory, the concept of the revolutionary legion ceased to be anathema.

As the struggle against the Willich group died away, Engels' interest in military science developed a momentum of its own. His military articles helped to buy Marx's bread, rendering the revolutionary cause an indispensable immediate service;[76] and even when his martial studies vanquished neither putschist delusions nor reactionary armies, they served as a tool for analyzing capitalist society. He continued to read and write on military questions (he discovered Clausewitz's theoretical work only in 1858[77]), and until his death in 1895 he was the principal military advisor of the revolutionary movement. Since he had no opportunity to try the role of revolutionary general, his military writings would have to stand alone as the product of his years of studying military science.

But what was the relevance of Engels' military writings to the

problems of revolution? His considerations of the practical
military problems of the revolutionary are few in number and
never programmatic. He produced a splendid paragraph on the
rules of insurrection, but it was more exhortation than instruction:

> Now, insurrection is an art quite as much as war or any
> other, and subject to certain rules of proceeding, which, when
> neglected, will produce the ruin of the party neglecting them.
> Those rules, logical deductions from the nature of the parties
> and the circumstances one has to deal with in such a case, are
> so plain and simple that the short experience of 1848 had made
> the Germans pretty well acquainted with them. Firstly, never
> play with insurrection unless you are fully prepared to face
> the consequences of your play. Insurrection is a calculus with
> very indefinite magnitudes the value of which may change
> every day; the forces against you have all the advantage of
> organisation, discipline, and habitual authority; unless you
> bring strong odds against them you are defeated and ruined.
> Secondly, the insurrectionary career once entered upon, act
> with the greatest determination, and on the offensive. The
> defensive is the death of every armed rising; it is lost before it
> measures itself with its enemies. Surprise your antagonists
> while their forces are scattering, prepare new successes,
> however small, but daily; keep up the moral ascendancy
> which the first successful rising has given to you; rally those
> vacillating elements to you which always follow the strongest
> impulse, and which always look out for the safer side; force
> your enemies to retreat before they can collect their strength
> against you; in the words of Danton, *de l'audace, de l'audace,
> encore de l'audace!*

And in the same series of articles, he laid down some revolutionary and military laws. "In war, and particularly in revolutionary
war, rapidity of action until some decided advantage is gained is
the first rule," he declared; so he had "no hesitation in saying that
upon *merely military grounds*" the Hungarians ought to have
rescued Vienna from the Habsburg forces. His other *dicta* also
stressed resolution and decisiveness: "In revolution, as in war," he
declared, "it is always necessary to show a strong front, and he

who attacks is in the advantage; and in revolution, as in war, it is of the highest necessity to stake everything on the decisive moment, whatever the odds may be." Similarly, "in a revolution he who commands a decisive position and surrenders it, instead of forcing the enemy to try his hand at an assault, invariably deserves to be treated as a traitor." Even a "well-contested defeat" was as useful as an easy victory, since defeats produced "a wish for revenge, which in revolutionary times is one of the highest incentives to energetic and passionate action."[78]

Despite their tone of assurance, these confident generalizations were not the ripe fruit of Engels' military learning, but were written in 1851 and 1852, as he *began* his studies in military science. And they were not a revolutionary textbook; they were parcelled out through a narrative that concentrated on the political and social aspects of the German revolutions of 1848-49.

Later, in a *Tribune* article of 1860, Engels hinted at a peculiarly revolutionary mode of warfare. He praised Garibaldi's insistence on seeking a victory to encourage his raw troops; a lesser and more conventional leader would have sought minor engagements to school his forces, but Garibaldi correctly saw the morale of his and the enemy's troops as the overriding concern. An audacious offensive was the only proper procedure in insurrectionary war.[79] But this only repeats some of the injunctions of 1851-52. These scattered quotations, and all the others that can be assembled, do not constitute a recipe for revolutionary success. Engels' instructions are simple and general: revolutions should not be begun unless they have a chance of succeeding; their leaders should proceed with vigor, and be neither traitors nor fools.

Much of the apparent irrelevance of Engels' military writings to the immediate, practical problems of revolutionary procedure can be laid to the market for which he wrote. Much of his writing was intended to earn money in the bourgeois press, or to impress the military establishment, and it would have been imprudent to fill the pages of the *Pall Mall Gazette* or *Manchester Guardian* with revolutionary training manuals.

Nevertheless, he could surely have written training manuals while he was *not* busy with the bourgeois press, and he did not. August Happich contends that Engels must have wished to channel his military expertise into useful handbooks, but refrained lest he be expelled from England. Certainly, Engels and Marx were convinced that their correspondence was being pried into, and that they were surrounded by spies; so fear of expulsion may have deterred them from practical revolutionary activity.[80]

Happich's assertion that Engels wanted to compose practical manuals is based, however, not on any of Engels' statements, but simply on the assumption that any revolutionary must want to do something practical and immediate toward accomplishing his revolutionary aims. It may be that when Marx and Engels ridiculed Franz Sigel for writing a revolutionary soldiers' handbook, they objected to Sigel's absurdly detailed and impractical text, and not to handbooks in general; and it may be that when they mocked the drilling of troops by Kossuth, Kinkel, and Garibaldi, they objected to the prospect that the troops so drilled would be squandered in a futile putsch, and not to the concept of preparatory training. However, despite his assertion that "insurrection is an art," Engels' general tendency is to derogate the importance of insurrectionary technique.[81]

Purely military factors were never really crucial; Milan's virtues as a scene for street fighting were irrelevant in 1853, and in 1857 Engels declared that the excellent guerrilla terrain in Berg and Mark was much less important than the stolidity of the population. He and Marx remarked that in demonstrations that remained short of open armed conflict, the masses seemed to improvise the right tactics, and Marx's suggestion that demonstrations would go better if crowds would make proper use of railings was perhaps the only case where he or Engels offered any concrete tactical advice.[82]

When Engels did discuss the methods of insurrection, his assessment of the purely military chances of revolution was almost always discouraging. Though in 1847, before he had studied military science or seen a revolution at first hand, he imagined barricades springing up spontaneously and irresistibly all over Paris, his judgments on the effectiveness of barricades in later years ranged from sober to dismal.[83]

In 1854 Engels reported that barricades had been successful in Spain, and that the successful employment of this revolutionary weapon, which had been considered obsolete after 1848, opened the prospect of a new era of European revolution. The troops of official Europe had been beaten by a popular rising just as they demonstrated their incompetence in the Crimea. But even in this cheery assessment there was a note of caution: barricades had succeeded only against the Spanish army, which was not much of an army. It might be, then, that the insurgents' success was a local phenomenon, rather than a turn in the tactical balance between rebellion and order. Two years later, commenting on the lessons of the Spanish revolution and its defeat, Engels (or Marx) pointed out some novelties in the street fighting in Madrid. Revolutionaries had allegedly assailed attacking columns with the bayonet; barricades had been used sparingly, at major intersections only; and houses had been used as strongholds of resistance. Whatever the workers had learned from Dresden and Paris in 1848, the soldiers had learned more, using artillery to crumble houses and flanking fire to replace headlong assaults. In a conflict between revolutionaries and a regular army, the odds continued to favor the army.[84]

Insofar as Engels' military studies produced practical advice, then, the advice consisted of warnings against foolishness. In this field as in others, the founders of Marxism took a morbid delight in dispelling illusions. Wishful thinking that might mislead the movement was to be discouraged, and any tendency to overrate the effectiveness of guerrilla warfare seemed to Engels a delusion. There is in Engels' work no trace of the modern school of revolutionary thought (Regis Debray, *et al.*) which makes the heroic guerrilla the originator and carrier of revolution.[85] For Engels, guerrilla war was simply a species of warfare, and not a particularly effective one.

His readings had taught him that guerrilla activity was no substitute for a regular army. Early in his studies, he had read Carl von Decker's text on secondary operations, which insisted that irregular campaigns must always be ancillary to the operations of a regular force. Napier's Peninsular War book, which Engels so admired, treated the Spanish irregulars as mendacious and unreliable, neglecting "the thousand narrow winding currents of Spanish warfare to follow that mighty English stream of battle, which burst the barriers of the Pyrenees, and left deep traces of its fury in the soil of France." Engels' own experience in Baden

probably supported his skeptical attitude toward the effectiveness of improvised forces, and he never repudiated Decker's
belief that irregulars could amount to nothing on their own.[86]

"The support of a regular army," Engels wrote in 1853, "is now-
a-days necessary to the progress of all insurrectionary or irregular
warfare against a powerful regular army." In 1852 he suggested
that, contrary to precedent, guerrilla tactics might be used to good
effect in densely settled country, but despite the prevalence of
poachers as a pool of guerrilla talent, he did not suppose that
partisan warfare alone would suffice to defeat a French invasion
of England.[87]

Though Engels was intensely interested in the appearance or
non-appearance of partisan war in the American Civil War, he
considered it mainly as a gauge of the morale and determination of
the belligerent parties. He complained that the civilian population
took less part in the war than the Russians in 1812 or the French in
1814. But a "white trash" partisan campaign would only have the
effect of making plantation owners appeal to the Union forces to
keep order. Anticipating that Beauregard's army at Corinth would
dissolve into guerrilla bands, he resolved to examine the odds of an
irregular campaign; but he found them unpromising for the
guerrillas, since his comments in late 1864 and 1865 foresaw only a
militarily insignificant fading echo of the regular war.[88] Engels'
considerations of Southern partisan war against the Union underline his view that there was nothing inherently revolutionary about
irregular activity. Reactionaries could use it as well, or as poorly,
as revolutionaries.

The dispersal of the Sepoy rebels' field forces in 1858 indicated
that the war was "gradually passing into that stage of desultory
warfare, to which, more than once, we have pointed as its next
impending and most dangerous phase of development"; but
though this change in the character of the war threatened the
British, Engels concluded that "by this change, the war loses much
of its interest." The impression that Engels considered guerrilla
warfare an inferior form of military activity is further supported
by his comments on Garibaldi's capture of Palermo, which proved
that Garibaldi was more than just a clever partisan leader—he had
real strategic gifts and was capable of directing serious military
operations. Garibaldi had raised himself to a higher plane.[89]

Engels' concentration on the conventional warfare of his day was entirely consistent with his devotion to the revolutionary cause. Since he could see no effective military shortcut to revolution, he restricted his practical advice to warnings against rashness and concentrated on analysis of the military activities of bourgeois society. Not only was this attitude consistent with Marx's predilection for studying phenomena that existed, instead of those that one might wish to exist (writing much more about capitalism than about socialism, for instance[90]), but it was the most useful way in which Engels' military studies could serve the revolution.

Military cleverness could not make a revolution; that had been the error of Willich and the military-putschist group. (Engels did develop what is discussed as the Theory of the Vanishing Army, Chapter Nine, but that was a means of predicting the revolution, not producing it.) Military skill would be useful not in making the revolution, but in defending it from hostile neighbors once it was made, and the defense would have to be carried on by conventional means.

Engels' 1851 essay on the defense of a revolutionized France predicted that eventually the proletarian revolution would change the very nature of war in unpredictable ways, since the greater productivity of the new society would provide commanders with unprecedented masses of unprecedented mobility. Nevertheless, on the morrow of the revolution, the revolutionaries would have to fight "with the methods and means of modern warfare in general." When Engels believed a crisis was imminent in 1857, and turned his studies to more "practical" channels, he concentrated on the organization and tactics of the existing European armies, which the revolution would have to face.[91]

Engels' ideas on these existing methods and means of contemporary war were in no way remarkable. He had no dogmatic preference for line or column formation, and although he criticized undue reliance on skirmishing tactics, he recognized that the introduction of the breech-loading rifle had increased the rate of infantry fire and necessitated an open order of attack. Operations on converging lines of operation, such as Moltke's novel maneuvers in 1866, violated the traditional Jomini-influenced reliance on interior lines and made Engels nervous.[92] Engels was a good, but rather conventional, military writer.

What *does* make his military thought remarkable is its integration into the vision of revolution that he and Marx developed. Engels' military studies were not a hobby or a diversion from his revolutionary mission;[93] they were central to the development of Marxist revolutionary thought. Engels and Marx were engaged in a continuing effort to understand the operation of bourgeois society and the forces that would, in due course, prepare that society's collapse. Engels' analyses of wars and their likely results shaped the Marxist outlook on the vital question of when European capitalism would break down; his views on the nature of armies showed how revolution could and could not be carried out, and furnished classical Marxism with its formulas for revolutionary tactics.

Now that the origins and purposes of Engels' military studies have been discussed, we must begin to consider what it was that Engels said. His ideas on military questions are centered around two great issues: the relationship between war and revolution, and that between armies and revolution.

PART II

War and Revolution

CHAPTER 3

War and Nations in Classical Marxism

Before we discuss in detail the evolution of Engels' ideas on the relationship between war and revolution, we must sketch the outlines of the basic attitudes of classical Marxism toward war and warring nations. Engels and Marx believed that violence was a likely, if not an inevitable, accompaniment to revolution. "Force," according to Marx, "is the midwife of every old society pregnant with a new one."[1] This expectation that revolution might involve violence did not lead Engels and Marx to abjure revolution or to glorify violence.

Especially in their later comments, they attempted to blame counterrevolutionary elements for any bloodshed that might occur,[2] and attempts to present the founders of Marxist socialism as advocates of violence for its own sake[3] are false. Certainly, however, they preferred the probable violence of revolution to the perpetuation of a social system built on oppression and misery. Kindhearted indecision on the part of the revolutionaries would cause greater suffering in the long run than decisive and successful brutality,[4] much as in warfare. In 1854 Engels demanded prompt and effective action in the Crimean War:

> Napoleon the Great, the "butcher" of so many millions of men, was a model of humanity, in his bold, decisive, home-striking way of warfare, compared with the hesitating, "statesmanlike" directors of this war, who cannot but eventually sacrifice human life and hard cash to a far greater amount if they go on as they do.[5]

Revolutionary leaders were likewise expected to pursue their work to a prompt conclusion.

Thus it is true that Marxists cannot logically condemn imperialist warmongers for brutality, since the revolutionaries will not themselves renounce the use of violence;[6] and in fact Engels and Marx did not register any absolute moral opposition to war.[7] It was one of the facts of capitalist life, and like the rest of the bourgeois order was to be studied, not decried.

References to war as a phenomenon that would vanish only with the destruction of capitalism[8] imply a disposition to see war disappear eventually, but Engels and Marx were not pacifists in any immediate sense.[9] They condemned bourgeois pacifism as futile, and considered that the free-trade pacifism of Cobden and Bright would mean only the substitution of the warfare of capital for the warfare of cannon, a change that would yield little advantage, even if it could be made.[10] Great historical changes, Engels said, commonly required force and stern ruthlessness.[11] Nevertheless Engels and Marx were far from advocating war for its own sake. Despite certain similarities between war and revolution, it is a monstrous oversimplification to claim that Engels and Marx considered war "nothing more than a revolution that attacks a social organism on its periphery and bores inward,"[12] just as it is preposterous to consider war and revolution as mutually exclusive.[13] Hermann Wendel has written that:

> the sun round which their world revolved was the social revolution in Germany, and eventually throughout the world; and they saw everything in sunlight or in shadow, according as it promoted or thwarted this idea;[14]

and Wendel's observation perfectly describes the shifting attitudes of Engels and Marx to war and to the nations engaging in it. War might appear to further the revolutionary cause or hinder it, and was praised or condemned accordingly.

If war is considered to be morally neutral, it follows logically that *resorting* to war is likewise morally neutral. Engels' and Marx's condemnation of Napoleon III as the aggressor in 1870 may be balanced against Engels' advocacy of pre-emptive measures by Austria against Napoleon in 1859. Napoleon's real crime in 1870 was not that he was an aggressor, but that his aggression was undertaken in behalf of a system of government that Marx and

Engels considered retrograde. The tendency of German Social Democracy to assume that defensive wars are just and aggressive wars are unjust is not a legacy from Marx and Engels.[15]

Nations, like war, were a fact of life under the existing system. It may be that Engels and Marx wished to see nation-states eliminated,[16] but their eventual inclinations in this direction did not lead them to ignore the existence of nations. Anyone who disregarded the existence of nation-states was a self-delusive fool, as Marx informed the Proudhonists who "declared war obsolete and nationality nonsense."[17] There was, however, nothing inherently virtuous in the principle of nationality, which Engels opposed even as he argued strongly for Polish independence.[18] Neither was there any virtue in national risings, if the objective effect of the rising in question was to hinder the progress of the European revolution. Therefore Engels and Marx supported or opposed the national aspirations of the several oppressed and divided peoples of the world with great flexibility. What Engels and Marx said in 1850 of the Rhinelanders could accurately be said of the revolutionary partners themselves: "In a decisive struggle between Revolution and Counterrevolution," they would "choose the revolutionary side unconditionally, be it represented by Frenchmen or Chinese."[19]

As they observed the wars of the later nineteenth century, Engels and Marx concluded that the "revolutionary side" was represented, more or less, by the Western allies in the Crimean War; the insurgents in the Sepoy Rebellion; the Austrians in the Italian War of 1859; Garibaldi in his campaigns in the South of Italy; Juarez in the Mexican Intervention; the Union in the American Civil War; the Germans in the Danish War; the Austrians in the Austro-Prussian War; the Prussians in the first stage of the Franco-Prussian War, and the French Republic in the second stage; the Communards in their struggle against the Republic; and the Turks against Russia. Engels and Marx were never neutral. In all these conflicts, as in the revolutionary struggles of 1848 and 1849, the revolutionaries supported as lesser evils regimes and movements that represented the revolution only imperfectly.[20] The reasoning behind these choices, and the various ways in which the wars were expected to affect the revolution's prospects, are discussed in this section. Here it is necessary only to point out the

facility with which Engels and Marx cast the several governments
of Europe now as heroes, now as villains, in their search for
temporary allies in the camp of their great-power foes.[21] Though
some nations were more often heroes, and some more often
villains, Engels and Marx assigned the roles according to revolutionary opportunism, and not primarily because of personal
predilections for one nation or another.

The flexibility of their attitudes toward the nations of Europe,
and the extent to which nations and their vicissitudes were
subordinated to the interests of the revolution, are perhaps
clearest in the case of Poland. Marx praised Poland as the
thermometer of European revolution, and Poland's position in his
and Engels' estimation rose and declined according to what
Poland seemed likely to do for the revolution. If an agrarian
revolution began in Russia, Engels wrote in 1851, Poland would
cease to be indispensable. But Poland usually appeared useful,
and consequently was usually supported.[22]

Some countries, however, may have been regarded less coolly
than Poland. In 1860 Charles Dana of the New York *Tribune* wrote
Marx a sort of testimonial. "The only fault I have to find with you,"
he said,

> has been that you have occasionally exhibited too German a
> tone of feeling for an American newspaper. This has been the
> case with reference to both, Czarism and Bonapartism, I have
> sometimes thought that you manifested too much interest and
> too great enthusiasm for the unity and independence of
> Germany.[23]

Dana's misgivings were not unique to him. Leaving aside the
allegation that Marxist thought is inherently Germanic in form,[24]
we find many authors who argue that Marx and Engels were
influenced, if not dominated, by German chauvinism. Marx, it is
said, was a "Red Prussian,"[25] and those who trouble to differenti-
ate between Engels and Marx agree that Engels was even more
patriotic and nation-conscious than his colleague.[26] The Red
Prussian thesis therefore requires a closer look: was Germany an
exception to the objective, uninvolved attitude that Engels and
Marx maintained toward nations such as Poland?

Some expressions of German national spirit were clearly tactical efforts to attract support by taking a patriotic line, as when Marx and Engels recommended a German-national stance during Austria's Italian difficulties of 1859, or when Engels (on Marx's advice) reviewed the first volume of *Capital* with the proud declaration that at last the Germans had produced an economist,[27] but it is also undeniable that genuine expressions of patriotic sentiment abound in Engels' earliest writings. He said that popular literature ought, among other things, to inspire the reader with love of his Fatherland, and in an obituary tribute to the patriot Immermann he vowed to become "as strong and firm and German" as the departed hero. But in an essay on Ernst Moritz Arndt, he praised Arndt principally for avoiding the chauvinist excesses of other *Deutschtümler* such as Jahn.[28] He had read and praised Börne's polemic against the superpatriots,[29] and his readiness to contribute to Ruge's *Deutsch-Französische Jahrbücher* tends to exonerate him from any charge of all-out chauvinism. As Engels wrote in 1891, he and Marx had always been more intimately bound up with the German workers' movement than with any other;[30] but this does not necessarily make them German chauvinists.

Engels' affection for Germany often showed itself in a kind of embarrassment over Germany's failings, which he regretted without denying. There is a note of injured national pride, for instance, in his complaint that the petty thievery of the German bourgeoisie made a poor showing alongside the grand larceny of the English and French bourgeoisie.[31] During the enforced vacation from revolutionary journalism in 1848-49, Engels walked through Burgundy and admired the richness and beauty of France, which he compared to Germany—"poor in wine, a land of beer, schnaps, and rye-bread, of silted-up rivers and revolutions!" He quoted with complete approval Georg Weerth's statement that no one since Frederick the Great had treated the German people so *en canaille* as the *Neue Rheinische Zeitung*.[32]

Engels' Germanophilia did not extend to the dynasties and governments of the existing German states. In common with many Rhinelanders, Engels and Marx detested Prussia and its rulers.[33] Germanophilia may have exerted some covert influence on their foreign policy preferences, but Engels and Marx rationalized their support of German powers by reference to the same criterion of revolutionary advantage that determined their frequent support of Poland.[34]

Engels' and Marx's antipathies may have been quite as important as their alleged pro-German sentiments in determining their positions on international rivalries. But examination of the racial and national epithets that they applied in their correspondence to third parties tend to indicate that they detested people with little regard to nationality, seizing on racial or regional labels in much the same way that they employed other dyslogistic terms.[35] Thus their opinions of the races and nationalities of the world do not suffice to explain their desire, from time to time, that one nation of fools and villains should defeat another. The special antipathy toward Russia and France (or Tsarism and Bonapartism) that Dana detected had other motives than simple prejudice.

Engels' Russophobia was almost as vehement as that of Marx, who saw Russian influences everywhere, almost as if no one could be stupid or reactionary without Russian prompting.[36] Engels wrote in 1849 that Europe had two choices: "whether to be free, or Russian"; and later he wrote that since 1789 "there had been in reality but two Powers on the Continent of Europe—Russia and Absolutism, the Revolution and Democracy."[37] His and Marx's detestation of Russia was based on their assessment of Russia's counterrevolutionary role, and it softened somewhat as Russia came to appear less irrevocably committed to reaction.[38] Like other nations, Russia was seen in the revolution's light; and it was Russia's usual posture in relation to the revolution that cast her in especially deep shadow.[39]

One alleged Russian agent was Louis Napoleon. In general his sins were separated from those of France,[40] in contrast to the early treatments of Russia in which the whole country was damned along with the Tsars; but Napoleon himself was a special threat. His exploitation of nationalist revolutionary aspirations was annoying, and in Marx's analysis his government was a bureaucratic and military apparatus that had drifted loose from its original purpose of administering the interests of the bourgeoisie and continued to exist as an independent entity, supported only by army and *Lumpenproletariat*—thus a frustrating anomaly in the Marxist analysis of the relationship between class and state.[41]

Opposition to Bonapartism took second place only to opposition to Russia, as in the Crimean War, where Napoleon was temporarily useful.

In addition to the themes of Germanophilia, Russophobia, and anti-Bonapartism that run through classical Marxist foreign policy, there is a persistent streak of antagonism toward small nations and would-be nations. Engels' attitudes toward the South Slavs in 1848-49 are most conspicuous, but he also objected to the Swiss[42] and the Danes,[43] as well as the Mexicans and others.[44] This exasperation with small nations that refused to cooperate with the course of progress by vanishing was, like the other phobias and philias, a product of Engels' concern with revolution. Even when the strict and rather arbitrary division of nations into revolutionary and counterrevolutionary camps ceased to be applied, large nations seemed more likely to facilitate progress than small ones,[45] and Engels (an early admirer of Friedrich List[46] as well as Hegel[47]) was quite ready to see some small countries absorbed by their larger neighbors.

Engels was "first and foremost a revolutionary,"[48] as he described Marx. Engels' and Marx's interest in war and foreign policy was a product of their interest in the revolutionary transformation of Europe and the world. Examples have been cited to illustrate this contention, and secondary authorities have been invoked in support, but we have made no attempt to display all the available evidence that revolutionary aims determined classical Marxism's attitudes toward both war and nations. Such an exhaustive study would fit awkwardly into the present work, and it would only belabor the obvious. Instead of reiterating on each page of Part II the importance of revolution in determining Engels' and Marx's views on war, we shall concentrate on the more interesting and less obvious question of precisely *how* war, or the victory of one side or the other in some particular war, was expected to affect the revolution's prospects. Just as nations might pass from hero to villain and back again, war could appear revolutionary, counterrevolutionary, or irrelevant to revolution. It appeared in all these roles, as circumstances changed and as Engels revised his analysis of the relationship between war and revolution.

CHAPTER 4

War the Bringer of Revolution: The 1793 Model, 1848-1851

Engels' first and most coherent analysis of the relationship between war and revolution was developed during the revolutions which swept over most of Europe in 1848 and 1849, raising the hopes of liberals, nationalists, and other opponents of the European order that had prevailed before 1848. War, Engels expected, would feed and intensify revolution; and revolution would inspire an embattled people to military triumph, as allegedly in the France of 1793.

War would surely follow the upheavals of 1848, Engels declared in the *Neue Rheinische Zeitung:* Germany would be involved, and would be forced to adopt revolutionary measures of centralization, vigorous in proportion to her previous fragmentation. A land containing twenty Vendées within its borders and situated among powerful neighbors could, in a time of general revolution, "escape neither civil war nor foreign war." The greater the indecisiveness of the people and their leaders, the longer and more dangerous the war; Germany's existing leadership might seem incompetent enough to guarantee a second Thirty Years' War, "but fortunately the force of circumstances, the German people, the Tsar of Russia, and the French people still [had] something to say about it."[1] This first vague, apocalyptic prophecy said only that war was inevitable, and should be conducted intelligently; it was not yet clear precisely who was to fight whom, or what the people, Tsar, or force of circumstances was expected to say.

Engels' vision of a great revolutionary war had little in common with most of the military actions that German powers actually undertook during the revolutionary period. Engels and the *Neue Rheinische Zeitung* defended the Poles in Posen and the Italians in

Italy against Prussian and Austrian interventions "despite the patriotic howling and drum-beating of almost the entire German press."[2] The suppression of demonstrations in Prague and Posen was opposed as likely to drive the Slavs into the arms of Russia and reaction,[3] and Hungary's cause against the Habsburgs was espoused with great vigor. Germans, said Engels, were everywhere justly regarded as oppressors, and he castigated the pseudorevolutionary pseudogovernment at Frankfurt for ratifying the sins of its predecessors.[4] The various feats of German arms were really attempts to drown the revolutionary spirit in a wave of chauvinism, and to train mercenaries for the eventual destruction of the German left.[5]

Germany's war against Denmark, however, was seen in a different light, and Engels' discussion of the Danish War led him to formulate the analysis of war's effect on revolution that served, during the revolutions of 1848-49, to organize his thinking on the subject. His initial attitude toward the war was simply one of exasperation: the new German *Bundesarmee* was exposed to general derision as it advanced and retreated in "a real quadrille, a martial ballet," conducted by the Camphausen ministry for its own amusement. The stage for this performance was "lighted by Schleswig's burning villages, and the chorus formed by the bloodthirsty shouts of Danish marauders and *Freischärler*";[6] but Engels displayed little real anger against the Danes, who had conveniently demonstrated "how Prussia, when she takes the lead, knows how to protect the honor and interests of Germany." The *Neue Reheinische Zeitung* had regarded the war with calm amid the prevailing patriotic imbecility ("schleswig-holstein-meer-umschlungenen Strohenthusiasmus").

Engels next assessed the Danish War when there was no longer any prospect that the elements governing Germany would resume the conflict. This time Engels offered belated but enthusiastic praise for the war and assailed the Danes; now he approached the Danish War as an instance in which war had served as a revolutionizing force, and as a possible introduction to a greater war which would powerfully assist the revolutionary cause in Germany and Europe. In contrast to the military actions in Posen, Prague, and Italy, he declared, the Danish War had been "popular from the beginning," because in Schleswig-Holstein German forces fought *on the side of revolution*. "What a pity that Germany's first revolutionary war is the most ludicrous war ever yet fought," Engels lamented.

War had transformed the movement in Schleswig-Holstein. The original intentions of the Schleswig German leaders had been reactionary; they had not intended to join Germany (what Germany? Engels asked—no unified nation existed to be joined) but merely to secede from Denmark and establish yet another petty, stagnant German principality. But the struggle against the Danes had driven the leaders to ever more radical measures, and the Schleswigers' fight had become progressive. Now the Kiel *Landesversammlung* was the only one in Germany elected not only by universal suffrage, but by direct vote, and the direction of the struggle had become national rather than particularist.[8]

That war should thus escape the control of those who began it, forcing those engaged in it to move left or perish, became the dominant theme in Engels' war commentaries in 1848 and 1849. There was good precedent for this hope that Germany would be purified and regenerated in the forge of war; certain of the Prussian reformers of 1813, notably Clausewitz, had hoped to bring about changes within Prussia through the war against Napoleon.[9] The changes desired by these "half-and-half reformers," as Engels had called them, were by no means identical with those that Engels intended, and Engels was not yet acquainted with Clausewitz; but Engels' view of the uses of war ran parallel to that of the reformers.[10] Like them, Engels based his expectations on the experience of France in 1792 and 1793, where revolution and defense had proceeded hand in hand.[11] 1793 became Engels' model of the relationship between war and revolution; revolution would lend increased vigor and effectiveness to war, and war would give to revolution, the "locomotive of history,"[12] an initial push and a continuing accelerative force.

If the German people and their representatives decisively rejected the armistice of Malmö that had ended the fighting in Schleswig-Holstein, the war would become the trigger for a world war that would activate the 1793 model on a larger scale, setting off a genuine German revolution. Repudiation of the armistice would pit Germany against "the three most counterrevolutionary powers of Europe: *Russia, England,* and the Prussian *government*." These three powers supported Denmark because in the event of a successful German revolution, Prussia would cease to exist, England would be unable to exploit German markets as well as she could in a divided Germany, and Russia would be faced with democracy on her very border.[13] The *Neue Rheinische Zeitung* had already called for a war against the principal bulwark of reaction:

> *Only war with Russia* is a war of *revolutionary Germany*, a war in which she will wash away the sins of the past, in which she will pull herself together, in which she will defeat her own autocrats and—as is proper for a people throwing off the chains of long and lowly slavery—advance the cause of civilization by the sacrifice of her sons, and make herself free within as she frees herself without.[14]

Now Engels argued that a war against England and Prussia as well as Russia would be even better:

> It is precisely such a war that the dormant German movement requires—a war against the three great powers of the counterrevolution, a war that would *really* dissolve Prussia in Germany, which would make unavoidable an alliance with the Poles, which would lead immediately to the emancipation of Italy, which would be directed precisely against the old counterrevolutionary allies of Germany from 1792 to 1815; a war to place "the fatherland in danger," and thereby to save it, by making *Germany's* victory depend on the victory of democracy.

If the bourgeois and *Junker* pseudorevolutionaries in Frankfurt chose war, he continued cheerfully, they would seal their doom as had the Girondins, swept aside in a war they began; and if they accepted the armistice, they would abdicate all semblance of power in favor of the Prussian government.[15]

When the Assembly chose the doom of ratifying the armistice over the doom of war, Engels declared that Frankfurt had pronounced its own death sentence, wished for a German Cromwell to disperse it, and temporarily shifted his hopes to France. Cavaignac might have to proclaim a red republic to ward off threats from his right, and events in France might then inspire a German revolution.[16]

The great war of Germany against the counterrevolution was not the only hope, but it was this war, or one somewhat like it, that Marx prophesied in his New Year's greeting for 1849. Writing the war cry in Engels' absence from Cologne, he enlarged upon Engels' picture of war as the bringer of revolution, and expected the war to transform England as well as Germany. England was "the rock on which the waves of revolution break," and a continental revolution would be a teapot tempest if England stood apart.

> And the old England [would] be brought down only by a world war, which alone [could] offer the Chartists (the organized English workers' party) the conditions for a successful uprising against their powerful oppressors.The Chartists at the head of the English government—at this moment the social revolution first emerges from the realm of utopia into that of reality.

Marx expected that the war would be set off by the triumph of proletarian revolution in France.

> England, as in Napoleon's time, [would] be at the head of the counterrevolutionary armies, but [would] be cast by the war itself to the head of the revolutionary movement, and [would] make good her sins against the revolution of the Eighteenth Century.

Marx continued: "*Revolutionary uprising of the French working-class, world war*—that is the table of contents for the year 1849."[17]

Marx must have expected his world war to involve Germany as well as England, and to transform Germany according to the process Engels had sketched out, but he did not say so. In addition to this less Germanic emphasis, Marx's account of war's effect on revolution differed from Engels' in one important aspect. Engels had concentrated on the case of a nation already launched on a revolution of sorts—or at least progressive in relation to its reactionary foes—which was driven into increasingly radical policies in the course of defending itself; he was attracted by the accelerative revolutionary effect of wars that were, in revolutionary terms, *justified*. Marx opened a different prospect, that a nonrevolutionary and unpopular war might drive the English populace into revolt. In a way, Marx's version looked forward to 1917, where Engels looked back to 1793; but Marx's line of thought was left undeveloped.[18]

Even in 1848 and 1849, when he was most inclined to see war as a force for revolution, Engels did not apply the 1793 model to all wars. Some might indeed be counterrevolutionary in their effect. When the Frankfurt Assembly declared that any attack on Trieste would be considered an act of war against all Germany (thus in effect sanctioning Austria's reconquest of Italy), Engels ridiculed a policy that would involve Germany in several wars at once. The Germans would find themselves "in the happy position of fighting at the same time the Tsar and the French Republic, the reaction and the revolution." So foolish was the Frankfurt Assembly that it had "arranged matters so that Russian and French, Danish and Italian troops [would] meet in the Paulskirche."[19] This disapprobation of a war on several fronts appears to contradict the calls for war against the three great powers of the counterrevolution, but the contradiction vanishes when the *ideological* fronts involved are considered. Supporting Austria against the Italians' justified revolt and its putative French supporters could hardly be a revolutionary struggle that would regenerate Germany; it would blur the issues and prevent the war from becoming truly revolutionary.

Even a war waged in a progressive and just cause might fail to lead to revolution, as Italian events demonstrated in the spring of 1849. On March 28, Engels wrote that the war against Austria was propelling Rome, Tuscany, and Piedmont into revolution; but three days later he decided that Italy's cause was hopelessly lost because of the intrinsic worthlessness of the Piedmontese monarchy. "It was a great blunder from the beginning," he wrote, "for the Piedmontese to oppose the Austrians only with a regular army that would fight an ordinary, bourgeois *honetten Krieg*." A people bent on winning its independence could not be restricted to "*ordinary* methods of fighting"—it was necessary to resort to "mass rising, revolutionary war, guerrillas everywhere." Only thus could a small people deal with a great one, only thus could a weaker army successfully oppose a stronger one. Spain, said Engels, had demonstrated this from 1807 to 1812, and Hungary continued to demonstrate it.

These invincible revolutionary weapons would allegedly have nullified such conventional military setbacks as the disaster at Novara, but Piedmont could not use them. "In a *monarchy*, even a constitutional one," Novara ended the campaign, and peace was made with the Austrians; in a republic, however, "*nothing at all would have been decided.*" In a republic, a mass rising would have menaced the Austrian Marshal Radetzky's communications and bases, and while Radetzky stood surrounded, confused, and uncharacteristically idle, the Piedmontese would have liberated Venice and marched on to destroy the Austrian army.

> But mass uprising, general rising of the people—these are means from which the kingdom shrinks in terror. These are the means which only a republic can employ—1793 proves it. These are means whose *employment* requires *revolutionary terrorism*, and where is a king who could resolve on this?

The army should have proclaimed itself the center of a popular rising, and "transformed the war of *armies* into a war of *peoples*, as the French did in 1793"; but monarchy could not permit it. Charles Albert might or might not be a traitor—"his *crown*, the *monarchy* alone, suffice[d] to ruin Italy." Only a republic could have resorted to "the irresistible force that saved France in 1793."[20]

The failure of the 1793 process to take hold in Italy prompted Engels to suggest other ways in which the revolution might begin. The very *defeat* of Charles Albert might inspire the proclamation of a republic in Turin, whereupon the people of Paris, "aware that France [could] not allow the Austrians in Turin and Genoa," would follow suit with a rising of their own, and the French army, "burning to cross swords with the Austrians," would join the Parisians.[21] There was no indication that France would be transformed in the ensuing war with Austria, perhaps because the likelihood of war seemed slight, perhaps because a workers' revolution in Paris could be counted on to be genuinely revolutionary without any need for the drastic prod of war. Engels' hints that defeat in one country might cause revolutions in other countries by a kind of vague contagion recurred in his later writings but were not developed in 1849; the 1793 model continued for the time to dominate his discussions of the subject of war and revolution.

In contrast to Piedmont, and thanks largely to superior leadership, Hungary did succeed in becoming truly revolutionary. Engels supported the Hungarians to the extent of opposing all national movements that threatened to interfere with the Hungarians' struggles. "Of all the nations and nationalities of Austria," he declared, "there are only three that are the carriers of progress, that are still capable of life—the *Germans, Poles,* and *Magyars.*" He concluded: "Therefore they are now revolutionary." On the other hand, "all the other greater and lesser tribes and peoples" had "the immediate mission of going under in the world-revolutionary storm," and were therefore counterrevolutionary.[22] This remarkable sorting of peoples into absolute, eternal categories of saved and damned was, as Roman Rosdolsky points out, based almost exclusively on the people's performance in the crucial revolutionary hour of 1848.[23] It ignored completely the Czech risings in Prague and Agram. Though Engels had warned against forcing the Czechs into alliance with the counterrevolution when the Frankfurt Assembly acquiesced in Austria's suppression of the Prague rising, revolutionary *Realpolitik* now led him to disregard all considerations of motive and to consider only the immediate usefulness of each nationality to the world revolution. His effort to represent the Magyars as a socially and economically progressive force in the Habsburg lands was untenable,[24] and the only defense for his statements is the argument that although the Czechs and others might have been subjectively revolutionary, they were nevertheless at that moment objectively reactionary, since the Magyars' military effort had to take precedence over all other considerations.[25]

Engels saw the Hungarians' glorious accomplishments as an echo of 1793: "For the first time in the revolutionary movements of 1848, for the first time since 1793," he declared, "a nation dares to oppose skulking counterrevolution with revolutionary passion, to oppose white terror with red terror"; he continued that "mass rising, the manufacture of weapons on a national basis, assignats, swift justice for those who impede the revolutionary movement, the Revolution in Permanence—in short, all the principal features of the glorious year 1793 [were] found again in Hungary, armed, organized, and inspired by Kossuth."[26] As a result of the Hungarians' exertions, "in place of the leaderless, unorganized mass of December [1848], the Imperial forces were suddenly faced with an army that was concentrated, brave, numerous, and well-organized, and extremely well led."

And as in Schleswig-Holstein and in the France of 1793, the dynamics of the struggle had carried the revolutionaries past their original objective. With the Hungarian declaration of independence of April 14, 1849, Engels felt that the movement had lost its original narrow, particularist character. Hungary was now firmly allied with the forces of revolution against the forces of repression, and Engels sketched the results that were to be expected:

> Hungary independent, Poland restored, German Austria become the revolutionary spark of Germany, Lombardy and Italy independent—with the fulfillment of these plans the whole Austrian state system [would be] destroyed, Austria vanished, Russia driven back to the borders of Asia.

In fact, he promised, other powers might well be drawn in, and in "a few weeks, perhaps a few days," the "French, Magyar-Polish, and German revolutionary armies" would celebrate their brotherhood on the field of triumph under Berlin's walls.[27]

There were no more issues of the *Neue Rheinische Zeitung*, and Engels' campaigning in Baden prevented him from following closely the remainder of the Hungarian war, and from explaining the Hungarian revolution's defeat. (As we have seen, he considered writing a history of the Hungarian campaigns, but never did.) When he next took up the subject of war and revolution, his faith in war's revolutionizing force had been considerably dampened by the failure of his predictions, and by his discouraging experiences in Baden and the Palatinate.

After he had watched the collapse of the 1848 revolutions, and had observed the failure of the 1793 model to operate in Baden, Engels could no longer place any confidence in the system that had given form to his pronouncements in the *Neue Rheinische Zeitung*. When the *Neue Rheinische Zeitung* was reincarnated as a monthly in English exile, Engels still had no system to replace the 1793 model, and in 1850 he dodged the issue of war's effect on revolution, discussing the prospect that the Porte's refusal to extradite Hungarian revolutionary refugees might produce a Russo-Turkish war without mentioning the consequences that such a war would have for the revolution. It would be an interesting war—all Europe involved, England defeating Russia, which would be a giant with its hands amputated once Odessa and St. Petersburg were taken—but it would apparently produce no revolutions in Russia, or in England, or anywhere else.[28]

But Engels could not indefinitely ignore the linkage between war and revolution. He began to analyze the 1793 model by disassembling it. To organize his and Marx's thoughts on the subject, and as a "sort of exercise" in his new specialty of military science,[29] he began an essay on the prospects that would confront a revolutionary French regime under attack by all the counter-revolutionary powers of Europe.

In the *Neue Rheinische Zeitung*, Engels had concentrated on the intensifying and accelerating effect that war would have on the political and social side of a revolution. It was assumed that a revolution would increase a nation's ability to defend itself. If a nation in desperate military straits could save itself only by resort to increasingly radical measures, those measures had to yield military dividends—else why could a "Fatherland in danger" be saved more surely by a revolutionary regime than by any other sort of government? Now that the dust of 1848 had settled a bit, Engels examined more closely this matter of what revolution might be expected to do for war, and his findings were not encouraging.

During the revolutions of 1848 and 1849, Engels had functioned to some extent as a cheerleader of revolution. In 1851, however, he had to be entirely cold-blooded and detached, lest he mislead himself, Marx, and the proletariat as to the prospects of a future revolution. "Now that we are not writing an *NRZ*, we have no need for illusions," he said, praising the generalship of Radetzky.[30] Even the accomplishments of the miraculous year 1793 diminished under Engels' critical scrutiny: Valmy was a trivial artillery duel,

Carnot a mediocrity, and the heroic volunteers, when not directly under the eye of Dumouriez, fought no better than the south German *Volkswehr* of 1849. The *levée en masse* was no panacea. It had increased the size of the French forces, but had not created an army out of nothing; only the allies' indecision permitted the French to train their levies in the *école de bataillon*. France had been saved not by an irresistible revolutionary force, but by the discord and incompetence of her foes.

Thus if the putative French revolutionaries of 1852 were to decree a mass levy and send two million men to the frontiers, in obedience to the tradition of '93, they would produce only confusion, "a senseless waste of all resources," which "would not increase the army's strength by one usable battalion." The best hope lay in expanding each existing battalion into a regiment, so that the officers on hand could be most productively employed. It was useless to try to train new officers in the two months that it would take for the counterrevolutionary onslaught to strike.[31]

Invoking his own experiences, Engels declared that something should have been learned from the Palatinate and Baden. He generalized: "It is a plain fact that disorganization in the armies and the total disorganization of discipline have been conditions as well as results of every successful revolution to date." France had required the whole period from 1789 to 1792 to assemble Dumouriez' army, which disintegrated; Hungary had needed the period from March, 1848, to the middle of 1849 to field an organized army. Engels concluded that "precisely the factor that enabled Napoleon to form gigantic armies rapidly, namely good cadres, is necessarily lacking in any revolution (even in France)."[32]

Engels never regained his lost faith in the military invincibility of a popular rising. "National enthusiasm," he wrote in 1866, "is a capital thing to work upon, but until disciplined and organized, nobody can win battles with it." Revolutions created disorder, and disorder was incompatible with military effectiveness. The Sepoy rebels, "a motley crew of mutineering soldiers who [had] murdered their own officers, torn asunder the bonds of discipline," and established no unified command, were dismissed in 1857 as "certainly the body least likely to organize a serious and protracted resistance."[33]

The legend of 1793 took its place among the optimistic illusions that the scientific socialists delighted in exposing. When in 1870 Gambetta attempted a *levée en masse*, Engels could consider that his predictions of 1851 had been confirmed. There were not enough officers; once the regular armies were lost, as in the capitulation of Metz, it became "extremely difficult to turn crowds of men into companies and battalions of soldiers." Engels continued:

> Whoever has seen popular levies on the drill-ground or under fire—be they Baden Freischaaren, Bull-Run Yankees, French Mobiles, or British Volunteers—will have perceived at once that the chief cause of the helplessness and unsteadiness of these troops lies in the fact of the officers not knowing their duty; and in this present case in France who is there to teach them their duty?[34]

Under the circumstances, he asked, "what are these 2,000,000 of men worth to France?" It was "all very well for the French to point to the Convention, to Carnot, with his frontier armies created out of nothing, and so forth"; but Moltke would not repeat the blunders of the 1790s, and would not grant the green French troops five years for practice.[35]

In the long run, to be sure, revolution would have enormous military utility. Engels' 1851 study examined the relationship between socio-economic structure and military organization, and condluded that since a rational socialist economy would increase the productivity of labor, a socialist nation would eventually be able to spare more of its manpower for military service than a bourgeois nation could. Greater masses would lead to new (and unpredictable) modes of warfare, and the socialist state would be much more efficient than the bourgeois state. But these advantages would not be available immediately. Indeed, much of the revolutionary proletariat would be needed on the home front to guard against counterrevolution. In the short run, therefore, the revolution would have to defend itself "with the means and methods of modern war."

The military possibilities of the bourgeois era had been discovered and elaborated by Napoleon, and the lessons of Napoleonic warfare had been thoroughly assimilated by the generals of the reactionary powers. Radetzky demonstrated this very clearly, and the chance of having superior strategy and tactics was "at least as good on the side of the coalition as on that of France." The revolutionaries could not rely on the unpredictable factor of military genius, and the big battalions would prevail.[36]

After Engels' reassessments, war seemed much less attractive. Should Cavaignac come to power in France and attack Prussia (so as to silence French socialists with a bit of *gloire*), the war would do the revolution no good either in Prussia or in France. Should a revolution occur in Germany, a most unpromising war would ensue; France, Italy, and Poland were all interested in Germany's fragmentation, and Mazzini had even made promises to the Czechs. "Apart from Hungary," Engels concluded, "there is only one possible ally, Russia, assuming [!] a peasant revolution is carried out there." Germany would at any rate "wage a *guerre à mort* with our noble friends in all directions," and it was "most dubious how the business [would] turn out."[37] It was clear that neither Germany nor the revolution would profit from a war.

Engels' gloomy reassessment of the military consequences of revolution had destroyed the symmetry of the 1793 model. The happy symbiosis in which war and revolution fed on each other ceased to work. Occasionally Engels reverted to the hope that war's exertions would somehow propel a belligerent power into revolution, but since revolution no longer promised to work any martial charm, the reciprocal relationship between war and revolution was gone, and the process became unstable. (Engels did not pursue the possibility that the *illusion* of revolutionary invincibility might serve as a sort of Sorelian myth to lead a beleaguered nation into revolution; rather he emphasized the folly of relying for salvation on the mystique of the *levée en masse*.) Occasional desperate attempts to resurrect the 1793 model lacked the consistency and conviction of the *Neue Rheinische Zeitung* articles. The image became tentative, cluttered with qualifications, a pale ghost of its original self. Engels' reexamination destroyed it in 1851.

CHAPTER 5

New Models:
The Revolutionary Uselessness
of Limited War, 1851-1859

If the 1793 model was dead, what was to replace it? The quest for a new interpretation of war's relationship to revolution was carried on in Engels' and Marx's comments on the European wars of the 1850s. The first of these, the Crimean War (1854-1856), grew out of the customary Russo-Turkish strains and pitted Turks, British, French, and eventually Piedmontese against Russians. The war remained limited in scope, with the principal action the allied siege of Sevastopol, on the Crimean peninsula. Sevastopol fell in September, 1855, and the Russians (prodded by neutral Austria) agreed to a settlement that permitted the Ottoman Empire to decay at its own pace. The other promising war of the 1850s was the result of the Plombières plot (July, 1858) between the Piedmontese diplomat Cavour and France's Napoleon III, who had recently been reminded by a bomb of his affection for the idea of Italian unity. The Austrians were to be pushed out of Northern Italy, and the French rewarded for their assistance in this project with the Piedmontese provinces of Nice and Savoy. Austria was duly goaded into war, but after two major battles Napoleon III withdrew from the war in the Peace of Villafranca (July 11, 1859), gaining Lombardy but not Venetia from the Austrians. Napoleon traded Lombardy for Nice and Savoy; the Piedmontese conducted plebiscites in the North Italian states and annexed them; and a free-lance campaign by Garibaldi took over the Kingdom of the Two Sicilies and moved up into the Papal States, leading to further plebiscites and the creation of the Kingdom of Italy in 1861. Neither the Crimean nor the Italian war led to the European revolution.

The military and diplomatic events of the Crimean and Italian

Wars concern us only insofar as they provoked Engels and Marx
into reassessing their view of war's revolutionary role. The wars
were important to Engels and Marx, bringing both hope and
confusion. In the revolutionary doldrums of the 1850s, the
revolutionary strategists clutched at whatever straws they found;
the wars promised somehow to shake up the existing order, but it
was by no means clear just how they would affect the prospects of
revolution. The analytical vision of the 1793 model, vivid but
distorted, had been discarded, and Engels and Marx confronted
the bewildering events of the Crimean and Italian Wars without
any reliable means of assessing their consequences for the
revolution. The abandonment of the 1793 model had left a
theoretical void, which an assortment of vague and groping
suggestions entered but could not fill. The relationship between
war and revolution, which in 1848 and 1849 had seemed locked
together in a precise, mutually supporting pattern, now seemed
erratic, almost accidental.

Engels had used the analogy of 1793 explicitly; his attempts to
replace it were much less coherent. This chapter sorts Engels' and
Marx's observations on the wars of the 1850s into models so that
they may be analyzed, but this order is imposed upon the material.
Engels and Marx did not move consistently from one set of ideas
to the next. They tried one, dropped it, picked it up again, tried
another. During the Crimean and Italian Wars (which are treated
together, as a single stage in the development of classical
Marxism's ideas on war), Engels and Marx shuffled repeatedly
through the same pack of ideas. They were anything but dogmatic
about war's revolutionary implications, and tried out whatever
seemed promising. But their reflections of the 1850s are more than
a study in confusion. Despite all the disorder, inconsistency, and
contradiction, one central conclusion arose from the dust of battle,
and that conclusion became the starting point for Engels' and
Marx's subsequent assessments of war. Eventually, by a variety of
routes, Engels and Marx arrived at the view that only a truly
monstrous war would suffice to produce the European revolution.

Sometimes the perplexing connection between war and revolution could be ignored. In the spring of 1854, Engels wrote to Marx

that a war between Prussia and England would be convenient—
not because it would bring about a revolution anywhere, but
because it would deter Engels' father from visiting Manchester
and discovering that his son had been pursuing revolutionary
journalism to the detriment of Ermen and Engels' business
interests. And even when Engels said that each step in the Crimean
War brought it closer to the point of escaping Aberdeen's and
Palmerston's control and escalating according to a purely military
dynamic of retaliation,[1] he did not try to connect the war's
expansion to any prospect of revolution. The war was interesting
to watch, but had no apparent revolutionary import.

In November, 1853, Marx compared the Crimean hostilities
with a strike in Wigan: "While the first cannon-bullets have been
exchanged in the war of the Russian against Europe," he declared,
"the first blood has been spilt in the war now raging in the
manufacturing districts, of capital against labor." But Marx drew
no causal connection between the two struggles, and suggested no
way in which one would influence the other; simultaneity was
their only common element. When the London *Times* did attempt
to link the Crimean War and revolution, Marx objected that the
paper had considered a war in behalf of the Turks less attractive
than one for the Poles or Hungarians, and a week later had feared
that "the first collision between British and Russian armies would
be a signal of revolution all over the continent." Thus, said Marx,
one day England should avoid war with Russia because it "would
defend the Turks, instead of the Poles and Hungarians; and the
next day because any war in behalf of Turkey would be
simultaneously a war in behalf of Poles and Hungarians."[2] But as
yet Marx only ridiculed the *Times*' inconsistency, without offering
his own interpretation of the war's significance.

He and Engels were still not sure how war would affect
revolution when the Italian War broke out in 1859. The war's
immediate effect might be reactionary, said Marx, though "perhaps it will bring us some opportunities too."[3] Engels was
delighted—"Vive la guerre!" he exclaimed—but he did not say
how the war would enable him to hunt Prussians instead of foxes.
Marx replied, "Pas trop de zèle,"[4] but he, too, was convinced that
the war must have *some* significance.

War was important enough to make a revolt in Spain seem a sideshow: Marx saw a Russian hand in Espartero's rising of 1854, which was "far from meaning a popular revolution," and "must prove a powerful agency in dissolving so superficial a combination as what is called the Anglo-French Alliance."[5] Marx was sufficiently interested in the revolt to dig into Spanish revolutionary history, examining especially the role of the Spanish Army, which he said had degenerated since the Napoleonic Wars, when it had been the most revolutionary part of the nation; now it fought only against the people and national guard.[6] Marx's comments are interesting for his occasional generalizations ("under revolutionary, still more than ordinary circumstances, the destinies of armies reflect the true nature of the civil government"[7]) and because he wrote them without relying on Engels' military expertise. But the Spanish revolution seemed unlikely to touch off the European revolution. Marx regarded it as a study in revolutionary processes, not as a forerunner of greater things. For the European revolution, the war in Russia was more promising, even though it was not clear *how* it would affect the revolution's chances.

There was one direct and obvious way in which the war (either the Crimean or the Italian one) might have revolutionary consequences: Napoleon III might unleash some of the nationalist revolutionists whom he maintained in order to make his brother sovereigns nervous. But Napoleon's agents were most useful against Austria, which was neutral,[8] and such instigated revolts did not seem promising. Engels and Marx disapproved, of course, of rebellions that might interfere with the war effort of Russia's enemies. Disorders among the Greek subjects of the Ottoman Empire (stirred up, according to Marx, by Stratford de Redcliffe, Britain's ambassador in Constantinople, to sabotage Turkish resistance) were deplored.[9] This disapproval was in keeping with the general principle, applied against the Czechs and Croats in 1848-49, that discontented groups should wait their turn and not interfere with the progress of revolution in more important theaters; in 1859 when Engels and Marx supported Austria against France and Piedmont, they were similarly annoyed by nationalist revolutionaries who allowed themselves to be used by Napoleon.[10] But during the Crimean War they showed little enthusiasm for Napoleon's revolutionary threats, even though

Napoleon was for once on the right side. They reported such
threats as mere incidents in the war.

As it turned out, Napoleon III abandoned his revolutionary
posturing in favor of "limited war" in the Crimea. The European
Revolution, said Engels, would not be conjured up by the man
who had crushed the Roman Republic[11]—not that it mattered who
or what got the revolution started, but Engels and Marx did not
expect Napoleon to accomplish anything, even if he tried. In 1859
Napoleon again threatened to play the revolutionary card, even
inviting the Hungarian revolutionary Kossuth to his headquarters,
but Marx argued that after the battle of Solferino Napoleon began
to fear the outbreak of a real revolution, and therefore pulled out
of the war.[12]

Why should Napoleon threaten to unleash his tame revolutionists only when things were going well for him, and he didn't
need them? It is not clear at all; the only thing clear is that
Napoleon was not the connection between war and revolution.
But what *was* the connection?

Sometimes Engels and Marx returned to the positions of the
1793 model. Even the rhetoric of revolutionary invincibility,
which Engels had repudiated in 1851, turned up on occasion. Once
France and Britain had committed their forces on Russian soil,
said Engels, Prussia and Austria might march on Paris. "If this plan
succeeds," he declared,

> there is no force at the disposal of Louis Napoleon to resist
> that shock. But there is a force which can "mobilize" itself
> upon any emergency, and which can also "mobilize" Louis
> Bonaparte and his minions as it has mobilized many a ruler
> before this. That force is able to resist all these invasions; it has
> shown that once before to a combined Europe; and that
> force, the Revolution, be assured, will not be wanting on the
> day its action is required.[13]

As in 1851, the situation pitted a revolutionary France against the
world, but this time Engels claimed that the revolution could win.
He did not say how this was to be done; no doubt Napoleon's

officers would try to organize the revolutionary levies, but France had possessed officers in 1851, and Engels had considered them inadequate to the task. Besides, he had a very poor opinion of Napoleon's army.[14] Probably the 1793 model was resurrected because nothing had replaced it. Engels had damaged it beyond repair with his analysis of 1851, but when the Crimean War promised somehow to affect the stability of the existing order, the old model was dragged out, gaps and all.

It was still there in 1859, despite Marx's admission that "revolution in Germany now, which equals the disorganization of her armies, would work out to the advantage not of the revolutionaries, but of Russia and Boustrapa."[15] ("Boustrapa" was a derisive label for Napoleon III, derived from his three coups, at Boulogne, Strasbourg, and Paris.) Here Marx accepted fully the conclusions that Engels had drawn in 1851: revolution would disrupt military effectiveness, and reactionary invaders would have an easy task. Marx's view of the poor odds facing an invaded revolutionary Germany did not entirely contradict his esteem for a Franco-Russian alliance that would dispose of "our lousy Prussian regime"—"the only dilemma that could cost it its neck";[16] he may have hoped not for a two-front war but simply for loss of the Russian support that he believed maintained *Junker* dominance in Prussia. On other occasions, however, the magic of war as a bringer of revolution was praised quite as extravagantly as in 1848.

Engels wrote to Ferdinand Lassalle in May, 1859:

> In general world events seem to be taking quite a favorable turn. A better basis for a thoroughgoing German revolution than a Franco-Russian alliance is hard to imagine. We Germans must have the water up to our necks before we are *en masse* consumed by the *furor teutonicus;* and this time the danger of drowning seems near enough. *Tant mieux.*

In such a desperate crisis all parties would successively come to power and ruin themselves until "the moment must come, when only the most ruthless and determined party is able to save the nation."[17] Perhaps Engels' rhetoric was deliberately exaggerated to dissuade Lassalle from taking the wrong line on the war;[18] while Engels and Marx considered Napoleon III the villain (his regime

of a few swindlers with military support lacked a proper class base
and had to seek foreign adventures to entertain the army and
distract the populace[19]), Lassalle saw in Austria the main obstacle
to German unification. Prussia should take advantage of Austria's
difficulties, he proposed, and unify Germany around Prussia's
"more liberal traditions."[20] Engels and Marx considered that the
socialists "absolutely must identify our cause with the present
German regimes,"[21] and Engels' exuberant plunge into the rhetoric of 1793 was surely an attempt to cure Lassalle's Bonapartist
flirtation.[22]

But not all of the Italian War reappearances of the discarded
model can be explained away. Engels and Marx told their readers
in the Berlin *Volk* that "*Prussia's armed mediation,* i.e., her alliance
with Austria, *means revolution.*" If Prussia entered the war,
"Bonapartist despotism and Habsburg tyranny would fight on the
Spree and Mincio," while "the battles of freedom would be fought
on the Order and Vistula," as Russia moved in.[23] The Prussian
government, beset by Russia, would have to appeal to national
spirit and class interests, setting loose a commotion that would
dwarf the wars of the first French Revolution. The war was clearly
expected to transform Prussia, though the related expectation that
the revolutionary state would be able to fend off all attacks was
not explicit. When Engels boasted that the German people could
take care not only of the French and Russians, but of their thirty-
three princes at the same time, he attributed the Germans' strength
not to any invincibility inherent in revolution, but to their
revolutionary education won in 1848.[24] Overthrowing the German
princes would not apparently unleash new forces against the
French and Russians, nor would the war topple the princes.
Instead the people would dispose of foreign and domestic foes
"simultaneously"; there was no clear causal link between the
internal and external struggles.

The 1793 model was simply less persuasive and coherent than in
1848-49, because one essential component, revolutionary invincibility, was lacking. Yet in a sense the model was applied even
more broadly than it had been when fresh: in 1848-49, it had
worked only for governments already entered on a revolutionary
course; monarchies (such as Charles Albert's Piedmont) were

ineligible for the process. In 1859, however, the monarchies of
Austria and Prussia might be transformed by military strains.

This prospect opened the possibility of a domesticated version
of the 1793 model, in which a government might adopt increasingly radical measures while remaining in control, democra-
tizing itself enough to satisfy public opinion and generate public
enthusiasm for the war. Engels and Marx themselves referred to
developments of this type as revolutionary, in their comments on
the American Civil War;[25] but such events as Bismarck's adoption
of radical programs in 1866 and the leftward shift of most
belligerent governments in the First World War[26] were not the sort
of revolution for which they lived.

The 1793 model was no longer good enough. It might be
brandished on occasion, for want of something better, but a
replacement was sorely needed. During the Crimean and Italian
Wars, some hints of new approaches began tentatively to emerge.

One way for war to produce revolution was what may be called
a 1905 model, developed during the Crimean War. Even if
revolution was not invincible on the battlefield, a war might be
carried on so incompetently as to annoy the people, leading them
to shake off an unpopular regime. (This is not to imply that the
blunders of the Russian Army and Government in the Russo-
Japanese War were the sole cause of the 1904-1905 uprising, but the
blunders certainly helped to release the accumulated discontents;
1905 probably came reasonably close to what Engels and Marx
had in mind.) The revolutionaries thus brought to power might
win the war or end it, not because revolution was invincible but
because the new leaders were bound to be less incompetent than
those they had replaced.

Engels declared on New Year's Day, 1855, that if Austria and
Prussia entered the war on Russia's side,

> the spring is likely to see a million and a half of soldiers
> arrayed against the Western Powers, and an Austro-Prussian
> army marching on the French frontiers. And then the
> management of the war is sure to be taken out of the hands of
> its present leaders.

He did not say that the revolutionaries would win; but no one could do *worse* than Napoleon III and Palmerston. Similarly, Marx predicted that the war, "coinciding with a commercial crisis," would enable the proletariat to recoup the losses of June, 1848, "and that not only as far as France is concerned, but for all Central Europe, England [!] included." The English aristocracy had shown itself incompetent to direct the war; the middle class was unwilling to continue the war and therefore unfit to govern; there remained the petty bourgeoisie and the workers. "Which of these classes will be the one to carry England through the present struggle, and the complications about to arise from it?" asked Marx.[27] Surely the proletariat would run the war better; but Marx used the war's mismanagement as an *argument* for revolution, not as something that would force Britain to revolt; and the workers' takeover was a military asset only by comparison with the aristocracy's blunders.

As the war and the bungling continued, Marx dignified the grumbling of Britain's unfortunate Crimean army with the title of "revolt," though he apparently expected the troops to do no more than continue to "direct thousands of letters to the London papers each week, to appeal from their superiors to public opinion."[28] The French troops were also said to resent the stupidity with which they were employed, and the French public was annoyed by war taxes.[29] A mismanaged war could create popular discontent; but what if it *did* bring revolutionaries to power? In 1859 when Marx suggested that a decisive Austrian victory in the Italian War might cause a mutiny and revolution in Paris, he stuck to the dismal conclusions that Engels had reached in 1851: if there was a revolution in Paris, a new Holy Alliance would crush it.[30]

The 1905 model, if it can be called that, was applied sporadically and without much conviction; it was not a satisfactory substitute for the 1793 model. The new analysis did provide a means by which war might lead to revolution, but the lack of invincibility posed a fatal problem. It would do little good if a bungled war brought revolutionaries to power, only to have them crushed by foreign invasion. Unless a revolutionary government could defend itself, what was the point of its taking power?

One possible source of hope was the principle of revolutionary contagion, which was sometimes offered as a substitute for invincibility. The Crimean stalemate made Austria the arbiter of Europe, Engels said, but

> there is a counterpoise against this Austrian supremacy. The moment France is launched again into the revolutionary career, this Austrian force dissolves itself into its discordant elements. Germans, Hungarians, Poles, Italians, Croats, are loosened from the forced bond which holds them together, and instead of the undetermined and haphazard alliances of to-day, Europe will again be divided into two great camps with distinct banners and issues. Then the struggle will be only between the Democratic Revolution on the one side and the Monarchical Counter-Revolution on the other.[31]

The promised triumph of the revolution depended not on any power inherent in a revolutionized France, but on the fragility of the Habsburg Empire. If contagion could disrupt the armies of the revolution's enemies, it could save the revolution; and Austria was not the only power vulnerable to contagion.

In September, 1853, Marx predicted that war with Russia would cause a general upheaval on the Continent, which would probably find a significant echo among the English masses. "If we cast a look at Europe," he wrote a year later, "we meet with symptoms of revolution in Spain, Italy, Denmark, the Danubian Provinces, Greece, Asiatic Turkey," and even in the French ranks at Varna.[32] A promising commercial crisis was under way,[33] and Marx hoped that the forces of revolution were everywhere ready to strike. Similarly, in 1859 Italy was such a hotbed of revolution that an outbreak would be no more surprising than a new eruption of Vesuvius; so energetic were the revolutionaries that Marx declined "to predict whether the revolutionists or the regular armies will appear first in the field." Marx attributed to the Italian revolutionaries the expectation that "a successful revolution in Italy [would] be the signal for a general struggle on the part of all the oppressed nationalities to rid themselves of their oppressors." And Marx's own somewhat Delphic prediction that "a war begun in any part of Europe will not end where it commences"[34] is at least compatible with the principle of contagion.

If contagion was to amount to anything, it required powerful revolutionary forces everywhere, ready to be released when needed; and sometimes Engels and Marx persuaded themselves that the world was ripe for revolt. Even Russia, which had seemed in 1848 and 1849 the monolithic incarnation of reaction, whose only use to the revolution was in frightening other states enough to make them appeal to their proletariats,[35] seemed promising in 1859. "In the next revolution," Marx commanded, "Russia will please to join the rebels"; and he predicted that if revolution broke out in Italy, explosions would follow in France, Germany, and *Russia*.[36] Engels likewise claimed that "we [Germans] have allies in the Russian serfs," whose struggle for emancipation menaced the traditional reactionary thrust of Russian foreign policy.[37]

"We must not forget," Engels warned the *Tribune*'s readers in 1854,

> that there is a sixth power in Europe, which at given moments asserts its supremacy over the world of the five so-called "great" powers, and makes them tremble, every one of them. That power is the Revolution. Long silent and retired, it is now again called to action by the commercial crisis and by the scarcity of food. From Manchester to Rome, from Paris to Warsaw and Pesth, it is omnipresent, lifting up its head and awakening from its slumbers. Manifold are the symptoms of its returning life, everywhere visible in the agitation and disquietude which have seized the proletarian class.

War's role in rousing this dormant monster was almost incidental; "A signal only is wanted," said Engels,

> and the sixth and greatest European power will come forward, in shining armour and sword in hand, like Minerva from the head of the Olympian. This signal the impending war will give, and then all calculations as to the balance of power will be upset by the addition of a new element which, ever buoyant and youthful, will as much baffle the plans of the old European Powers, and their generals, as it did from 1792 to 1800.[38]

War was "a signal only," and that was the difference between the situation envisaged here in the 1850s, and the 1793 model of

1848-49. In place of a revolution intensified by military pressures within a single beleaguered country, we find revolutions springing up all over the map.[39]

Contagion provided some hope, but it was a poor substitute for the revolutionary invincibility of the original 1793 model. Engels had, after all, observed in Baden the failure of revolutionary slogans to disperse Prussian troops. If contagion failed to work, as Marx and Engels sometimes feared it might,[40] a revolution anywhere in Europe was likely to remain isolated, and doomed to be crushed by counterrevolutionary neighbors. Though Marx and Engels adopted the Paris Commune of 1871, after its failure (a revolution which remained isolated, save for minor demonstrations of sympathy, in a single city), the value of a dead or doomed revolt was limited. Without invincibility or contagion in good working order, most revolutions seemed likely to be doomed.

But during the Crimean and Italian Wars, Engels and Marx began to develop another line of approach. Partly promising, partly ominous, this new analysis of war's relation to revolution saw war as more than just a signal. A big war would be required; the Crimean War would not do unless the German powers were added.[41] A thorough holocaust would devastate Europe, exhausting the existing governments and blasting a path for the revolution. Engels sketched the process in August, 1854:

> The grand actions of 1854 are, we dare say, but the petty preludes of the battles of nations which will mark the annals of 1855. It is not until the great Russian army of the West, and the Austrian army come into play, no matter whether against each other or with each other, that we shall see real war on a grand scale, something like the grand wars of Napoleon. And, perhaps, these battles may be the preludes merely of other battles far more fierce, far more decisive—the battles of the European peoples against the now victorious and secure European despots.

By December he thought that Austria's intervention was near; "at any rate," he concluded, "it cannot be doubted that the moment for war to swell into more gigantic and terrible proportions, and to wrap all Europe in its flames, is now close at hand."[42] Once the existing governments had burned themselves out in war, in this 1917 model, the revolutionaries would take charge of the ashes.

This was a somewhat less heroic picture than the 1793 model, to be sure, but it did not require either invincibility or contagion to work. Like the other models suggested here, the 1917 model is a construction assembled from ideas that Engels and Marx expressed in asides, never troubling to work out the principle explicitly. It is less clear and less precise than the 1793 model, in part because Engels and Marx did not have the Russian Revolution before their eyes to serve as a type case; chronology interfered. Nevertheless, something like a 1917 model came to shape their views.

Only an earthquake of a war, in which governments would shake one another to pieces, would lead directly to revolution. And despite Engels' predictions that an expanded war, with consequent revolution, was imminent,[43] the Crimean War remained limited. Engels and Marx complained that the British aristocracy waged the war halfheartedly, urged on by an impatient populace; even the *Times* admitted that the directors of the war effort were unfit for their tasks. Engels insisted that others would have to take the direction of the war out of the incompetent hands of Napoleon III; new and more vigorous policies were required, since all actions so far had been exercises in futility.[44] But he did not predict that a new and more determined policy *would* necessarily be initiated. In March, 1855, he mentioned only the diversionary "revolution" that the Tsar might stir up in Austria in the event of Austrian intevention against Russia; and in February, 1856, he predicted that no new campaigns would be undertaken.[45] Far from expanding into a full-scale holocaust, the war was running down, and Engels' hopes with it.

From the first, gloomy predictions had been mixed with hopeful ones;[46] already in August, 1854, Engels and Marx had suggested that instead of the war's destroying the belligerent governments, the governments might suffocate the war. Engels complained that France, England, and Russia could "carry on their war for six months, and unless by mistake, or on a very shabby scale, they have not even come to blows"; there they were, "the French doing nothing and the British helping them as fast as they can." It was a miserable war on esthetic grounds. "The fact is," Engels complained,

> that conservative Europe—the Europe of "order, property, family, religion"—the Europe of monarchs, feudal lords, moneyed men, however they may be differently assorted in different countries—is once more exhibiting its extreme impotency. Europe may be rotten, but a war should have roused the sound elements, as war should have brought forth some latent energies; and assuredly there should be that much pluck among two hundred and fifty millions of men, that at least one decent struggle might be got up wherein both parties could reap some honour, such as force and spirit can carry off even from the field of battle.

It was a frustrating picture; "with Governments such as they are at present," said Engels, "this Eastern War may be carried on for thirty years, and yet come to no conclusion."[47]

Similarly, Marx wrote that the Tsar was said to have doubted "that England, with a *bourgeois* Parliament, would carry on a war with glory." Marx concluded "that the Czar knows his Cobdens and his Brights, and estimates at its just value the mean and abject spirit of the English middle class." And even Engels' *Tribune* article of February 2, 1854, which depicted the revolution as the sixth and greatest European Power, ready to appear instantly, invincible in shining armor, contained a cautionary note: so long as the war remained "confined to the Western Powers and Turkey on the one hand, and Russia on the other, it [would] not be a European war such as we have seen since 1792."[48] Even in this most enthusiastic assessment of the war's revolutionary potential, he hinted at the possibility that the war might remain limited, and therefore unproductive of revolution.

This new emphasis on the necessity of *large-scale* war modified some of the reappearances of the 1793 model during the 1850s. Only a very dangerous military plight would suffice to raise "the water up to the necks" of the Germans;[49] naturally it would take more of a threat to terrify Prussia into calling on the German people than it had taken to drive Holstein's leaders to the left in

1848, but the emphasis on scale sets some of the 1850s comments apart from the applications of the 1793 model during 1848 and 1849. In June, 1859, Marx predicted that war would escape both the confines of the Italian peninsula and the bounds of conventional warfare; once Russia entered the war, central Europe would be consumed by a revolutionary conflagration.[50] Only when the war grew larger could it make the revolution.[51]

After the smoke and dust settled, the confused and contradictory commentaries that Engels and Marx composed on the Crimean and Italian wars led to a new analysis of war's relationship to revolution. A very large war was the only sort of war that could produce revolution. This conclusion was usually incorporated in the 1917 model, which continued to shape classical Marxist thinking on war until Engels' death in 1895. Engels and Marx continued to expect a world war—in 1888 Engels predicted "the devastations of the Thirty Years' War compressed into three or four years and extended over the whole continent"[52]—though their opinion of its desirability changed. (See chapter seven.)

The premise that only a huge and terrible war would suffice to produce revolution led to two important conclusions: a war that remained limited was irrelevant to the revolution in any immediate sense; and if there was a path to the revolution that did *not* lead through the bloodbath of a world war, the peaceful path should be taken.

CHAPTER 6

War Remote from Revolution, 1857-1871

As Engels' and Marx's analysis of the connection between war and revolution evolved, their attitude toward war necessarily changed. Even in 1848-49, when war had seemed the midwife of revolution, Engels and Marx had advocated wars somewhat different from those that were actually fought. In the 1850s and afterward, the discrepancy between the wars that they might have wished to see and the wars that actually occurred became greater and more conspicuous. Since only a catastrophic world war promised to produce the revolution, and since the wars of the later nineteenth century remained limited, Engels could regard the wars, in their immediate effects, as almost irrelevant to revolution.[1]

No people or state was considered intrinsically revolutionary or counterrevolutionary; all were judged not on what they had done for revolution in the past, but on what they might do in the future. If no nation would revolutionize itself while fighting, and none was revolutionary to begin with, wars would remain contests among the existing bourgeois and aristocratic states; the revolutionary's choice among the contenders would be a choice of lesser evils. Engels and Marx always did make choices; Engels' reference to *"militaria,* where one is always on the side of the victor"[2] was facetious and concerned past military history as fashioned into encyclopedia articles, not current events. But the choices they made were not the passionate commitments of 1848.

If the side that Engels and Marx favored lost a war, the approach of revolution would be delayed, the course of history impeded; if the side that they supported won, revolution would not therefore follow immediately, but a setback would be avoided. Conditions favorable to social, economic, and political progress would be created—or at least would not be destroyed—and progress, in the fullness of time, would bring the revolution.

All the wars of the period from the 1850s till 1871 failed to make a revolution of useful proportions, or to make necessary any change in the classical Marxist view of war's revolutionary role. As we examine what Engels and Marx had to say about these wars, we see the world revolution's General Staff applying the formula developed in the previous chapter. But examination of these wars does more than just demonstrate that no new theory was developed (fortunately, since proving a negative is seldom very interesting); it reveals the intensity with which Engels studied the military events of the period. His disappointed comments on the wars that occurred reveal the outline of the greater war that he might have liked to see, and the failure of other wars to change Engels' and Marx's view of war points up the importance of the Franco-Prussian War, which—though it did not make the revolution—did make a difference.

Even the Italian War, which had on occasion evoked such enthusiastic echoes of the 1793 model, was often discussed in terms of its immediate, nonrevolutionary consequences. To be sure, the publics for which Engels and Marx wrote may have exerted a calming influence; the *Tribune*'s readers might not have appreciated or paid for daily prophecies of revolution, and certainly Engels' strategic pamphlets, intended to establish him as a military critic, would serve their purpose better if they bore no trace of revolutionary exhortation. But the fact that Engels thought it worthwhile to make a name in bourgeois-aristocratic military circles indicates that he expected those circles to survive for a while; and he and Marx discussed the war in their own candid correspondence, free from considerations of audience, as if they expected no revolutionary result. Surely, had Engels pinned serious revolutionary hopes on the war, he would not have greeted the Armistice of Villafranca with such good cheer. "Apart from the continuation of the war, we could have wished for nothing better than *this* peace," he informed Marx. "Prussia disgraced, Austria disgraced, Bonaparte disgraced, Sardinia and Italian vulgar liberalism disgraced, Kossuth disgraced . . . ," a host of villains had been embarrassed, and the only gainers were "the Russians and the revolutionaries."[3] Small enough gain from a war, if the war had really amounted to something.

The first of Engels' calling cards to the military establishment, *Po und Rhein* (written in February and March, 1859) maintained that Napoleon III needed a war, preferably for the Rhine, to bolster his position in France. Since a Bonapartist attack was imminent, it would not do for Austria (which in this instance represented German interests) to abandon northern Italy. "On the eve of war, as in war itself," Engels declared, "one occupies every useful position from which one can threaten the enemy and injure him" without regard to large moral issues. Nevertheless, Engels' intention of "defending the Rhine on the Po" was not to be confused with "the tendency of many German military and political figures to declare the Po, *i.e.*, Lombardy and Venetia, an indispensable strategic element and, in other words, an integral part of Germany."

Engels' principal target was this natural-frontiers theory. In commenting on Engels' pamphlet, Marx said that the nationalist tone of the opening was justified because in general the argument was a "victory for Mazzini" over the Frankfurt Assembly's support for Austria's hold on Italy; Engels had "enabled Germans for the first time to support Italian emancipation with a clear conscience."[4] Engels assailed the theory of natural frontiers as inimical to German interests. If Germans could demand the Adige and Mincio with the bridgeheads Peschiera and Mantua, France could reasonably demand the Rhine from Basel to its mouth, together with all the bridgeheads on the right bank; and the "natural frontiers" of Reuss-Greiz-Schleiz-Lobenstein might stretch from the Po and Mincio to the Vistula. The languages and sentiments of the great European peoples must determine the frontiers; "military considerations," Engels argued, "can have only a secondary relevance."[5] Germans had conquered Italy before they held the Adige and Mincio (in 1848 Engels had derided comparisons of Frederick Barbarossa and "Radetzky Barbabianca"; now he appropriated the successes of both to strengthen his argument), and could do so again if necessary. Only if German armies would be beaten wherever they showed their faces was it necessary to hold the passes permanently.[6]

Contrary to the fears of the natural-frontiers theorists, an independent and united Italy would not fall under French domination. France could be relied upon to alienate the Italians, and whether or not Germans held Lombardy, they would have significant influence in Italy *"so long as we are strong at home."* Engels advised German patriots that "instead of seeking our strength on foreign ground and in the oppression of foreign nationalities, we should do better to take care that we be *united and strong at home."* Engels concluded as he had begun, sweetening his recommendation that Italy be relinquished to the Italians with a dose of patriotic bluster, and even a quotation from Frederick the Great. Once Germany was united, "'our genius' will again be 'to attack'; and there will yet be rotten places where this will be necessary enough."[7]

When Engels composed his sequel to *Po und Rhein*, the war was over, and there was no longer any point in holding Austria's Italian possessions, even temporarily. But although it was fine for Austria to lose something, it was most undesirable that France should gain. Here Engels differed with Ferdinand Lassalle, who considered Austria the real villain; *Savoyen, Nizza und der Rhein* was a chance to "come to grips" with Lassalle on the Italian question. The partial unification of Italy, with payoffs to Napoleon III for his assistance, had to be opposed as a false solution.[8] To Engels, the real villain of the piece, as so often, was Napoleon III, who plotted with the Russians to overrun the Rhine. "Has the Rhine-land no other purpose than to be subjected to war, so that Russia may have a free hand on the Danube and Vistula?" Engels asked. He hoped that Germany would answer the question "sword in hand." Nice and Savoy might join France eventually, but it made a difference

> whether Savoy becomes French voluntarily, when Germany and Italy have achieved political and military unity and thus have greatly raised their standing in Europe, or whether a ruler bent on conquest, like Louis Napoleon, swindles it away from a still-divided Italy, in order to perpetuate his dominance over Italy and to establish at the same time a precedent for the theory of natural frontiers.[9]

As in *Po und Rhein*, Engels avoided the topic of revolution, mentioning only that unrest in Russia might hobble the onslaught from the East. Germany's chief enemies, the Tsar and Napoleon III, were also the revolution's principal foes, but Engels refrained from pointing this out to his audience of military experts. As we have seen, the two strategic pamphlets made a satisfactory impression, though some of the military felicities of *Savoyen, Nizza und der Rhein*—such as the predictions that France could best be invaded by way of Belgium, and best defended on the Marne—have become more striking to post-1914 readers than they were in 1860.[10]

While the Austrians were losing their war against Piedmont and France, Engels doggedly predicted Austrian victories and explained away Austrian defeats. With the single exception of Garibaldi's operations in the Alps,[11] Engels discussed the war in terms of opportunities presented to the Austrian forces. He set the tone on May 12, 1859: all the railroads in the world could not deliver the French to the scene of the action till the Austrians had battered the Piedmontese army for two full weeks. Unfortunately the Austrians wasted their chance.[12]

The Austrian loss at Montebello would never have occurred but for the chance arrival of a French division by train; the defeat had no results, and the Austrians had not wanted a victory there anyway; the French had been compelled to divide their forces, and the withdrawal had been carried out superbly.[13] Palestro on the Sesia (May 30) was insignificant, and Engels dwelt on the silliness of Victor Emmanuel's personal participation and on the poor composition of the Italian victory communiqué. Magenta (June 4) was almost an Austrian victory, strategically speaking. Even after Engels admitted that Magenta was a defeat, he reminded his readers that there had been no pursuit, so it was not *much* of a defeat.[14]

After discussing a series of glorious and promising Austrian disasters, Engels predicted a week before Solferino that soon the "lightning hidden in the clouds" would have to let go; the Austrians' superior position would have to take effect. At Solferino the lightning struck the wrong way; Engels concluded that the Austrian Emperor Franz Josef bore the sole responsibility. He had managed to outblunder Napoleon III.[15] But Engels did not abandon hope; on the day before the Armistice of Villafranca, the *Tribune*'s readers were informed that the Austrian position promised an Austerlitz, with the Austrians on the winning side.[16]

The Italian War was too short to drive Engels to the point of impatience and frustration that the long Crimean stalemate had achieved, but his comments on events in Italy showed some of the same connoisseur's disgust that marked his Crimean outbursts. Before Magenta, he complained that the war continued "to maintain its pre-eminence in the annals of modern warfare for slowness." He declared, "we almost seem to be transported back to those antediluvian times of pompous and do-nothing warfare, to which Napoleon put such a sudden and decisive end."[17] Despite the effusions discussed in Chapter Five, the Italian War was on the whole a poor affair, and not much missed.

When Garibaldi's volunteers, and eventually the Piedmontese government, moved to follow up the gains that had been made in the North, Engels backed the Italian nationalist cause without hesitation. No longer was the cause tainted by alliance with Napoleon III, or directed against a German power. Indeed, an increase in Italy's strength would make her less subject to French domination. Engels' letters to Marx expressed trepidation at Garibaldi's apparent rashness, while his journalistic comments radiated confidence; but his support for Garibaldi was entirely consistent.[18] Garibaldi had come in for his share of abuse as a putschist, vulgar democrat, and associate of Willich, but in action he was superb.

Although Garibaldi's enterprise was admirable, it did not promise to produce the European revolution. If Franz Josef tried to rescue the Neapolitan Bourbons there would be disorder in Austria, but even if the Austrian state collapsed, no revolution seemed likely.[19] The unification of Italy was a useful thing, since it would remove one more tiresome national issue from the world agenda, making room for social and economic issues; but like other limited wars, it fell far short of the level needed to demolish the existing world order.

Italy and the Crimea had roused contradictory pangs of hope, but rebellions and repressions in the colonies did not offer even the illusion of revolution. The great Indian Mutiny of 1857 remained a remote affair. To be sure, Engels practiced his riding, and in

November, 1857, assured Marx: "in 1848 we said, Our time has come, and in a certain sense it did come; but this time it is coming completely—this is it"; but the source of Engels' optimism, and of Marx's hope that "the 'mobilization' of our persons" was imminent, was a promising commercial crisis.[20] When the crisis faded and Engels admitted that "it all looks damned optimistic," he pinned his faint hopes for a new commercial setback on Indian and Chinese overproduction. India was peripheral, important only as it affected the European situation.[21] A revolution there would distract England, so that the British would not be able to move against a European revolution; "India, with the drain of men and bullion it will cost the English, is now our best ally," Marx declared.[22]

Unable to defend the atrocities committed by his Sepoy allies, Marx recounted the iniquities of East India Company rule, and declared that "the outrages committed by the revolted sepoys" were

> in a word, such as respectable Englishmen used to applaud when perpetrated by the Vendeeans on the "Blues," by the Spanish guerrillas on the infidel Frenchmen, by Serbians on their German and Hungarian neighbors, by Croats on Viennese rebels, by Cavaignac's Garde Mobile or Bonaparte's Decembrists on the sons and the daughters of proletarian France.[23]

But Engels' military reportage approached the struggle entirely from the British viewpoint. British commanders were praised when they moved correctly and criticized when they moved slowly or ineptly; the emphasis was always on what the British ought to do.[24] And save for some derision at the self-proclaimed heroism of the British, the private comments ran parallel to the public ones.[25]

Despite their sympathy for the Indians, Engels and Marx considered the revolt futile and doomed. Marx pointed out that the Indian Army gave the Indians their first instrument for nationwide resistance to the British, but Engels judged the rebel forces incompetent, capable only of a superficial imitation of Western military science. As the rebel field forces dispersed,

Engels declared that the remaining scattered resistance was devoid of military interest.[26] Indian events that would produce no immediate impact on Europe were not worth very grave regrets.

An encyclopedia article on Afghanistan reflected the same orientation as the Indian Revolt pieces. Engels criticized Lord Elphinstone's leadership in the First Afghan War, but expressed no sympathy for the Afghans. No doubt he worked from British, rather than Afghan sources; but in any case, he and Marx had developed no arguments that would make the struggles of colonial peoples against their oppressors practicable—or even, in the long run, justifiable. Engels had supported the right of progress against stagnation in the *Neue Rheinische Zeitung,* and although he and Marx might rail against the colonialist powers' brutality and hypocrisy, they did not argue that these unfortunate conditions might be abolished.[27] Engels and Marx did not waste time or tears on causes that they deemed to be lost, and the colonial peoples were written off for the time being. Maximilian's ill-fated adventure in Mexico, even more than the Indian Rebellion, was considered a sideshow, important only as an episode in the career of Napoleon III, "the most classical conclusion to the farce of the lesser Empire."[28] As usual the European consequences were all that mattered, and they were not very great.

The American Civil War was taken much more seriously than the other extra-European conflicts. Engels wrote to Joseph Weydemeyer in 1864: "Your war over there is one of the greatest things that could happen in one's lifetime," and in 1867 Marx proclaimed hopefully that "as in the 18th century, the American war of independence sounded the tocsin for the European middle-class, so in the 19th century, the American civil war sounded it for the European working-class." To turn from the American war to Prussian politics was "to descend from the greatest to the smallest." Nevertheless, the war had little immediate relevance to revolution. It was important, but its importance was long-range, like that of Russia's emancipation of the serfs. In 1863 the outbreak of revolution in Poland could banish American events from the Marx-Engels correspondence for more than a month.[29]

Like the Indian Rebellion, the Civil War contributed usefully to economic distress in England; its prolongation was "highly desirable in the interest of Europe," and if England was so foolish as to intervene, John Bull would lack for corn as well as cotton.[30] Marx and Engels supported the progressive, industrial North against the reactionary, agrarian South, and helped to organize demonstrations against pro-Confederate tendencies in British policy.[31] Apart from the war's possible leverage on European economic conditions, the importance of the Civil War lay in the preservation of the Union, so that economic progress might continue unobstructed.

Sometimes Marx and Engels applied the 1793 model vision of war as a radicalizing force to the Union's war effort, but in this context they expected only a shift toward more resolute war measures. "To date we have experienced only the first stage of the war—*constitutional warfare*," Marx wrote in August, 1862; "the second act, revolutionary warfare, lies ahead." Chief among the "revolutionary" measures desired was the abolition of slavery; and, said Marx, "a single nigger-regiment would work wonders on the southern nerves." If Lincoln balked at abolition, "a sort of revolution" might be necessary, but New England and the Northwest would eventually prevail. "Revolution" throughout meant something different, and much less sweeping, than it meant in Europe; it was a means to victory, rather than a great social transformation.[32]

Even this unrevolutionary sort of revolution was not assured, and Engels feared that slack leadership might lose the war. In June, 1861, he predicted Union victory because the North had an edge in military manpower, and "the belligerence of the Southerners [was] significantly alloyed with cowardly backstabbing"; but soon he complained of "brave old Scott," and of "the slackness and stupidity that manifest[ed] themselves throughout the North." Where, he asked, could one find "revolutionary energy anywhere among the people?"[33] The trivial, nitpicking criticisms that the Forty-Eighter Fritz Anneke directed against the Union armies were insignificant, but it mattered that the South appeared to be more determined. The Confederate embargo on cotton and Southern guerrilla action in the border states showed determination, whereas "defeats don't spur these Yankees on, they put them to sleep." Engels complained that "the Southerners, who at least know what they want, seem like heroes to me in comparison with the flabby management in the North." He asked Marx, "or do you still think that the gentlemen in the North will put down the 'rebellion'?"[34]

Marx did think so. He had held aloof from Engels' orgy of pessimism, and though some of his observations (such as seeing General Pope as a "man of energy" and therefore a hopeful sign) went amiss, he clung to the larger shape of things more successfully than did his partner. "It seems to me," he cautioned Engels, "that you let yourself be guided a little too much by the military aspect of things." The South had an initial edge because of its very backwardness, and because it possessed a class of unpropertied adventurers who could be assembled rapidly into a warlike militia. As for the North, "a *bourgeois* republic, where swindling has so long ruled supreme" would naturally require time to find itself. The American events were earthshaking despite everything.[35]

Engels continued to grumble through 1862. In eighteen months of war, he said, the Union had succeeded only in demonstrating the incapacity or treason of all its military and civil authorities; though no doubt it was useful that the bourgeois republic had so thoroughly disgraced itself that it could never again be advocated seriously, save perhaps as a transitional device. By the end of December, however, Engels discounted the Northern disaster at Fredericksburg. Perhaps Marx's admonitions had taken effect, or perhaps Engels had by this time become inured to Union defeats. As late as February, 1863, he considered that despite increases in Northern armaments, "it look[ed] rotten in Yankeeland." And even in the summer, when Grant's operations at Vicksburg brightened the picture, Engels feared to predict success: "we have so often seen American generals operate well for two weeks, and then once more commit the greatest asininities," he complained, "that one can predict nothing as to their future movements."[36]

Finally in September, 1864, Engels expressed to Marx an unqualified optimism as to the war's outcome; and in November, he sent Joseph Weydemeyer a cheerful war commentary that echoed many of Marx's admonitions of 1862, generously excusing the Union's early difficulties on the ground that America's officers and much of her arms had been snapped up by the Confederacy at the beginning of hostilities.[37] Why had Engels sunk so deep into pessimism? In a decade of war watching, he had seldom seen the victory of the side he favored, so he was conditioned to expect disappointment; but Marx had observed the same wars, and shared Engels' distaste for the hypocritical aspects of bourgeois democracy, and Marx kept his head. Probably Marx's diagnosis was right: Engels paid too much attention to the purely military aspects of the war. He had cultivated an interest in war as a sort of game, and it offended him when the game was badly played. Eventually content won out over style (and the Union's military style improved, too).

Engels' sparse published comments on the Civil War revealed little of his distress and apprehension; making the best of things, he compared Bull Run to the early setbacks of the French revolutionary armies of the 1790s.[38] In the public discussions of the war, as in the letters, the North was the more progressive side; and in all the comments, the war promised only the most remote and eventual services to the cause of revolution.

An exception to the general pattern of wars that might, but more likely might not, launch the revolution, was the Polish rebellion of 1863. For once revolution was not a possible by-product of the struggle, but an inherent part of it. The conflict's location in the midst of Europe, the fact that it menaced the Russian citadel of European reaction, and perhaps the Poles' long identification with revolutionary movements convinced Marx that "the era of revolution" had been "fairly reopened." Marx renounced the "fond delusions and almost childlike enthusiasm" with which he and Engels had greeted the outbreaks of 1848, but he was clearly delighted. "Hopefully this time the lava will flow from East to West and not the other way around," he said, "so that we may be spared the 'honor' of a French initiative." Even Russia might be vulnerable to revolution this time. Engels agreed: "The chances of victory now outweigh those of defeat," he declared.[39]

This optimistic assessment was based, apparently, on the assumption that a sort of revolutionary contagion would occur. Poland would touch off local grievances all over Europe, as had the February, 1848, rising in Paris. If the unrest did not spread and the Poles remained isolated, they were doomed. After the Poles had held out for four months, and no sympathetic revolutions occurred, Engels suggested that a rising might still take place in

Berlin, where "the best possible kindling" was heaped up by the struggle between Crown and Reichstag over the military budget. (Bismarck was then collecting taxes without parliamentary authorization, and was not popular.) "As much as I despise the courage of our old friends the democrats," Engels declared, something might happen. If half the Prussian forces were on the Polish border and half on the Rhine, Berlin would be vulnerable to a coup. And here we come to the remarkable part of Engels' analysis of the situation: such a coup would be a *bad thing*. "Bad luck for Germany and Europe if Berlin comes to the head of the movement!" Engels exclaimed.[40]

Here was the prospect of a revolution controlled and tamed by those who began it. None of the processes by which revolution was to radicalize or replace its instigators seemed to apply. When Engels blamed the collapse of the Polish revolution on "the baseness of the German liberal *Spiessbürger*," and condemned "the dogs in the Prussian Chamber" for their lack of "perception and courage," he seems to have wished from the Berliners only a parliamentary resolution of some sort in favor of the Poles. A German revolution was simply not in the cards.[41]

Marx—not long after he had tried to dispel Engels' excessive pessimism about the American Civil War—clung to a misguided optimism about Poland. As late as September, 1863, he hoped that the Poles might set off the rest of Europe, particularly Germany. "Nothing can be accomplished with these dogs without bashing them from outside," he declared. In order to provide the requisite bashing, he endorsed the project of a Colonel Lapinski, who hoped to raise a symbolic legion to carry the German nationalist black-red-gold banner against the Russians in Poland. This would embarrass the Parisians, who had long been generous with lip service to Polish independence, and would determine if it was "still possible to bring the Germans to their senses."[42] Engels appears to have made no comment on Lapinski's scheme. After the first enthusiasm of February, 1863, his own assessments of the Poles' prospects were not encouraging. On Poland, Engels took a more sober and sensible stance than did Marx, whose optimism in this instance depended on unhatched revolutions that might distract the Russians. Engels summarized the Polish situation in November, 1864, in a letter to Weydemeyer: "It will be a long time before Poland is able to rise up again, even with help from outside, and Poland is absolutely indispensable to us."[43] Where wars had failed to rouse the revolution, so too the Polish uprising failed, worthy though it was.

Since the European revolution was proving remarkably difficult to ignite, it is not surprising that the Danish War of 1864 passed without arousing the least hint of optimism. Marx's prescient *Tribune* article of December 27, 1858, had suggested that "a little private war with Denmark as to Schleswig-Holstein" might "prove an exceedingly clever diversion, and create popularity at the cheap price of bleeding the mob."[44] Despite this perception of the Danish War as a counterrevolutionary diversion, undertaken with the Tsar's assent, Engels backed the German cause. He admired the needle-gun's effectiveness and the Prussians' valor, and when Palmerston threatened to intervene in Denmark's behalf, Engels set about advising the German military community as to British line tactics with the same thoroughness that he usually devoted to warning the British about potential French invaders. He was pleased to report that Krupp coastal batteries could pierce any ship in the British fleet.[45] Although he did suggest in 1863 that the struggle for the Duchies might be linked with an anti-Russian crusade in aid of Poland,[46] the Schleswig-Holstein question in 1864 seemed a minor episode in the politics of capitalist Europe. The excitement and revolutionary importance that the Schleswigers' struggle against the Danes had seemed to possess in 1848 could not be recaptured. The situation had changed, and so had Engels.

The approach of the Austro-Prussian War of 1866 aroused revolutionary enthusiasms second to none, but as the war turned out differently than Engels and Marx had expected, the hopes vanished swiftly. After the war ended, they reverted to the usual custom of considering it and its results in terms of the long-run prospects of revolution. All the immediate revolutionary expectations preceded the fighting, which upset them; and the predictions themselves were erratic as to the mechanism that might produce revolutionary results. As the war approached, it seemed to Engels most promising, almost an opportunity to end all opportunities. "If this chance escapes without being used, and if the people let this happen," he declared, "then we can quietly pack our revolutionary bags and commit ourselves to the study of abstract theory."

How was this great opportunity to present itself? Engels hoped that the Prussians would be thoroughly beaten, in which case either the Austrians would dictate peace in Berlin, toppling the Prussian regime; or Berlin would see an uprising before the Austrians arrived.[47] The martial exertions of the 1793 model and the general devastation of the 1917 model were both absent from the prognoses that Engels and Marx delivered in 1866. Apparently the regime was to vanish in a cloud of embarrassment as the Prussian Left, frustrated by four years of constitutional conflict, took advantage of the government's discomfiture. "If the collision really comes, then for the first time in history the development depends on what Berlin does," Engels concluded. "If the Berliners strike at the right time, everything can turn out well—but who can rely on *them*?" If war came and the Berliners proclaimed a republic, all Europe could be "overturned in two weeks," said Engels; "But will they?" Engels thought they might, and he looked forward to trying the authorities who had mistreated the revolutionaries captured after the Dresden rising of 1849. In the circumstances, even a triumph of the parliamentarians would have a revolutionary character, and would lead further.[48]

Engels was much less particular as to who began the revolution than he had been in 1863; presumably the same parliamentary democrats whom he had despised and feared to see in the lead three years before were now to set in motion great events. What mattered was that *someone* should begin; revolution was by no means an automatic consequence of war. Indeed, inactivity on the military front might generate unrest among the Prussian *Landwehr* troops, whom Engels believed to be unenthusiastic about the war. Left idle for three or four weeks, they would be "capable of anything"—their discipline would vanish, rebellion would spread like a forest fire, if only Austria refrained from attacking. Even after the war began, Engels saw the *Landwehr* as an impediment to Prussian operations, and a force that might "rebel after the disaster."[49]

Engels' belief that a Prussian defeat might lead to revolt explains his preference for an Austrian victory; in addition, he thought that the Austrians could win quickly, avoiding a prolonged stalemate that would benefit Napoleon III as the two German *Schweinehunde* bid against each other, proffering German territory in exchange for French support. Marx expressed a similar fear when he suggested: "Unless a revolution sweeps away the Habsburgs and Hohenzollerns (it is unnecessary to mention the lesser dung-beetles), we shall end up with a Thirty Years' War and a new partition of Germany."[50]

In examining the consequences of a bloody stalemate or a Prussian defeat, Engels and Marx overlooked the possibility of a sudden and overwhelming Prussian victory. Marx contended that since the "second Jena" that Engels had promised *might* have happened, Engels had proved himself a prophet,[51] but Engels' prophecies in 1866 were singularly inaccurate in terms of what actually occurred. Reviewing the approaching conflict in the *Manchester Guardian*, Engels said that the Prussians would lack a united command, while the Austrians were "under the unconditional command of General Benedek, an experienced officer who, at least, knows his mind." Despite the Prussians' better logistics and armaments, the Austrians' experience and their more open tactical formation gave them the edge.[52]

News from the front persuaded Engels that Prussian morale was better than he had expected. Convinced that they were fighting for the unification of Germany, "the hitherto sullen and sulky men of the reserve and Landwehr then crossed the frontier of Austria with loud cheers." Nevertheless "the greater portion of whatever success they have had" was due to their superior rifle. "If they ever get out of the difficulties into which their generals have so wantonly placed them," Engels said, "they will have to thank the needle-gun for it."[53]

Engels marveled at the speed with which the Prussians followed up their initial successes. Even allowing for the needle-gun's terrible effectiveness, the Prussian feats were remarkable. He continued, however, to condemn the Prussian strategy, which divided forces and carried out the invasion of Bohemia along widely separated routes. Engels said that such a scheme ought to have disqualified its proponent from a lieutenant's commission; it was the same blunder that had led to the Italian disaster at Custozza in 1849. Moltke's policy of dividing his forces and operating on exterior lines of communication would be justified only if Bohemia were entirely unoccupied by Austrian forces. Engels' denunciation of the Prussian strategy was published on the day of Königgrätz, and he had to remark wonderingly afterward that the Austrians had so managed things that for practical purposes Bohemia was indeed unoccupied. Austria's blunder, plus the needle-gun and the "terrible tactical energy" of the Prussians, had nullified Moltke's "signal strategic blunder."[54]

Once the war had come to its surprising conclusion, Engels and Marx turned promptly to the political consequences of the Prussian triumph. The now-or-never aberration of Engels' June 11 letter was forgotten, and Marx assessed the war's results in terms that recalled the ungrudging acceptance of the Italian War's end. "Next to a great defeat of the Prussians, which perhaps (but for the Berliners!) would have led to a revolution, nothing better could have occurred than their tremendous victory." At least the war had been quick, and Napoleon had therefore been unable to meddle in German affairs.[55]

Besides, the new arrangements in Germany would eventually force Bismarck to rely on the bourgeoisie as well as the army, and might lead to a reopening of the social question.[56] Marx and Engels despised those who fawned on Bismarck after his success,[57] but it was necessary to accept the *fait accompli,* "we may like it or not." They objected to Wilhelm Liebknecht's staunch refusal to acknowledge the fact of the Prussian triumph; it was unfortunate that Germany should be submerged in Prussianism, but the new centralization would eliminate the need for risings in all the petty capitals. "Thus," Engels concluded, "in my opinion we have no choice but to accept the situation, without approving it, and to use as much as we are able the greater facilities which must necessarily be offered for *national* organization and unification of the German proletariat."[58] The Austro-Prussian War ended, after all, as another episode in the history of capitalist Europe. Its ultimate role was to smooth slightly the path of revolution—in the future.

The Franco-Prussian War destroyed the Empire of Louis Bonaparte and touched off the Paris Commune, rearranged the European balance of power, and greatly modified the classical Marxist view of war's relationship to revolution. But despite the scale and impact of the war, it aroused in Engels and Marx no more hope of an immediate general European revolution than the Sepoy Rebellion. In assessing previous wars, Engels and Marx had eventually resigned themselves to accepting gradual, eventual consequences in place of an immediate revolutionary payoff. In 1870 they applied a patient, cautious analysis from the beginning.[59]

The stance of Engels and Marx on the war is at first sight somewhat confusing: they began by supporting Germany (or at least opposing France), and then became the most vigorous supporters of the French in the war's second stage. But if we bear in mind that Engels and Marx dealt in terms of lesser evils as they confronted the power struggles of the capitalist world, the reasons for their modified position are obvious. Save perhaps for the Tsar, who was farther away and beset with internal problems, Napoleon III had been Europe's prime bogeyman for two decades, and anyone who opposed him was a lesser evil; once he was gone, the French Government of National Defense became the lesser evil as compared to Bismarck.

The primary role ascribed to Napoleon III in whatever was happening in Europe explains the belief that confusion over the Spanish throne made war *less* likely.[60] Confusion in Spain was expected to distract Napoleon III from his long-plotted assault on the Rhine. When the war broke out, Marx declared in his First Address on the War that "the war plot of July 1870 is but an amended edition of the *coup d'état* of December 1851." Already Marx accused Prussia of a counterfeit Bonapartism of its own, and of collusion with Russia; he warned that if the German workers allowed the war "to lose its strictly defensive character and to degenerate into a war against the French people, victory or defeat [would] prove alike disastrous." Having issued that warning, Engels and Marx continued to support the war till Sedan. Engels blamed French chauvinism for allowing Napoleon III to start the war, and said that the French needed the chauvinism knocked out of them.[61]

Engels praised the exploits of "our soldiers," and Marx agreed that the French needed a beating. A Prussian victory would represent "the centralization of state power, useful to the German working class," and the international preponderance of Germany would shift the center of gravity of the international workers' movement from France to Germany, establishing the dominance of Marxist theory over Proudhonist.[62] It should be noted that these notorious remarks, so beloved by the Red Prussian school of Marx criticism, justified support of Prussia in terms of the advantage of the world revolutionary movement, as did Engels' similar obser-vations three weeks later. Germany's defeat would secure the position of Bonapartism for years, said Engels, while Germany would be *kaputt* for years, perhaps for generations—no hope of an independent workers' movement, all energies absorbed in the national struggle. If Germany won, on the other hand, the German workers could "organize themselves on a much different national scale than before," while the French, "whatever sort of govern-ment [might] result," would "surely have a more open field than under Bonapartism."[63]

All these speculations on the likely postwar balances among the workers' movements demonstrate very clearly that Engels and Marx expected the workers' movements to remain *movements* after the war. Marx wrote cryptically to Paul and Laura Lafargue that the war would have consequences unexpected by the officials on either side, but the consequences did not, apparently, include a general revolution. A German victory would be a good thing, since the fall of Napoleon III would produce a revolution in France, said Marx; but since he mentioned the revolution so casually, as a minor argument in favor of a German victory, he clearly meant a republican revolution, not a socialist one. A German defeat would cause a twenty-year setback. Marx thought it useful that workers in both countries protested the war; the class war was so developed that war could not turn back the wheel of history.[64] War appeared as a species of misfortune, which threatened to impede the course of progress by stirring up chauvinism—and this was a preview of Engels' and Marx's subsequent thinking on the subject of war and revolution. The theoretical implications were not yet followed up, since the events of the Franco-Prussian War demanded too much attention.

If a German defeat would be a bad thing, so too would an excessively great German victory. Although building a policy around opposition to Bismarck's national achievements—as Wil-helm Liebknecht tried to do—was foolish, Engels suggested even before Sedan and the proclamation of the French Republic that Liebknecht's quixotic stance (*Prinzipienreiterei*) had its uses. Whatever his faults, Liebknecht held himself aloof from wartime chauvinism. Though the movement in Germany could not preach total abstention from a defensive war, it must oppose annexations and work for an honorable peace as soon as a nonchauvinist, republican government appeared in France.[65] It became less and less likely that the war would end as Engels would have liked, in a standoff with each belligerent admitting its inability to subjugate the other,[66] and as the war progressed the danger of a total German triumph loomed ever greater.

When Paris proclaimed a republic on September 4, 1870, Prussia ceased to defend Germany against Napoleon III. Marx's Second Address to the General Council of the International immediately demanded "an *honourable peace for France,* and the *recognition of the French Republic.*" Marx expressed his and Engels' position even more emphatically when he wrote that France fought not for independence alone, but for the freedom of Germany and Europe. (As Marx pointed out, the International was the only ally that the Republic found.)[67]

Just though her cause was, however, France did not fight for these things well enough. Though Engels and Marx supported the Republic strongly, their support was by no means uncritical. In the first place, the Republic was timed wrong. Engels wrote to Marx on August 10 that the Prussians might be bright enough to make peace with a republic, lest they bring upon themselves a new 1793, though "for the *élan* of 1793 to reproduce itself, and *effectively,* it would take the *enemies* of 1793, and—as you rightly say—other Frenchmen than those just emerging from the *bas empire.*" He wrote again on August 15 that a republic could cause the Prussians some trouble if, and only if, it was proclaimed promptly. But a revolutionary regime coming as late as August 20 would only "make a fool of itself by parodying the Convention"; now there was no reason for Bismarck to resist annexationist pressures and his own foolishness, and there was "no limit to German ambition except the doubtful limit of German moderation."[68]

As to the real military utility of a republic, Engels had no illusions. He was "curious" as to whether the military disasters would produce a revolt in Paris, but it was an idle sort of curiosity. A rising would do no real good; Paris could not be held. Once the republic was proclaimed, Engels complained that becuase German victories had "*given* them a republic—*et laquelle!*" the French demanded that the invaders should leave the sacred soil of France or face *guerre à outrance.* The notions of soil forever sanctified by 1793, and the "holiness of the word Republic," annoyed him. He shared Marx's view that the French suffered from an excess of memory and would have to rid themselves of their cult of the past.[69]

The glorification of 1793 that now confused the French was something that Engels himself had shared, and had fought free of with some difficulty. As he assailed the self-delusion and wishful thinking of the Republic, he recapitulated and elaborated on his repudiation of the 1793 model, nearly two decades earlier. He complained that the myth-intoxicated French had not yet had enough beating to satisfy them, and the Germans had already won far too much. As Engels saw it, prolonging the war would only underline the German triumph. "A couple of forts once taken," he said, Paris should "desist from a hopeless struggle," and capitulate to prevent "useless sacrifices."[70]

The defense of Paris promised only sacrifice, out of all proportion to the benefits gained. Engels compared its situation to that of Saragossa in 1808-9, since there was no real regular army force to defend the city.[71] In any case, the defense was a farce, as Marx claimed—conducted by Orleanists to exhaust and distract the populace.[72] The besieged city's commander, Trochu, had always advocated a long-service professional army, and Engels watched with ironic amusement as Trochu attempted to manage a force of untrained rabble.[73] Nothing useful should come of it.

To be sure, a "real national enthusiasm" on the part of the French might cause the invaders trouble (and here Engels praised the Spaniards of 1808); but such "national fanaticism" had "dried up in the money-making West of Europe," and "the twenty years during which the incubus of the Second Empire [had] weighed upon France [had] anything but steeled the French character." Therefore, Engels said, one could see "a great deal of talking and a minimum of work; a great deal of show and an almost total neglect of organization; very little non official resistance and a good deal of submission to the enemy; very few real soldiers and an immense number of Francs-tireurs." The reserve armies being raised in the provinces would be uselessly green, and in one *Pall Mall Gazette* article Engels confined himself to a discussion of the German forces on the ground that the "character of the [French] troops, who prove[d] themselves in all engagements more or less unfit for the field," took away "almost all interest in either their organization or their numbers."[74]

Engels' pessimism as to the Republic's military outlook did not make him and Marx cease to support the French. Great Britain's intervention against Prussia was demanded; the British could damage German maritime trade, and perhaps a British expeditionary force could stiffen the raw French levies, much as Wellington's forces had worked in Spain.[75] And as civilian resistance to the invaders increased, Engels defended the population's right to take arms and condemned the German reprisals, invoking the Prussian resistance to Napoleon in 1813.[76]

Finally, cautiously, Engels began to concentrate on the military possibilities still available to the French. In October, 1870, he had contended that in the unlikely event of a great outburst of national enthusiasm, "everything might still be gained" by raids harassing the invaders' long lines of communication and supply, and forcing Moltke to detach large enough numbers of troops to let Bazaine escape from Metz. (Prince Friedrich Karl also thought the German forces overextended, and said that if Bazaine had not capitulated, he would have had to raise the siege of Paris.)[77] Metz fell, but Gambetta's exertions raised up new armies and new hopes. Engels did not again suggest that everything might yet be gained, but in contrast to his earlier belief that the French should spare themselves needless sacrifices, he began to suggest that continued efforts might be worthwhile.

The fortifications around Paris had given France "some two months of breathing time, which, under less disastrous circumstances, would have been invaluable and [might] even now turn out so," Engels said, and had in addition "given her the benefit of whatever chances political changes may bring on during the siege." Furthermore, the new Army of the Loire must be more formidable than expected, judging from the caution with which Moltke moved against it; a new spirit showed itself in the French nation and army.[78]

Through December, 1870, and January, 1871, Engels contended that time was working in favor of the French. The Prussians were tiring,[79] and in the race of reinforcements which the war had become, the French chances were "immensely more favourable" than they had been in September. "If we could say with safety that

Paris will hold out till the end of February," Engels said, "we might almost believe that France would win the race." The new *Landwehr* call-ups would be both older and younger than usual, and the German philistine might lose his appetite for conquest when personally summoned to the colors. "Thus," Engels told his readers,

> we make bold to say that, if the spirit of resistance among the people does not flag, the position of the French, even after their recent defeats, is a very strong one. With the command of the sea to import arms, with plenty of men to make soldiers of, with three months—the first and worst three months—of the work of organization behind them, and with a fair chance of having one month more, if not two, of breathing-time allowed to them—and that at a time when the Prussians show signs of exhaustion—with all that, to give in now would be rank treason. And who knows what accidents may happen, what further European complications may occur in the meantime? Let them fight on, by all means.[80]

This was far from an enthusiastic invocation of the *levée en masse*. It was not expected that the Prussians would be thrown out of France; but perseverance in the conflict might enable France to gain better terms and mitigate her disaster, and Europe's.

Engels later pointed out one way in which the situation might have been improved. The two weeks after the fall of Metz (October 27, 1870) were "the critical period of the war," for the 120,000 Germans formerly occupied around Metz could now be sent to tighten the ring around Paris. The French ought to have struck at the besiegers of Paris, even with "such young troops as France then had available," before the additional German forces arrived from Metz. Raising the blockade of Paris "would have exerted a pressure on Europe, and could have meant an honorable peace." Moral and material consequences would have been enormous—Paris could have been reprovisioned, and time won for the formation of the new armies in the provinces.[81] Had the opportunity not been missed, no great French victory would have resulted—only the limitation of the defeat.

But limiting the extent of the disaster was important enough that

Engels apparently sent the Government of National Defense a plan for the relief of Paris. The nature of Engels' plan remains obscure, since Paul Lafargue's mention of the plan in 1891 upset both Engels and the German socialists, and after Engels' death his literary executors destroyed the relevant papers lest they serve as pretext for a renewed persecution of the Social Democrats in Germany.[82] Nicolaievsky and Maenchen-Helfen conclude that Engels' "underlying idea must have corresponded exactly with the plan that Bourbaki's army tried to carry out in December, 1870," and that "the coincidence may have been more than accidental." Since Engels had emphasized the length and vulnerability of the German supply lines, it is entirely possible that his suggestion coincided with Bourbaki's effort to relieve Paris by swinging north to threaten the Prussian rear.[83] It is also possible that the Government of National Defense arrived at the Bourbaki offensive's direction by process of elimination, after efforts in all other directions had failed. Whether or not he deserves the credit (or blame) for Bourbaki's offensive,[84] it is significant that Engels supported the French Republic so strongly that he probably tried to render it military assistance.

A week before the fall of Paris, Engels still contended that the French would get more reinforcements than the Prussians in the next two or three months, and he took a similar line while admitting that Bourbaki's defeat was a decisive setback, and the fall of Paris imminent. The article that appeared on the day of the capitulation of Paris asked whether France should now give in, but gave no answer. Finally, after assessing the results of the armistice and of the passage into Switzerland of the last shattered fragments of Bourbaki's army, Engels concluded that the moral constitution of the French nation was broken. There could be no further resistance, and he announced the end of his "Notes on the War." Even after this final article, he raised the possibility that brutal peace terms might incite renewed resistance; and he judged that the situation was not entirely hopeless, at least from a material standpoint.[85] As in 1849, Engels was reluctant to give up.

But never, in his articles on the Franco-Prussian War, had Engels held out false hopes. He had painstakingly listed the possibilities open to the French, but he had not predicted that the French *would* grasp them. He had pointed out initially that the French could expect to win the war only if the long-service Bonapartist army scored quick successes before the Prussians were fully mobilized, and as Sigmund Neumann points out, he was "the only European observer to predict the strategy which led to Moltke's decisive victory at Sedan."[86] The cheery confidence in his own powers of analysis that Engels expressed as he sent the first *Pall Mall Gazette* article to Marx ("Enclosed please find the Prussian plan of campaign") was fully justified. Not only did Engels avoid embarrassing predictions, such as those of 1866, but the London press paid him the compliment of plagiarism,[87] and Marx's daughters dubbed him "General."

Throughout the war, Engels and Marx had envisioned the war's effect on the prospects of revolution as remote and eventual. They feared that the Parisians might not agree, and might attempt a workers' revolution before the war ended. If the Paris uprising thus committed itself to national defense, Engels said, the workers would be uselessly butchered by the Prussians, and the revolutionary movements would be mired in chauvinism for twenty years. (Engels' own efforts to stave off the defeat of the Republic, in contrast, had not submerged the revolutionary in the national cause.) Marx was outraged by the follies of the International's branch which threatened to set up a commune in Paris; he might grumble that the Government of National Defense believed it could "conduct a revolutionary war without a revolution,"[88] but he did not seriously contend that a real revolution would do better in battle. The myths of 1793, which flourished so vividly in Paris, remained unacceptable to Engels and Marx.

Even after the war's end, when national issues ceased to blur the class lines of the struggle, the Commune seemed a hopeless cause. To be sure, Marx defended the Commune vehemently, and in a famous letter to Kugelmann he argued that revolutionaries could not always wait till they were absolutely sure of success. He also blamed the Commune's defeat on inadequate leadership, which might indicate that he thought better leaders might have achieved success. But a decade afterward, Marx contended that a compromise with the Versailles government was the best that could have been obtained, "with a little common sense."[89]

Engels' *Pall Mall Gazette* articles ended with the war, and his comments on the prospects of the Commune were sparse. We cannot determine whether he shared Marx's opinion, expressed on April 12, 1871, that an immediate march on Versailles might have saved the Commune. His own analysis of the military situation, presented to the International's General Council on April 11, was sober, picking out a few bright spots in a generally grim picture: since the Communards had their own artillery, Haussmann's broad streets (allegedly designed for the convenience of artillery-men dealing with riots) presented no tactical disadvantage; the insurgents could not be starved out; they were better organized than their counterparts in June 1848, and had already held out longer than in the June Days.[90] The Commune seemed already dead, ready to be set on a shelf next to the June Days in the revolution's collection of heroic defeats. Despite its importance as a laboratory of revolution and an inspiration to later revolution-aries, it offered little prospect of expanding into a general European revolt.[91]

The verdict on the Franco-Prussian War and its consequences has been rendered while the conflict was in progress. There were some benefits: the German workers had not been swept up completely in wartime chauvinism; the French proletariat had been schooled in the use of arms; and the center of gravity of the European workers' movement had been shifted to the German working class.[92] But the greatest change that the war brought was the annexation of Alsace and Lorraine to Germany. Engels and Marx had consistently opposed the annexation; now that it had occurred, European politics and the face of war itself assumed a new and more ominous aspect. After 1871, the revolutionaries could no longer regard war as an essentially neutral phenomenon, which might accelerate or delay the revolution in a remote, eventual way. After 1871 war became a Bad Thing for revolution, and a new period in classical Marxism's evaluation of war began.

CHAPTER 7

War an Impediment to Revolution, 1871-1895

After the Franco-Prussian War and the German annexation of Alsace and Lorraine, Engels and Marx regarded war as a threat to the progress of socialism. War had previously seemed undesirable on occasion;[1] now it was consistently deplored and feared. A war in Europe would almost certainly pit against each other Germany and France, the two nations with the most promising workers' movements. The revolution's hopes would be submerged, at least for a time, in a flood of wartime chauvinism. If Germany made an honorable peace with France, Marx and Engels predicted in 1870, then all would be well. Germany's new prominence would produce a German war with Russia, ending reactionary Muscovite domination of Europe. But if Alsace and Lorraine were annexed, France would side with Russia in the inevitable confrontation, and it would be "superfluous to enumerate the unpleasant consequences." The socialists were unable to prevent the annexation, and for the remainder of their lives they enumerated the unpleasant results that a war would bring.

The Franco-Prussian War made war more likely, as well as less desirable. Just as the Austro-Prussian War of 1866 had made inevitable the war of 1870, so that war bore a new conflict in its womb. Prussia ought to have learned from Tilsit that a great power could not be kept down, and that annexations would not ensure peace.[2] Marx and Engels predicted that Alsace-Lorraine would become a "western Poland,"[3] and despite all their past and future declarations of support for the Poles, it was clear that a *new* Poland, which would unsettle the peace of Europe, was not a welcome thing.[4]

Although a clash between France and Germany was the

ultimate nightmare, Engels and Marx spent little time worrying that a French war of revenge would touch off the conflagration. Instead, they feared that France would be drawn into a conflict instigated by the perennial menace to the East. Russia had long been the arch-villain in international relations; now Napoleon III was no longer able to upstage her. The likelihood of a Russian war against Germany appeared so great that Marx could write of it as something that might as well be concluded promptly. A Russian War might finally terminate the series of events, all unprofitable to revolution, that had occupied Europe since the foundation of the Second Empire of Napoleon III. Everything in that period had served, unwittingly, to "work out the 'national' goals of 1848—Hungary, Italy, Germany!" It seemed to Marx that "this sort of movement" would end only when Germany and Russia had clashed.[5]

Making a virtue of necessity, Marx declared in 1870 that war with Russia was the *"best result"* of all the Franco-Prussian War's consequences, for it would end Russian support for reactionary Prussian policies within Germany. Once Russia ceased to back the *Junkers,* Germany would cease to be dominated by Prussianism. And even after the annexation of Alsace and Lorraine, Marx could regard the "general European war" as unavoidable. Unavoidable things are to be analyzed, not regretted; "we must go through it," declared Marx, "before any decisive foreign effectiveness of the European working class can be thought of."[6] Engels, too, tried to look on the bright side: another war and another German victory would at least complete Bismarck's Bonapartist triumph and allow decline and disillusionment to set in. Even so, it would be better if a Berlin revolution broke out before new Sedans were won.[7]

Even here, as Marx and Engels came closer to advocating war than at any other time after 1870, they saw war as something to be endured. It was not desirable in itself, and would not speed the revolution; but if it was inescapable, Europe might as well get it over with. Usually, however, Engels and Marx were less resigned to war's inevitability. Even in 1870 they suggested that war might be avoided in "the unlikely event of the previous outbreak of a *revolution in Russia*."[8]

Two decades later, Engels was more sanguine as to the likelihood of a Russian revolution, and declared:

all this danger of a general war will disappear on the day when a change of things in Russia will allow the Russian people to blot out, at a stroke, the traditional policy of conquest of its Tsars, and to turn its interest to its own internal vital interests, now seriously menaced, instead of dreaming about universal supremacy.

Thus Engels, who had formerly preached war as a stimulus to revolution, now praised revolution as a means of avoiding war. The Russian Revolution would deprive Germany of her allies against the French Republic (Austria and Italy having been driven into German arms by their fear of Russian encroachments on Constantinople); Germany would be forced into a conciliatory settlement on Alsace-Lorraine, and Europe could disarm.[9] Peace might be preserved even without a revolution, since Russia's ability to make war was lessened by financial difficulties, poor rye harvests, and cholera.[10] Engels studied all these phenomena with great interest, though he would have preferred a revolution.

Two more factors worked to postpone the outbreak of war: "First, the incredibly rapid improvements in firearms, in consequence of which every newly-invented arm is already superseded by a new invention, before it can be introduced into even *one* army," and second, "the absolute impossibility of calculating the chances, the complete uncertainty as to who will finally come out victor from this gigantic struggle." Engels told interviewers that war's unpredictability helped to maintain the peace,[11] and he was glad of it. "If only peace lasts, thanks to the general fear of the war's outcome!" he wrote to Bebel in 1891. As in 1848 and 1849, he counted on war's ability to escape the control of those who began it; but now he hoped that the diplomats would recognize the perils that confronted them, and would avoid war. "A war? It is child's play to start it. But what will become of it, once begun, mocks all calculation," he warned. Peace was preserved only by the continuing revolution in military technology and the uncertainty that it produced.[12]

No diplomat wanted more than a sham war, Engels wrote to Sorge in 1888, "but once the first shot is fired, control is at an end, the horse can bolt." It seemed most unlikely that a war could remain localized.[13] A peripheral war that did stay on the periphery, such as the Russo-Turkish War of 1876-78, could be analyzed with the detachment that had pervaded Engels' war commentaries before 1871. Engels grumbled at the Turks' incompetence; they had a modern army for battle, but moved and provisioned it like a swarm of Spahis.[14] The only relevance of the war for the revolutionary cause lay in the prospect that the Russians' incompetence might generate enough disgust with the Tsar's government to accelerate developments in Russia.[15] Remote and minor military events might affect the revolutionary situation (as the Sino-Japanese War of 1893-94 might result in the inundation of the European labor market with a flood of coolies, disrupting the economic system[16]), but the most likely war was a big one.

A major war *would* produce the revolution. Marx saw the Russo-Turkish War as the start of "a series of wars ('localized' and finally 'general')" that would speed the development of the social crisis, and Engels spelled out the future with admirable clarity. The only possible war that could involve Germany, he said, was a world war:

> indeed, a world war of unprecedented extent and violence. Eight to ten million soldiers will strangle one another, and in the process will eat all Europe more bare than any swarm of locusts. The devastations of the Thirty Years' War, compressed into three or four years and extended over the whole continent; famine, pestilence, general barbarization of armies and peoples alike through extreme want; irreparable derangement of our artificial machinery in trade, industry, and credit, ending in general bankruptcy; collapse of the old states and their traditional wisdom, such that crowns by the dozen will roll in the streets and none will put them on; total impossibility of predicting how it will all end, and who will emerge victorious from the struggle; only one result absolutely certain: general exhaustion and the establishment of the conditions for the final victory of the working class.[17]

Here was the collapse theory, presented in striking detail. The revolutionaries would take over the rubble, their triumph assured by war's devastation. War would bring the revolution; nevertheless Engels did not hail the war, but feared it.

The war would mean unprecedented slaughter; it would be the last war as well as the end of the capitalist system. Politically, militarily, economically, and morally, the class state would collapse. "*Après nous le déluge*," bourgeois politicians were accustomed to declare; but after the deluge would come the socialists. The apocalypse would bring the revolution and would end at last the miseries of the exploitative system. But Engels concluded, "It is not necessary."[18]

War was unnecessary because *peace* would bring the revolution just as surely, and much less painfully. "We are advancing so famously everywhere that a world war now would be inopportune for us," Engels wrote in 1885. The movement needed no particular New Year's wishes for 1886, for it was "going forward everywhere—differently according to place and people—but everywhere famously forward." Fortunately, said Engels, continued peace seemed likely.[19] "It is to be hoped that the war clouds will blow away," he wrote in 1888;

> everything is going so nicely according to our wishes that we can get along very well without the disruption of a general war—and such a colossal one as there has never been before—although in the long run this too would have to work out in our interest.

Wishing Wilhelm Liebknecht a happy 1888, Engels hoped for peace on both foreign and domestic fronts: "I want neither war nor *putsch*, everything is going too well for that." In Germany, he declared four years later, peaceful development would mean a socialist victory "under the *most favorable* conditions"; in a war, the socialists would have to take undesirable risks. Engels' analysis remained constant throughout his later years; war, he concluded, "may after all delay our victory, and the other road is safer."[20]

This "other road," leading to a revolutionary victory without the need to pass through a world war, will be explored in detail in Chapter Nine. At this point it should be sufficient to note that the peaceful alternative existed. Promising signs abounded; Engels awaited the death of Wilhelm I in Germany, delighting in the prospect that the reign of Friedrich III would be rendered short and uncertain by throat cancer (the disease that killed Engels

himself eight years later).[21] In 1890 he noted that the departure of
the old triumvirate of Wilhelm, Moltke, and Bismarck left the
Reich in wonderfully shaky condition. He had already predicted
that Wilhelm II would make the German Empire ridiculous.[22] The
Russian monarchy was also wavering at the top, and the only
question was which socialist party would have the first opportunity—possibly the Austrians, usually the French formed the
advance guard, but the disciplined mass of the German party
would strike the deciding blow.[23]

The German Social Democrats had weathered Bismarck's
antisocialist law (in force 1878-1890), and could not be stopped
unless new measures, "intellectual *mitrailleuses* and Maxim guns"
could be devised; but if Germany became involved in a two-front
war against Russia and France, the resulting "struggle for national
survival" would produce a wave of chauvinism and destroy the
German socialist movement for years.[24] Not only Germany, but all
the belligerents would be fighting for their lives, and France, too,
would be swamped in chauvinism. "Such a war," Engels declared
in 1882, "would, I believe, postpone the revolution for ten years,
after which, to be sure, it would be more thorough."[25] War might
provide a temporary respite for the beleaguered defenders of the
capitalist order; it would push back the revolutionary movement
all over Europe, destroying it completely in many countries and
stirring up national hatred; it would offer the revolutionaries only
the opportunity to start over from the beginning, "though on an
even more favorable basis than today." Especially the German
movement, Engels' special pride and joy, would be demolished in
war, while peace meant almost certain victory. "If there is a war,"
Engels wrote to Lafargue in 1889, "then—socialist movement, so
long for a while!"[26]

Even Russia, which had so often seemed a monolithic bastion of
counterrevolution, was the scene of promising developments that
war would interrupt. A Pan-Slavist war to save Tsardom would set
back the movement in both Germany *and Russia;* "the whole
achievement of the revolutionaries in Russia, who [were] on the
eve of triumph, would be useless, destroyed." Only war could
save the Russian monarchy, which tottered on the brink of its 1789.
"So I should want war? Certainly not," Engels declared.[27]

Everywhere war would disrupt useful developments. But war

would affect different nations in different ways. France, for example, would be unable to make a revolution once she engaged in war. France relied on the Russian alliance against Germany, and any French revolutionary initiative would be squelched by the Russians—who would, if necessary, join with Germany to restore "order" in France. Any wartime revolutionary movement in France would appear as treason, and would be futile.[28] On the other hand, Engels sometimes suggested that war might bring radical democrats to the fore in France, and that the rule of the radical democrats would disillusion the French workers and do wonders for their political sophistication. But if the French thus took the political lead in Europe, their chauvinist self-infatuation would grow to intolerable proportions. The revolutionary cause in France would not benefit from war, and the French must be made to see that a war against Germany, in alliance with the Tsar, was a war against the strongest socialist party in Europe.[29]

Engels did his best to persuade the French that a war against Germany would be a counterrevolutionary act, and in the process he revealed that wartime Germany would be governed by different forces than an embattled France. Writing in the French *Almanach du Parti Ouvrier pour 1892,* he promised that if no war occurred, the German socialists would come to power in ten years, begin the restoration of Poland, and allow the people of Alsace-Lorraine and northern Schleswig to determine their own destiny. But if Germany was attacked prior to the socialist takeover, the German workers would have to defend their country against the Russians and their allies. Engels quoted the *Marseillaise,* and said that the German workers would greet invaders as had the French *sans culottes* a century earlier.[30] This rhetorical flourish, directed at a French audience, was something less than a serious revival of the 1793 model, but in letters to Bebel and Sorge Engels suggested that although war might set the European socialist movement back twenty years, the German party might also come to the helm to expel the invaders, *à la Marseillaise,* and "play 1794" (or 1793).[31] Engels' resurrection of the 1793 model was extremely reluctant; attempting to seize power during a war was an undesirable risk. "I hope, above all, that peace lasts," he wrote to Bebel. The socialists did not need to go for broke, and war would force them to do just that. Much better to await the inevitable developments of peace;

but "if war came and brought us prematurely to the helm," it was necessary to be prepared.[32]

Engels declared, with some irritation, that of course he accorded the French socialists the same right of self-defense that he asserted for the Germans, but he saw no prospect of a German attack on France. If war came, the aggressor would surely be Russia, no matter how the outbreak of hostilities was managed, and Germany's defense would require the use of all available positions, including Metz and Strasbourg.[33] The importance of the German socialist movement led Engels to a genuinely defensist position. "Little as I want new Sedans," he wrote, "still less do I yearn for the victory of the Russians and their allies, even if the latter are republicans and have good reason to object to the Frankfurt peace." In war the German socialists, unlike their French counterparts, had a chance of coming to the helm, making Germany the "revolutionary center." If a Russian attack seemed imminent, the German Social Democrats would have to vote for military appropriations, embarrassing as it would be.[34]

Despite his reluctance to see Cossack hordes overrun Germany and demolish the German socialist movement, however, Engels' emphasis did not shift "from peace to the defense of the fatherland," as Bertram Wolfe contends.[35] Engels regarded his defensist article for the *Almanach du Parti Ouvrier* as a thankless task, undertaken to set the French workers straight as to the grievous results of a Franco-Russian assault on Germany. He declined to contribute to the 1893 *Almanach;* only the dire threat of war had compelled him to write the previous year's article, he said, when the French Republic had bowed down to the Tsar at Kronstadt.[36] (A French naval squadron had visited the Russian naval base in July, 1891, cementing Franco-Russian relations.) Thus his emphasis in defense was an effort to *preserve* peace, by warning potential aggressors and their potential accomplices.

As usual, the chief potential aggressor was Russia; France was cautioned as Russia's ally. Russia, like France, appeared immune to a revolutionary takeover in the course of war. In 1875, Engels described the outbreak of a Russian revolution as "very likely" during a Russo-German war, but he did not predict that the Russian left would take over the war effort. Instead he concentrated on the results that such a shock would have in Germany.

Usually a wartime rising in Russia was "to be expected only after very severe defeats of the Russian Army."[37]

Thus the 1905 model, in which military embarrassment would lead to revolt, was prescribed for Russia, while the 1793 model applied to Germany and no model at all applied to France. On one occasion Engels wrote that the workers of *whichever* nation lost the war would be duty-bound to start the revolution, and he once wrote that defeat would produce a "change of system" in Germany;[38] but he generally maintained his triple standard in evaluating war's consequences. His views were supported by revolutionary calculation, and cannot be dismissed as simple Germanic chauvinism: the Russian revolutionaries might stave off the war by a prompt success, but their real strength lay in the fragility of the government they opposed. They stood no chance if the Tsarist regime could strengthen itself by victory in war. In contrast, the victorious German rulers would confront the inexorably expanding German socialist movement, its hand strengthened by the wartime expansion of the army (as explained below in Chapter Nine, "Engels' Theory of the Vanishing Army"). After a German victory, Russia would be broken in the dust of defeat, perhaps in revolt, and would no longer be available as a potential savior of reactionary order in Germany.[39] Since the German revolution was inevitable, and was due sooner than any other, Germany's victory was the victory of the revolution.[40]

This emphasis on Germany's defense shaped Engels' uneasy ruminations on the course that war would take if no belligerent power enjoyed a revolution. War should be averted if possible, of course; but if the catastrophe occurred, a stalemate on the Western Front was the least of the evils. As in 1870, he hoped that Germany and France would fight to a standstill. He assured himself that the French were reasonably strong, propped up by their fortifications, and that there would be no quick triumphal march to Paris or to Berlin.[41] Germany could fend off a two-front assault for some time, and a deadlock in the West would let the German powers move against Russia; loss of the Polish forts would produce a rising in St. Petersburg, and all would appear in a new light to the *Herren Kriegführenden*.[42] Russia, though offensively weak, appeared "strong to impregnability on the defensive side," and in one fascinating letter of 1891 Engels approached Schlieffen's view that

France, more vulnerable to a knockout, should be dealt with first, leaving the more tedious Russian campaign for later. Unlike Schlieffen, Engels proposed that once France had been tamed, she should be given at least (!) Alsace and Lorraine as a peace offering, while Germany swept East and restored Polish independence, employing "revolutionary means."[43] Engels also differed from Schlieffen in expecting a long war, which England's control of maritime trade would eventually decide.[44]

Whether the world war would produce revolution by means of the 1793 model, the 1905 model, or the 1917 model—or not produce it at all—Engels hoped fervently that the war would not happen. His aversion to the needless devastation and unpredictable chances that war would mean is massively evident, and on a personal level he resented the time that renewed military studies, taken up at each crisis, robbed from his weary labors on the third volume of *Capital*. "I hope it doesn't come to war," he wrote to Sorge in 1888, "even though my military studies, which I've recently had to take up on account of the war-scare, will be for nothing."[45] He so feared war that in 1892 he wrote seriously on the desirability of European disarmament.[46] War, which had been so often and so variously invoked as the midwife of revolution, had become entirely unwelcome.

But Engels did not know how to stop it. The general strike, which Marx had referred to as "Belgian nonsense," seemed entirely ineffectual as a means of preventing war.[47] Engels, like Bebel, could only point out the impracticability of the general strike, without proposing an alternative. His activity was limited to warning all who would listen of the dangers of war, and to hoping vigorously that war would not occur. But disliking war was not enough; as Friedrich Adler said in 1912, "it unfortunately does not depend on us Social Democrats whether there is a war or not."[48]

Engels' emphasis on the need to protect Germany and its socialist movement from Tsarist assaults, and his tendency to make defensist statements to encourage the maintenance of peace, raise the question of what he would have done had he been faced with the dilemma of war. It is entirely possible that he would have supported the German war effort, though surely without the unconditional and embarrassing alacrity of the Social Democratic

Reichstag delegation in 1914.[49] When in 1891 Engels reluctantly advocated voting new military appropriations against the Russian threat, he insisted that the new monies be used to make the army more democratic, as well as stronger.[50] It is difficult to imagine him forgetting the revolutionary movement in the *Burgfrieden* and rallying round the flag. The defense of Germany was one thing, the defense of the Bismarckian state was another. And surely the defense of Germany would have seemed less pressing once the Russian advance was checked—Tannenberg, Brusilov's collapse, certainly the March Revolution in Russia would have changed the situation. Military disaster, on the other hand, would have driven him to contemplate a wartime seizure of power.

Perhaps, too, he would have remained detached, watching with regretful fascination as the war assumed the massive and devastating form that he had so clearly foreseen, and waiting for exhaustion to create a revolutionary situation. The prospect that war would burn itself out, permitting the forces of revolution to take over the ashes of Europe, had occurred often enough in his comments. The only conclusion that is virtually certain is that Engels, however he approached the war, would not have lost sight of his revolutionary goals, and would not have responded to the general collapse of Europe by attempting to revive bourgeois rule in Germany.

Since Engels died in 1895, before the catastrophe occurred, it is not possible to determine how he would have responded to the World War. His analyses of war's effect on revolution offered no clear program for use in case of war; the only real consistency in the war studies of Engels' last quarter-century is the constant conviction that the world and the revolutionary movement would be better off *without* war. Perhaps Engels' failure to formulate a coherent plan of action shows how totally the prospect of war baffled and terrified him: he feared the dilemma so much that he shunned it.

PART III

Armies and Revolution

CHAPTER 8

Military Forms and Military Efficiency

Engels and Marx saw armies as social phenomena, and often took care to place military developments in social context. Engels' anthropological work, for instance, stresses the importance of military organization in various tribal forms and in the transition to the state. Social forms produced corresponding military organizations, aptitudes, and styles. "This is what men and society were before the division into classes," he wrote, praising the courage of African tribesmen in combat against the British.[1] Athenians, he said, were ideal light infantry because of their intellectual development, while Spartans were fit only for the phalanx—a formation which in most of Greece was eventually made obsolete by "the influence of commerce and wealth, which undermined the ancient contempt for death."[2] Engels also discussed Marius' reforms of the Roman Army and the effect of *latifundia* on the Roman legion, and contended that the burden of service in Charlemagne's wars had destroyed the Frankish free peasantry.[3] In a passage foreshadowing Sombart, Marx observed that armies had pioneered in cash salaries, the division of labor, the employment of machinery, and other areas; he hoped that Engels would one day elaborate more fully the contributions of armies to economic history,[4] but Engels never did. Other applications of his military studies were more pressing.

Technology, as well as the broad social arrangements of a nation or era, affected the nature of warfare. Engels discussed the relationship between weaponry and tactics in his *Anti-Dühring*,[5] and paid close attention to the effects of technology on the warfare of his day, discussing the excellence of the needle-gun as a temptation to Prussian adventures,[6] the wretchedness of Russian railroads as a deterrent to Russian aggression, and the uncertainties of the arms race as a force promoting peace.[7] Occasionally he went wrong, as when he wrote that "all further improvements" in weaponry after the Franco-Prussian War would prove "more or less unimportant for field warfare," but his general emphasis on the material conditions of war was more important than his judgment in detail. The social and technical conditions of a period determined the possible modes of conflict:

> It is not the "free creations of the mind" of generals of genius which have revolutionised war, but the invention of better weapons and changes in the human material, the soldiers; at the very most, the part played by generals of genius is limited to adapting methods of fighting to the new weapons and combatants.[8]

There were, of course, a number of ways in which the new weapons and combatants of the later nineteenth century might be arranged. Since the effectiveness of armies affected international constellations of power and the revolutionary calculations based upon them, Engels' role as the General Staff of the revolutionary movement required him to study armies and their organizational systems with great care. And since the armies of the existing states formed the principal barrier to insurrection, Engels had to examine them as obstacles—and perhaps, as we shall see, as means—to revolution.

One answer to the problems of national defense under prevailing economic and technical conditions was the militia system, the favorite military scheme of nineteenth-century liberals. The militia was distinguished from other military forms by short-term universal service and by a tendency on the part of its advocates to assail alternative systems as "standing armies." Liberals' advocacy of the militia had been directed originally against the mercenary professional armies of eighteenth-century absolutism; pro-militia rhetoric against the "standing army" persisted despite a certain want of clarity as to what was "standing" about the Pussian-style mass army, most of which was demobilized in peacetime.[9] This semantic imprecision led in 1898 to a violent controversy in the German socialist press over the definition of the terms "militia" and "standing army."[10] Length of service and the nature of the officers were among the chief points of difference between militia and mass army; but the difference was a matter of degree, as Franz Mehring pointed out,[11] and the idea of the militia was less a set of institutions than an attitude, a determination to deprofessionalize the army.

Numbers and spirit were to make up for lack of training,[12] and the French *levée en masse* of 1793 and the German wars of national liberation against Napoleon were invoked to demonstrate the powers of relatively untrained enthusiasm. Advocates of militia systems also pointed to the absence of standing armies in Switzerland and the United States to demonstrate the practicality of their ideas; but military considerations were in general secondary to political ideals. Armies were to be civilianized, and defense was to become the affair of the nation rather than the business of a special caste or professional elite.[13]

In his very first discussion of army organization, the Elberfeld speech of 1845, Engels espoused the militia system. Unlike the liberals, Engels did not advocate introducing a militia in the existing bourgeois society; instead, he contended that one of the principal benefits to be expected from the introduction of communism would be the abolition of standing armies. A communist society, he explained, would wage no wars of aggression, and therefore would need no army to attack its neighbors; and in the event of a foreign attack, no standing army would be required for defense, "since it [would] be an easy matter to train every able-bodied member of society, in addition to his other occupations, to a practical, not parade-worthy, familiarity with arms, adequate to the defense of the country." Since any such defensive war would be waged *"only against anti-Communist nations,"* the citizens would fight for their freedom with such desperate passion and tenacity that the mechanical precision of conventional armies would be helpless against them. The French from 1792 to 1799, said Engels, had demonstrated the miracles that revolutionary enthusiasm could perform in defense of an illusion, a sham-fatherland that did not really benefit the workers; how much more powerful would be the defense of a tangible reality, a genuine workers' fatherland![14]

In this early assessment, Engels discussed the militia only as it would operate in a communist society, but he did not always rule out its employment in a bourgeois state. While a noncommunist state might not be able to rouse the same enthusiasm that Engels promised for a revolutionized system, a militia might nevertheless serve—less efficiently than in a communist society, but the difference would be a matter of degree. In its reliance on enthusiasm as a substitute for training and organization, Engels' 1845 Elberfeld speech shared the essential elements of the liberals' view.

Although Engels might conceivably have adopted the liberal position on armies in order to appeal to his largely bourgeois audience in Elberfeld, there is nothing in his writings of the next few years to indicate that his 1845 speech was insincere. The *Neue Rheinische Zeitung* of 1848-49 often expressed faith in the powers of untrained, spontaneous masses, though an element of prop- agandist cheerleading sometimes crept into the paper's military analyses.[15] Communist calls for arming of the people may be discounted as expressions of Engels' judgment on army questions; as Höhn suggests, they may have been intended to rally liberal support by annexing a traditional liberal demand, and they certainly served to embarrass the bourgeois liberal revolutionaries by forcing them either to arm potential enemies to their left, or to admit their dread of the masses.[16] Armament of the people was a political demand, not a military program, and amid the pre- occupations of the revolutionary year Engels did not take time to argue the case for a militia system as a means of national defense. Nevertheless, insofar as Engels' and Marx's statements touched on army organization, they expressed an inclination toward popular enthusiasm and toward militias.

In 1851, however, Engels reappraised the relationship between war and revolution, debunking the legends of 1793 and forsaking all reliance on unorganized enthusiasm. Revolutions, he observed, produced disorder, and disorder interfered with military effec- tiveness.[17] Engels' new stress on organization as essential to military success made him doubt the practicality of a system that relied on spontaneity and spirit as substitutes for order, and after 1851 he considered militias virtually useless under existing condi- tions.

The Swiss archetype of the militia system was singled out for dispraise in 1851. "Whoever has seen the awkward gait and uncomfortable appearance of a Swiss squad, or heard the jokes they crack with the drill sergeant while under drill," he declared, "must at once see that the military qualities of the men are but very poorly developed." The Swiss, "being rather slow-headed," required a good deal of drilling. Engels said that the army was no better at fighting than at marching; the low casualties on both sides in the Swiss civil war, the *Sonderbundkrieg* of 1847, proved that the army was not serious. Prussia's *Landsturm,* composed of the leftovers from the line army and the *Landwehr* reserve, was likewise useless: "if it should ever have to assemble, it would not be found fit for anything but police duty at home, and for a tremendous consumption of strong drink."[18]

The amateur Volunteer Movement in Britain was treated more kindly. Engels wished the Volunteers well, not because he hoped "that one day the English bourgeoisie and not the French *chasseurs* would have to face [their] rifles,"[19] but because they might be useful in repelling a Bonapartist invasion. "There has been one thing wanting to the volunteer movement, and that is a fair and intelligent, but plain and outspoken criticism by competent outsiders," Engels declared, and he undertook to provide the necessary criticism. His comments in the *Volunteer Journal* pointed out deficiencies, particularly among the officers, though in 1862 he told German readers that Volunteer maneuvers were no worse than European exercises directed by officers grown gray on the maneuver field.[20] The English were more fortunate than the Americans in having a competent regular army to provide leadership in the event of war, but Engels did not insult the Volunteers by "the stupid piece of flattery that they were fit to fight any troops in the world." Most specifically, he considered the Volunteers inferior to their prospective opponents, the French light infantry, though he was generally sympathetic to the Volunteers' efforts.[21]

As for the American version of the militia, Engels concluded in 1891 that all the wars that the United States had conducted with volunteer forces demonstrated the folly of inadequate organization. The supreme example was the Civil War, in which militia units had disappeared entirely by the end of the war, giving way to regular forces. Engels had come to this view long before;

criticizing a militia scheme proposed in 1868 by Cluseret (later one of the Commune's generals), he insisted that "the American War—militia on both sides—proves nothing but that the militia system demands unheard-of sacrifices in men and money." He asked "what would have become of the Yankees, if instead of the Southern militia they had faced a solid army of a few hundred thousand men?"

From his condemnation of militias in America he drew general conclusions. In a militia system, officers could be neither good nor respected by their men; training raw troops in action had been possible for Napoleon only because Napoleon had good cadres to start with, while the Yankees, who began without such a reliable core, had inadequate cadres even at the end of the Civil War. Certainly since the introduction of the breech-loader (whose rate of fire rendered obsolete the column deployment of the French Revolutionary period) the pure militia was obsolete. "Which is not to say that the rational military organization does not lie somewhere between the Prussian and Swiss systems—where?" He concluded: "That depends on the circumstances. Only a Communist society can approach the militia system, and that asymptotically."[22]

At the opposite pole from "the fantasies of a militia army with, as it were, no period of service at all," was the long-service professional force. Engels' dismissal of the militia led him to appreciate the advantages, "undeniable and beyond dispute," of its antithesis.[23] The pure form of the mercenary volunteer army was obsolete, possible only in such exceptional cases as England's (even there it had undesirable side effects, lowering the standard of the army's raw material and requiring longer training and more brutal discipline than in conscript armies).[24] So when Engels referred to the "cadre system," he meant the various "conscriptions and lotteries," essentially incomplete versions of universal service, which furnished the manpower for long-service armies such as the French.

The cadre system elected to train a limited number of men for several years, in preference to training a larger number of men for a shorter period. The cadre system's relatively small, elite force was of course less susceptible than a mass army to becoming infected by popular enthusiasms; and in addition to being a reliable counterrevolutionary force, it offered some military advantages. Particularly at the beginning of a war, the men of a standing force knew one another better than members of a newly mobilized reserve or militia unit, and would therefore have more cohesion when first coming under fire.[25] An army such as Prussia's, which depended on short-term training and a large reserve, would be "inferior to the old battalions and squadrons which, in the first onset, any of the great European powers can bring forward against it." Since a third of every Prussian line regiment had less than three years' experience, another third less than two years', and the last third less than a year's, it was not be expected that:

> an army composed like this can have those military qualities, that strict subordination, that *esprit du corps*, which distinguishes the old soldiers of the English, Austrian, Russian, and even the French armies.

English experts, he observed respectfully, considered "that it takes three years completely to break in a recruit."[26]

Engels expressed great respect for the cadre system, particularly during the years between his first serious military studies in the early 1850s and the Austro-Prussian War of 1866. When Prussia mobilized in 1859 in response to the war in Italy, Engels said that the first month of war would be highly dangerous to the Prussians, whose army would at first be inferior to the Austrians'. Prussia would be facing the long-service French army, which Engels considered even better than the long-service Austrian force.[27] The professionalism of the English army also attracted Engels' admiration; he pointed out that the "lads" of the Crimea averaged at least twenty-seven years of age.[28] The initial advantage conferred by the cadre system was the main reason for Engels' unfortunate forecast of an Austrian victory over Prussia in 1866; but by 1870 Engels had changed his mind about the relative merits of military systems. This time he picked the long-service French army to lose to the short-service mass army of Prussianized Germany.[29] The French professionals might still concentrate quickly and strike before Prussian mobilization was complete, but this initial advantage no longer seemed decisive. It offered the French their only chance of victory, and that chance was slight.

Even before the events of 1866 demonstrated that a Prussian-style army might work very well in practice, Engels had expressed some misgivings about the cadre system. "While it gives the troops actually serving a high degree of efficiency," he observed in 1855, the French system "does not prepare any drilled reserves for a case of emergency." Therefore:

> a great continental war, in which France would have to act with two or three large armies, would force her, even in the second campaign, to bring into the field many raw levies, and would show, in the third campaign, a very sensible deterioration of the army.

The Prussian policy of relying on large trained reserve forces, in contrast, made a country half again as strong as the French or Austrian system of recruitment. Only by means of such a universal service system could Prussia maintain herself as a power on a level with more populous (in 1865) neighbors such as France, Austria, and Russia. Engels went so far as to say that universal service was "such a tremendous advance beyond all previous military arrangements" that wherever it had existed, even in an incomplete form, it could never be abolished.[30]

After 1866, there was no question about it. In 1870 it appeared that the only way for Prussia's foes to outdo her was by imitating the Prussian system of army organization and carrying it to its logical conclusion:

> If a nation equally populous, equally intelligent, equally brave, equally civilized were to carry out in reality that which in Prussia is done on paper only, to make a soldier of every able-bodied citizen; if that nation limited the actual time of service in peace and for drill to what is really required for the purpose and no more; if it kept up the organization for the war establishment in the same effective way as Prussia has lately done—then, we say, that nation would possess the same immense advantage over Prussianized Germany that Prussianized Germany has proved herself to possess over France in this present war.

If humiliated by the peace, France would surely follow the course that Engels recommended, and might soon "astonish Prussia as much by the crushing number of her soldiers as Prussia has astonished the world this summer."[31]

Thus the Prussian universal service army, in a completed and idealized form, set the pattern for future armies (except perhaps in backward places such as Russia, whose educated classes were insufficient to provide officers for a mass army[32]). In Prussia itself, the army failed in practice to fulfill its professed role as the military school of the nation in arms,[33] but Engels hoped to see it evolve toward the rational arrangement that lay somewhere between the Prussian and Swiss systems, closer to the unattainable ideal of the true militia system. He complained that "Prussia, when adopting the principle that each citizen was to be a soldier, stopped half-way, and falsified that principle, thereby falsifying all her military organization." Once universal service had been adopted,

> mere cadres of officers and noncommissioned officers should have been maintained, through whose hands the young men should have passed for instruction, and the period of instruction should not have lasted longer than was necessary for the purpose.

The advantages of universal service recruitment were essentially incompatible with the precision of the long-service cadre system, and Prussia's insistence on drill ground polish could be met only by intense and tedious effort, even with three-year service.[34]

These comments on the Prussian universal service system show Engels, even before 1866, dismissing all considerations of spit and polish. The contrast with his criticism of imprecise marching by Swiss militia and British Volunteers is obvious. At times Engels came perilously near to that fetishism of useless ornamental drill and dress that Alfred Vagts considered the essence of militarism; at other times his views were entirely in accord with Vagts' "military way" of effectiveness rather than show.[35] Engels seems to have leaned toward the long-service professional force, with its shiny buttons and parade ground precision, under the influence of the orthodox military writers whom he studied, and as a result of his own reaction against the cult of unorganized enthusiasm; at the same time, he was drawn toward some of the advantages of the universal service mass army. His ambivalence was resolved by the Austro-Prussian War, which demonstrated that the Prussian mass army was the wave of the future. What remained was to consider variations of the Prussian model, and to discover the consequences that the general introduction of the Prussian system would produce for the revolutionary movement.

Within the general framework of the Prussian system, Engels consistently favored the shortest term of service compatible with military efficiency. Though he refused to consider the Prussian army-organization dispute of the early 1860s a matter of principle, Engels made it clear that he saw no strictly military need for more than two years' training. It made no difference to the workers whether soldiers served for two years or three, he said; the third year, which conservatives believed necessary to instill an obedient, disciplined spirit, taught the soldier only the art of cadging drinks from newer recruits and the habit of making fun of his superiors. Moreover, the extra year had no permanent effect on his politics.[36]

A precipitate reduction of the term of service below two years might be dangerous, he admitted in 1865. But eventually, as he had argued a decade earlier, no more than a year should be "necessary to the purpose" of training infantry. In a country without a ready-made supply of horsemen, cavalry would require four years' experience. They would inevitably be reactionaries, but since they would be unable to carry out coups on their own, their politics did not matter.[37]

The great value of the Prussian army system lay not in what it was, but in what it might become. As it stood, the system pretended to arm the whole nation for its defense; but, said Engels, that was a lie. In practice, the eligible citizens were divided into two categories, the first serving in the line (and thereafter in the reserve) while the second group went straight into the reserve or *Landwehr*, receiving little or no real training. The contingent doomed to active service spent two or three years with the colors, "a period sufficient to make of them an obedient army, with the will drilled out of it, ever-ready for foreign conquest or for the forcible suppression of all domestic popular movements."

(This was a more than usually pessimistic view of the power of military service to mold soldiers' attitudes; Engels was engaged in painting the existing system in the worst possible light.)

So long as a single man escaped service, the nation's total resources were not employed, and the mad, costly competition to have the biggest army would continue. Only the introduction of a true people's army would end the contest and eliminate militarism, which Engels defined as "the introduction of the Prussian military system in all the great powers of the Continent." The first nation to introduce a true *Volkswehr* would simultaneously double its defensive strength and halve its military budget.[38] (Here the *Volkswehr* appeared as an alternative to the Prussian system, not as an extension of it—no contradiction, really, since the Prussian army system can be seen as producing its own antithesis as it arrives at its ultimate complete development.)

Engels might reasonably have wished to preserve the arms race; he predicted that militarism, and the unbearable strain of supporting huge "standing" armies with longer terms of service than Engels' *Volkswehr*, would combine with the growing cost and increasingly rapid obsolescence of weapons to ruin the capitalist governments. But just as he had renounced war as a preferred route to revolution, Engels chose to forego the bankrupting of the capitalist states in favor of a cheaper, truly universal service militia.[39] All the revolution really needed to prosper was peace and quiet.

It was partly in the hope of preserving peace that Engels came forward in 1893 with his scheme for introducing the *Volkswehr* into practice, and thereby guaranteeing the peace of Europe. Germany should propose to the world a gradual reduction in the term of service, so that there would be a "general transition from the standing army to the general armament of the people, organized as a militia." Engels, who had been so harsh in his estimate of existing militia systems, insisted that his version was distinguished from all other forms, such as the Swiss, by its emphasis on physical training of the youth as a prerequisite to shorter military training.[40] He had previously recommended more stress on physical education in the schools;[41] now he argued that better physical training would make it possible to decrease the term of military service without endangering the country.

An agreement to maintain two-year service would begin the process, and service would be reduced by stages to a year: "and then. . . ? Here begins the future, the genuine militia system, and we shall have more to say about it once it is finally gotten under way." If France and Germany agreed to the gradual reduction, the other, lesser powers would have to follow suit, and militarism would be at an end.[42]

Engels had not changed his mind about the difficulties of a militia. Instead, some of the disadvantages had come to appear as advantages. He had long considered the mass army superior in defense, since it provided more trained men than the cadre system;[43] his proposed *Volkswehr* was the ultimate mass army, and should be invincible in defense. A truly universal service army had little aptitude for offense, but that was no real disadvantage. "It should be recalled," Engels wrote in 1865, "that the headlong offensive of the cadre system led [in the Napoleonic Wars] from Jena to Tilsit, and the careful defensive of the *Landwehr* system with universal service led from Katzbach to Paris." The mass army was best suited to defense, or to counterattack following a broken invasion;[44] so much the better.

In Engels' later years, when war threatened to disrupt the progress of socialism, it was precisely this offensive incapacity of the militia system which inspired Engels to call for the progressive shortening of terms of service. The more an army depended on the mobilization of the whole population, the less readily it could be used for aggression,[45] and if all the powers had purely defensive armies, no war could interrupt the advance of socialism.

Engels' calls for a diminishing term of service went unheeded. His opinion that all the powers would have to adopt the Prussian mass army as their model, and would have to approach ever closer to true universal suffrage, on the other hand, was very widely shared. As he had predicted, so it came to be, though the increasingly monstrous armies were not rendered unfit for the attack by decreasingly lengthy training. Internationally, the mass armies faced one another; domestically, they faced the socialists. Even more important, from the revolution's point of view, than the army's efficacy as a means of national defense (or offense) was its function as a defender of the existing political and social order.

The most important purpose of all Engels' studies in military science was to provide a basis for revolutionary strategy and tactics.

CHAPTER 9

The Military Key to Revolution: Engels' Theory of the Vanishing Army

The army was, of course, more than a means for nations to defend themselves against one another; it was bourgeois society's ultimate defense against the revolution.[1] Marx even argued on several occasions that armies were maintained *primarily* as a bulwark of internal order; since there were not always barricades to bombard and strikers to shoot down, international conflicts were threatened, sometimes fought, to keep the armies alert. The bourgeois fear of the workers was the secret cause of Europe's standing armies, whose existence would mystify future historians; the Belgian army, for example, had no defensive purpose at all, existing only in order to conduct periodic massacres of the workers.[2] Engels agreed that all contemporaneous armies played this counterrevolutionary role, whether they were organized as a bourgeois militia or national guard,[3] or formed a long-service professional force, as in England.[4] He noted that both the British Army and the American National Guard built barracks and armories resembling fortresses, betraying their true function as garrisons against the populace.[5]

Thus the army was the enemy of the revolution; but in all his years of study Engels could see no chance of defeating it. From the beginning of his serious military education in the 1850s, he considered that training and organization gave armies such a decisive advantage over insurrectionary masses that discussing revolutionary tactics was a waste of time. In any open clash the forces of order were almost certain to prevail. Marx shared Engels' view, writing in 1871 that "Paris could resist only because, in consequence of the siege, it had got rid of the army, and replaced it by a National Guard, the bulk of which consisted of working men.'"[6] Even there the struggle against the army of the Versailles government was an unequal contest, and the circumstances of Paris in 1871 were unlikely to recur. The general strike provided no solution. Despite its success in compelling suffrage reform in Belgium, Engels said in 1893, the strike had been only a fortunate bluff, even against the "*very shaky*" Belgian army.[7]

The technical developments of the later nineteenth century swung the balance of force even further to the right. "An unarmed people against a present-day army is, in military terms, purely a vanishing quantity," Engels wrote to Bebel in 1884. No longer was there a sympathetic national guard to supply the people with arms, as in the bourgeois French rising of 1848. New, more effective high explosive shells had ended the day of barricades and street fighting forever. "*If the troops fight,*" Engels declared, "resistance is madness." It was therefore necessary to discover new tactics, he said; but in 1892 he had not yet solved the problem,[8] and he never did.

In his 1895 introduction to a new edition of Marx's *Class Struggles in France,* Engels elaborated further on the technological difficulties that had arisen since 1848 to make the revolutionary's task more difficult. While cities had increased in population, armies had grown at a greater rate, and railways made possible rapid concentration of government forces. Explosive shells and dynamite had replaced solid shot and pickaxes for breaking through barricades and walls; perhaps the most inauspicious development was in infantry armament, where the muzzle-loading musket had been replaced by a magazine rifle with four times the range, ten times the accuracy, and ten times the rate of fire of its forerunner. Sporting weapons were no match for military rifles, even at close range; and it was no longer possible for insurgents to make their own ammunition, even if they acquired rifles. Engels' last completed piece of writing was not an encouraging message to the revolutionary movement.[9]

Engels was convinced that the governments, aware of their advantages in a clash with the workers, hoped to provoke an uprising. Whatever their differences on other issues, he wrote in 1890, Wilhelm II and Bismarck agreed on the necessity of shooting down the socialists at the earliest opportunity.[10] Since the brutal suppression of a revolutionary attempt would enable bourgeois society to delay its own doom,[11] the socialists were obliged to avoid any action that might provide the regime with a pretext for repression. On the expiration of the German Anti-Socialist Law in 1890, Engels proclaimed that even if the party was outlawed again, the socialists would not do their foes the favor of building barricades and lining up behind them to die. The workers would not be taken in by any provocations, he said: "The Anti-Socialist Law has trained our workers too well for that, and besides, we have too many old soldiers in our ranks, and too many of them who have learned to wait out the rain of bullets, *Gewehr bei Fuss*, until the moment is right for the attack." (The government did intend that the army should impose disciplined habits on those who passed through its ranks, but it was not the government's intention to produce better-disciplined socialists.)[12]

Arming the people would help to redress the technical imbalance between army and people; but until every worker had a repeating rifle and a hundred cartridges in his home, any attempt at insurrection would be madness. If every French worker possessed a Lebel rifle and fifty cartridges, the Republic would be safe from a military coup; so long as the soldier had his rifle and the worker had none, the Republic would always be in danger. Only an armed people could make a revolution, or prevent a counter-revolutionary coup. But Engels never really expected any bourgeois government to provide the workers with the arms they would need to meet the army on equal terms, so he concentrated on the need to avoid any clash between workers and armies. "I want neither war nor putsch," he wrote in 1888; just as a war would arrest the progress of socialism, so would an uprising that would inevitably be crushed, dying without hope of success as in Paris in 1871.[13]

Engels' certainty that an untimely rising would end in disaster explains the cautionary tone of his later writings, which has been used to enlist him posthumously in the ranks of Marxist revisionism. But Engels was never completely converted to a belief in gradual legal progress as the road to socialism. It pleased him to argue that the socialists thrived on legality, and to cast the blame for any resort to violence on the forces of "order," but he expected an outbreak to occur. "Shoot first, *messieurs les bourgeois*," he taunted his enemies. "No doubt, they *will* shoot first," he continued; one fine morning the bourgeoisie would tire of watching the ominously rising spring-flood of socialism, and would resort to force.[14] His disapprobation of premature revolutionary attempts did not mean that he had abandoned his commitment to revolution, and it had little to do with his cheerful *bonhomie;*[15] it was a tactical decision, the product of his decades of military study. Engels insisted that the fighting should take place on ground favorable to the revolutionaries, and should be postponed until the moment was "right for the attack."

The general introduction of universal service in modern European armies helped to relieve the discrepancy in training between government and revolutionary forces. Unavoidably necessary on military grounds and useful in reducing the danger of war, universal service also trained the workers in the methods of combat. Therefore, universal service was in the interest of the revolution, and in Germany "should be used, above all, to learn to fight, especially by those whose education permits them to choose officers' training as one-year volunteers." In the same spirit, he wrote to Natalie Liebknecht that the year's training would be good for her son Karl; if August Bebel was the son of a noncommissioned officer, why should not Wilhelm Liebknecht be the father of a couple?[16] On the twenty-first anniversary of the Commune, Engels observed that the children born in 1871 were full-grown, and "thanks to the stupidity of the ruling classes," were soldiers, learning to defend themselves.[17] The military education of the working classes was one of the strongest motives for Engels' persistent advocacy of military service. But the workers would not be fully trained in arms for some time, and Engels never suggested that they were ready for a trial of strength against the armies.

When would the moment be right for revolution? The answer was implied in Engels' letter to Lafargue of November 3, 1892: under prevailing conditions, resistance was madness—*"if the troops fight."* The army's invincibility in any conflict against unarmed masses forced Engels to concentrate on developments that might split or dissolve the army from within. He wrote to Bebel in 1884 that those in power could rest easy for the time being: "With the military relationships as they are, we shall not strike until the armed force itself *ceases to exist as a force against us."*[18] Only the disintegration of the existing armies could make possible a successful revolutionary attempt. Training the workers, in the army or otherwise, always remained secondary to the disruption of the legions of order.

How might the armies be disrupted? Occasionally Engels and Marx considered the possibilities of dissension within the officer corps. Thus in 1889 Engels was pleased to report that Russia's "younger *educated* officers [were] constitutional through and through"—more advanced than their Prussian counterparts—so that the Russian government was compelled to distract them by threats of war. In 1874, Marx and Engels objected to the form of Bakunin's appeal to the Russian officers and to the attempt to make the officers swear unconditional allegiance to Bakunin, not to the idea of subverting the officer corps.[19] Especially in Bonapartist France, which Marx and Engels regarded as a country ruled by its army,[20] Napoleon's marshals appeared to be his rivals, and at every hesitation or setback in the Second Empire's foreign policy, Marx and Engels entertained hopes that Napoleon III would be deposed by the army that had made him.[21] Only the Guard was reliable, and if Napoleon survived a revolutionary attempt, the loyal Guard would be elevated to new heights, giving rise to new plots in the rest of the army.[22] Usually a military coup against the Second Empire was not expected to lead immediately to a proletarian revolution; it was sufficient that Napoleon would be disposed of, though Engels sometimes suggested that more might happen, as in this scenario of 1858:

> as soon as their distress at Bonaparte has made the troops so unreliable that an insurrection *must* succeed, their distress at the proletarians will again work at them till they are ready to beat the insurrection down—too late!—the stream rushes over them, the troops look on open-mouthed—and then we shall see how much water has accumulated since the last deluge, of 1848.

Discord among the officers might sometimes seem promising, but even the long-service army of Napoleon III was troubled by reds in the ranks as well as by legitimists in the officer corps.[23] If the French army was reformed in the direction of universal service, as seemed likely after the Prussian mass army did so splendidly against the Austrians in 1866, Napoleon III found himself in a "comical dilemma":

> either he leaves everything as it is, and then is no match for the Prussians; or he carries the thing through, and then he breaks his own neck, first by the colossal unpopularity of it, and second because he completely *debonapartizes* the army. From the moment when some sort of universal service is instituted in France, the pretorian system ends automatically, and the 25-30% re-enlisted fellows who now serve in the French army disappear for the most part.[24]

In 1868, when Engels declared that the Parisians had "not the ghost of a chance" without a military revolt, he placed his hopes on the reserve formations that the French reforms were intended to create. "Not until at least the *garde mobile* stands between army and people, in my opinion, can a coup be dared."[25]

Here was the great revolutionary consequence of universal military service. It might prevent an inconvenient war and it would surely provide the proletariat a military education; but most important, it would ruin the armies of Europe as agencies of social repression.

Like the collapse of capitalism itself, the coming of the mass army seemed both inevitable and desirable. Engels was satisfied that no government could avoid introducing the mass army, and most of his later military writings were concerned with working out the revolutionary implications of this system of army organization. He was not willing to wait patiently for military competition among the nations to bring the mass army, however, and he called for the speediest possible transition to the *Volksheer*. In 1891, for example, he used a German-Russian war scare to recommend that the German Social Democrats demand the *"immediate compulsory training"* of all those who had not done military service. The armament and enrollment into existing units of these new troops was the most effective counter to the Russian threat, since neither the upgrading of the army's weapons nor the creation of new army units could be carried out quickly. This "approach toward our *Volkswehr*" was also the only sort of defensive measure that the Social Democrats could support without embarrassment, in view of their refusal to vote a single man or penny for the existing military system; the push toward true universal service was the best possible policy for both the national defense and the revolution.[26]

During the Prussian army organization controversy of the early 1860s, Engels declared that "the only point which interests the German working class in the Prussian army organization" was "the increasingly thorough realization of universal service." The sooner universal service was achieved, the sooner the conscript workers and peasants could become conscious of their true position. As Engels predicted in the *Anti-Dühring*, "the machine refuses to work, and militarism collapses by the dialectic of its own evolution."[27]

Until this process was completed, Engels was not entirely sure what might be expected of Europe's armies. One of the great accomplishments of the French Third Republic was the creation of a republican army, he wrote in 1878; MacMahon's setback in the elections of 1877 had been possible only because the army, now that paid substitutes were abolished, was "a representative selection of young men of all classes," and could not be relied upon to crush the people and undo the election.[28] The French army, "no longer the *Soldateska* of the Empire," as Engels noted in 1887, progressed toward Engels' ideal of genuine universal service, and by 1914 French conscription was more thorough than the German.[29] Yet Engels regarded the French army with suspicion. Despite its democratic conscript base, it might threaten the Republic, and Engels' most pressing concern was whether the army would or would not support a coup.

This was his fear during the Boulanger crisis of the late 1880s; he wrote to Paul Lafargue that since the soldiers with two or three years' service had not yet stood against the people, it was impossible to predict what they would do. It would help to learn the composition of particular regiments—from what areas recruited, how many Parisians, and so on. In May, 1889, Engels feared that Boulangism was stronger among the common soldiers than republicanism had been during the MacMahon crisis.[30] Boulanger's fierce nationalism seemed to menace the peace that socialism needed, and Engels deplored the Boulangist success among some elements of the French Left;[31] while he believed that the Boulanger affair "ought to make our people demand again and again l'armement du peuple as the only guarantee against Caesaristic velleities on the part of popular generals,"[32] the popular, radical nature of Boulanger's appeal seemed able to infect even a people's army.

Occasionally the French army seemed to promise more positive contributions to the revolutionary cause; Engels was cheered in 1891 by a report that soldiers had refused to fire on a May Day demonstration, and in 1887 he considered the selection of Sadi Carnot as president of the Republic a favorable omen, a triumph of army and people over monarchists and opportunists. "What was the attitude of the soldiers?" he asked Paul Lafargue. "I mean the *line* troops. These peaceful victories are the best way to accustom the soldiers to the superiority and infallibility of the masses." A few more such days, he predicted cheerfully, "and the soldier will surely turn his rifle around."[33] But this was a rhetorical flourish. More often Engels expected that France would remain quiet. In 1892 he assured August Bebel that the unreliability of the army, in which universal service was still new and unfamiliar, prevented a coup, and the unarmed state of the masses prevented an uprising.[34] He was content to settle for a stalemate.

In Prussianized Germany, the situation was quite different. The French Republic, for all its faults, was worth defending from a military coup. In Germany, however, Engels endorsed Wilhelm Liebknecht's description of the Bismarckian constitution as the "fig-leaf of absolutism,"[35] and he saw no reason for reactionaries to violate the constitution, or socialists to defend it. He did occasionally commend the Prussian mass army as unsuited to counter-revolutionary activity, as when he said in 1865 that the peacetime army might be so used, but "the wartime army, certainly never." But his more usual emphasis had been clear twenty years earlier, when he told the readers of the Chartist *Northern Star* that Prussia's military system gave the people "a tremendous power, and which some time or other [would] be used against the government."[36] Instead of menacing a republic, the German army defended a despotism; and when universal service undermined the German army, it would mean revolution.

As the socialists increased their numbers in the electorate, they increased their numbers in the army. Engels considered universal service the necessary complement of universal suffrage; a majority in the polls might gain the socialists only a massacre, but a majority in the army was another matter entirely.[37] Engels touched upon the themes of war prevention and proletarian military training when he told an Italian correspondent to admire "the army-corps of German socialism, which pass in review on election day"; he was not using figurative language, he said, since at least half the socialist voters had served two or three years in the army, were adept in the use of needle-gun and rifled cannon, and belonged to the reserves. Soon the German reserves and *Landwehr* would belong to the socialists to such an extent that aggressive war would be impossible.[38] But the prevention of war was a secondary consideration. As important as it was to avert the interruption of socialist progress that a war would bring, it was still more vital to prevent the army from firing on the workers.

It was in this context that elections were truly useful. When the German socialists gained three and a half million votes, Engels said in 1893, half the army would be on their side; and in November, 1892, he assured Paul Lafargue that universal suffrage showed with absolute precision the day when it would finally become appropriate to reach for weapons and make the revolution.[39]

Many socialists who served in the ranks failed to show up in the electoral totals, since men were drafted at twenty and voted only at the age of twenty-five, creating a "reserve" of young socialist soldiers.[40] "The principal strength of German socialism lies by no means in the number of its votes," Engels declared in 1891. Soldiers were younger than voters, "and since it is precisely the younger generation which provides our party with the most recruits, it follows that the German army is more and more contaminated by socialists." He continued cheerfully:

Today we have one soldier in five; in a few years we shall have one in three, and in about 1900 the army, formerly the most Prussian element in the land, will be socialist in its majority. This is coming, as inexorably as a decree of fate. The Berlin regime sees it coming just as clearly as we do, but it is powerless. The army is slipping away from it.[41]

Particularly promising were developments among the East Elbian agricultural workers, traditionally a reliable counterrevolutionary element. "The electoral returns prove that the socialists are making headway rapidly even in the country districts, while the large towns already as good as belong to them," he wrote in 1890; "and, in a country where every able-bodied male is a soldier, this means the gradual conversion of the army to Socialism." What he said in print he reiterated in private, in a letter to Paul Lafargue. Socialism was gaining the agricultural laborers and day workers, the pillars of the status quo; they already had one soldier in four or five, perhaps one in three with the army on a war footing—in three or four years there would be no more Prussia.[42] With the farm workers would come the "core-regiments" of the Prussian-German army, the mainstay of Prussia. A bad harvest would accelerate developments in the area, and once the socialists had the agricultural workers, the army would be theirs. The East Elbian estates determined the Prussian character of the *Reich*; there was the decisive battleground against *Junker* rule, and the battle was going well.[43]

The socialist penetration of the army terrified the ruling circles more than anything else, according to Engels. The increasing numbers of socialists in the army formed the cutting edge of the general socialist advance which would probably drive the existing military and political elites to seek temporary salvation in a military coup. It was clear, Engels wrote in 1877, that the Prussians could not stand aside while their whole army was "infected with socialism"; surely they would take forceful countermeasures. When he told F. A. Sorge of progress in the East Elbian agricultural districts and therefore among the soldiers of the "core-regiments," he concluded that success was near: "then the entire old system collapses [*ist Kladderadatsch*] and we rule." But, he said, "the Prussian generals must be greater asses than I can believe, if they fail to see that as well as we do; and they must therefore burn with the desire to render us harmless for a while by means of a sanctimonious massacre." Thus it was doubly necessary to proceed with caution,[44] and resist provocations. Bismarck's only salvation lay in a major bloodletting, and it was essential for the socialists to avoid a premature and disastrous clash.[45]

Here is the reason for Engels' warnings, which can appear so "revisionist" when taken out of context. There was a time and a place for everything, particularly revolution; and it was the state of the army, above all, that determined the practicability of a revolutionary effort. Ernest Belfort Bax reported that he "more than once heard [Engels] say that as soon as one man in three, i.e., one-third of the German army actually in service could be relied upon by the party leaders, revolutionary action ought to be taken." According to Bax, Engels "to the last held the view that the social revolution could not be inaugurated otherwise than by the methods of forcible insurrection—least of all in Germany."[46]

While Bax seems to have missed Engels' occasional suggestions that in the absence of a counterrevolutionary coup the socialists might take power legally, his emphasis on the army's crucial role in Engels' tactical vision was correct. Legally accomplished or not, the revolution's success required the army's neutralization. Engels told Karl Kautsky that when the army was sufficiently socialist (a third to two-fifths), even the old fashioned barricade might be of use, since it would be only a matter of presenting the troops with opportunities for disruption. To Paul Lafargue, Engels insisted that "*demoralization* (from the bourgeois standpoint) must spread precisely in the ranks of the army; under the conditions of modern military technology (rapid-fire weapons, etc.), the revolution must begin in the army." At least, he said, "among us [Germans] it will begin that way." If revolution began in Germany, Engels wrote to August Bebel, it could begin only in the army.[47]

The army would have to be captured or crippled before any sort of revolution could succeed; its importance in getting the revolution launched is clear. Perhaps, however, its importance in a later stage of the revolution might be even greater. Marx and Engels concentrated on first things first, and were more intent on getting revolutionary movement under way than on mapping out in detail the developments that would follow eventually. Sometimes they used the term "revolution" to mean any marked advance past the existing state of affairs. In this limited sense, it might require a revolution to install in office the more progressive representatives of bourgeois democracy. Somehow, the leftmost bourgeois politicians (Clemenceau, Dilke and Chamberlain, Richter) should have a turn, so that they would be discredited.[48] A revolution (by context, a socialist revolution) aimed directly against the existing regimes would be suicidal, like Babeuf's well-meant but ill-timed effort of 1796.[49] Ultimately, the socialists' turn would come, and the reorganization of society would begin.

Marx and Engels considered it utopian and unduly speculative to try to peer too far into the future, and they left only very sparse instructions as to what to expect in the later stages of the revolution. Nevertheless, the army's importance in the ultimate, socialist phase of revolution was clear. The military training that the workers received in the mass army would be most useful both in the initial destruction of the existing military-bureaucratic state, and in the revolt against the ensuing bourgeois regime; and Engels told Bebel in 1884 that the dissolution of the army as a force against revolution was essential: "Any earlier revolution, even a successful one, would bring to power not *us,* but the most radical of the bourgeois or petty-bourgeois." If the army *began* the revolution, on the other hand, it might be quite different: "In this case—where our reserve aged twenty to twenty-five, which does not vote but is drilled, would come into action, pure democracy could be bypassed."[50] In the vaguely sketched final stages of revolution, as in the initial phase, the army's role would be crucial.

Engels' discussions of the army as the key to beginning and continuing the revolution ignored a whole range of problems that had occupied his attention in earlier years. He did not say, and did not wonder, how a revolutionized nation was to defend itself against its neighbors' counterrevolutionary assaults. An army infiltrated with socialists and paralyzed so that it could not oppose revolution would not be the most reliable instrument for defense, and Engels had long since renounced any faith in unorganized enthusiasm as a military force. Perhaps he assumed that the universal-service armies of the neighboring countries would not permit themselves to take part in counterrevolutionary crusades. If revolution broke out in Russia, Engels wrote in 1890, "the German Emperor might perhaps be tempted into sending an army to restore the authority of the Tsar—than which there could be no better way to destroy his own authority."[51] In general, the danger of foreign intervention did not seem worth mentioning.

Much of Engels' analysis of the army's revolutionary role was worked out in his discussions of developments in Germany, but he considered the process of military disintegration applicable to all the great European powers. For twenty years, he told the French socialists in 1891, the workers of Paris and their comrades in all the great civilized nations had been disarmed, while their enemies and exploiters had maintained a monopoly on the control of armed force. But what was the result of these two decades of counter-revolutionary military supremacy? Only that, since every able-bodied man now passed through the army, "the army reflects more and more the feelings and opinions of the people; that this army, the principal instrument of oppression, becomes day by day more unreliable." (Universal service was not yet universal enough to satisfy Engels, but here he was composing a message of uplift.) Those at the head of *all* the great nations watched in horror the approach of the inevitable day, when the troops would refuse to fire upon their fathers and brothers. With the dawn thus visible in the armies, the end of the old world could not be far off. Engels contended that the first hopeful sign had occurred in France, when the army's position had prevented Ferry from becoming President of the Republic, and that the apprehension of the German ruling classes was shown by Caprivi's attempt to get noncommissioned officers to serve longer terms as a protection against the socialist penetration of the army.[52]

It was a handsome picture, this Theory of the Vanishing Army—international in scope, logically coherent, and, perhaps most of all, hopeful. It enabled Engels to reconcile his hard won, realistic appreciation of the grim prospects facing a revolutionary attempt launched against an intact, resolute military force with his unflagging faith that the revolution *would* nevertheless succeed. It provides the essential link between his persistently cautious, moderate counsel on immediate, short-run matters and his equally persistent conviction that eventually the revolution would come. The Theory of the Vanishing Army was classical Marxism's solution to the great tactical problem of *how* the revolution was to be made.

But on what was it based? How did Engels know what the socialists who filled the ranks of Europe's armies would actually do in a confrontation between army and proletariat? He could refer to the French army's alleged role in the Ferry affair and, somewhat ambiguously, in the Boulanger crisis; and he could point to the very real apprehensions of the governing circles who feared the very developments in the army that fed Engels' hopes. In general, Engels seems to have felt no need for empirical demonstration, but to have assumed, as in the *Anti-Dühring*, that socialism would have no trouble in creating the class conscious- ness and revolutionary will that would induce the workers and peasants in the ranks to defy their masters. When in 1893 a French interviewer expressed doubt that the socialists in the German army could be relied upon to do their revolutionary duty, Engels replied: "on the day when we become the majority, that which the French army did instinctively, when it refused to shoot at the people, will be consciously repeated among us."[53]

Unless Engels' heirs in the movement could share his faith that socialist soldiers would be more socialist than soldier at the decisive moment, they could not logically rely upon the vanishing of the army. And in fact they did not; leading figures in both the German and the French socialist movements wrote extensively on military questions without endorsing Engels' prophecy. Accord- ing to a British reporter, Engels' disciple and close associate, August Bebel, watched a battalion of Prussian Guards march past in 1892 and said, "Look at those fellows! Ninety per cent Berliners and eighty per cent Social-Democrats! But if there was trouble they would shoot me or anyone down at the word of command from above!" The whole nation, he said, was "still drunk with military glory," and there was "nothing to be done until some great disaster [had] sobered it."[54]

While Bebel never challenged Engels' view of the futility of a rising *against* the army, he lacked his master's assurance that a revolution could be made *with* the army. He campaigned doggedly for the conversion of the German army into a *Volks- wehr*,[55] but his concern for the lot of the common soldier[56] and for the efficacy of German defenses[57] seems at times only dimly related to Engels' concentration on the army's revolutionary role. A National Liberal critic warned that the Social Democrats' demand for a militia system as a protection against militarist oppression was only a ruse, that an army effectively controlled by the workers would not remain defensive but would lead imme- diately to a proletarian terror;[58] Bebel seemed less sure.

He deplored the army's obsession with the "inner enemy," namely the socialists, who fulfilled their military duties at least as well as did the alleged friends of society; and he expressed gratification at the words of a general who assessed the workers' military qualities as superior to those of peasants. This praise, said Bebel, was more useful than all nonsense about barricades, street fighting, and the like, whose time was long gone by. *"The revolution ripens in material things and is transplanted from there into men's minds,"* he declared, *"with a speed and precision that leaves nothing to be desired."*[59] Apparently, the socialists' dutifulness in the ranks was to impress their social betters so much that socialists would be accepted into society.

It may be, of course, that the militia Bebel advocated was intended to facilitate the revolution, and that Bebel simply found it inexpedient to say so in public. But his antimilitarism[60] focused on the need for adequate defenses and for peace, so that socialism could arrive without the interruption of war.[61] All this was perfectly compatible with Engels' defensism and dread of war; but Bebel, despite his stout opposition to revisionism, could propose no method by which revolution could succeed.[62]

The French socialist leader Jean Jaurès, whose energy in promoting the militia system rivaled Bebel's, shared Bebel's emphasis on defense and peace. Socialism appeared in Jaurès' *Armée nouvelle* principally as a morale-building force, useful in inspiring the army.[63] Eventually, under the militia system, all would come to realize the beauty of military service, dedicated to the *"protection of national independence for the free development of social justice."* Jaurès, who made no pretense of being a revolutionary, did not discuss the army's role in revolution; indeed, one of the virtues of a rifle in every home was in discouraging irresponsible revolutionary rhetoric about resorting to arms.[64]

Thus Engels' doctrine of the vanishing army failed to become the doctrine of his successors. The prospect of a continuing peaceful increase in the proportion of socialists among voters and soldiers, leading to a situation where revolution would at last be possible, was in any case interrupted by the outbreak of war in 1914. This is not the place to examine the ways in which that war led to the opportunity for Lenin's personal variation on Marxism to seize power in Russia, though some analogies with Engels' predictions are obvious. The exhausting struggle that Engels had foreseen and deplored did produce a demoralized and divided army, whose condition facilitated both the March and November Revolutions; but Lenin's timely actions in November were most likely dictated by the circumstances, and arrived at independently of Engels' precepts. (Surely if Lenin had been aware of Engels' emphasis on the army and its place in the revolution, he would have emphasized strongly all similarities between Engels' advice and his own practice. He was always concerned to prove himself an orthodox Marxist.) Among most socialists, Engels' emphasis on resisting provocations, standing *Gewehr bei Fuss* till the appropriate moment, was taken out of context. There ceased to be any expectation that the right moment *would* arrive, so passivity ceased to be a temporary, tactical stance. When the army began to crack in Germany, the response of the Majority Social Democrats was to ally themselves with, and help to rebuild, the military machine whose collapse Engels had awaited as the beginning of the revolution.[65]

But even in Engels' own formulation, the Theory of the Vanishing Army was essentially a passive doctrine. The undermining of the army was something that would occur naturally. The revolutionaries would have to wait until the army contained the necessary number of socialists; then the army, the chief obstacle to revolution, would disappear. Lenin's emphasis on "the desperate, frantic struggle for the troops"[66] seems foreign to Engels' view. To Engels, the revolutionaries should be able to count on the troops before attempting a revolution; the subversion of the army was a prerequisite to successful revolt, not something that could be accomplished by the revolutionaries' efforts.

The Theory of the Vanishing Army was Engels' closest approach to a solution of the puzzle of how a revolution was to be made. From the 1850s till his death in 1895, he believed that the forces of order would surely defeat the forces of revolution in any violent confrontation, and he saw no point in attempting to drill and equip the revolutionaries to bring them up to their opponents' level of competence. The prospect of a steady and inexorable permeation of the mass army by socialism gave Engels and Marx an alternative to the conspiratorial, putschist approach that they opposed. Universal service would eventually make the revolution possible. Thus Engels' concentration on the composition of the

European armies was perhaps less a revolutionary tactic than an attempt at analysis and prediction; the percentage of socialists in the army would determine when the objective conditions for revolution were present.

Engels and Marx spent their lives in the study of economic and political phenomena (including the wars discussed in Part II above), hoping to determine when the conditions would be right for revolution, assuming that the force of circumstances would generate the appropriate movement of the masses at the appropriate time. Engels' studies of the army as the key to revolution were an attempt to understand one especially crucial indicator. Engels retained to the end his belief in the necessity and inevitability of revolution—and his belief that revolution was not be be brought about by the efforts of revolutionaries.

It is not surprising that revolutionaries should find in this point of view a source of frustration. For all their dedicated efforts, Engels and Marx had not bequeathed to the revolutionary movement a recipe for success. Unless a socialist accepted the full Theory of the Vanishing Army—as no socialist did—he was presented by the Marxist founders with a tactical vacuum. Bereft of the assurance that the army would disappear, which had enabled Engels to reconcile his warnings against putschism with his faith in the ultimate triumph of revolution, some of Engels' heirs—Bebel, for example—could do no better than to combine revolutionary goals with moderate, legal activity, while ignoring the contradictions. Others, more intent on logical consistency, were disturbed by the absence of any convincing means of making the revolution happen. Some searchers for consistency followed Eduard Bernstein in his course of abandoning the revolutionary goal as impossible and unnecessary; others, more determined to maintain the expectation of revolution, proposed new schemes for effectuating the revolt. Sorel's general strike and Lenin's activist, vanguard party fall into this category. While it would be foolhardy to claim that the perceived inadequacy of classical Marxism's tactical legacy caused all these subsequent developments in Marxism singlehandedly, it seems clear that the vanishing of the vanishing army was among the circumstances that permitted these variants to arise.

Notes

A Note on Documentation

The multiplicity of collections and editions available to the student of Marxism creates certain problems for both reader and writer. If a note documents some statement of Engels or Marx by referring the reader to some page of some collection, the reader is lost unless he happens to have that particular collection at hand; in addition, the status of preferred editions changes constantly.

While the research for this book was being done, the handiest and most nearly complete edition was the *MEW* (*Karl Marx-Friedrich Engels Werke* [Berlin: Dietz, 1960-74], 41 vols. plus supplementary volumes). Therefore most of my primary citations refer to the *MEW*; but it is being superseded both by an all-original-language *Gesamtausgabe* and an all-English *Collected Works*. Future scholars will not have to seek out articles that Engels wrote in English in their original newspapers and magazines if they wish to avoid retranslating from the *MEW's* German.

Since anyone now writing on classical Marxism will soon find his documentation obsolete, I have used the most convenient editions, and have tried consistently to specify both where I found the cited statement, and what letter, book, or article contained it originally. Thus the notes may be pursued by the reader in whatever collection he has on hand.

Since all of Engels' and Marx's letters are cited from the *MEW*, I have attempted to lighten the typographical burden of the notes by omitting repetition of *MEW* when citing letters of Engels or Marx; letters are identified by date, recipient, and the volume and page numbers from the *MEW*.

Abbreviations Used in the Notes

AMZ: *Allgemeine Militär-Zeitung*

EMC: *Engels as Military Critic*

FIWI: *The First Indian War of Independence*

IWK: *Internationale wissenschaftliche Korrespondenz zur Geschichte der deutschen Arbeiterbewegung*

MEGA, 1: *Marx-Engels Gesamtausgabe.* Series 1 (works) (Moscow: Marx-Engels-Lenin Institute, 1927-1935), 7 vols.

MEW: *Karl Marx-Friedrich Engels Werke*

MS: Engels' *Ausgewählte militärische Schriften*

NRZ: *Neue Rheinische Zeitung*

NRZ-Revue: *Neue Rheinische Zeitung. Politisch-ökonomische Revue*

PMG: *Pall Mall Gazette*

ZfMG: *Zeitschrift für Militärgeschichte*

Notes to Introduction

[1]Marx, "Theses on Feuerbach," *The German Ideology* (New York: International Publishers, 1947), 199.

[2]Robert Michels, *Political Parties: A Sociological Study of the Oligarchical Tendencies of Modern Democracy,* tr. Eden and Cedar Paul (New York: Dover, 1959), 44. Marx's daughters bestowed the "General" on Engels after his Franco-Prussian War articles, and almost always addressed him by it. See Eleanor Marx-Aveling, "Karl Marx, löse Blätter," *Österreichischer Arbeiter-Kalender für das Jahr 1895,* in *Mohr und General. Erinnerungen an Marx und Engels* (Berlin: Dietz, 1964), 272; also her "Friedrich Engels," *Sozialdemokratische Monatsschrift,* 2 (1890), *ibid.,* 452-53. Marx seldom referred to Engels by the title except when writing to his daughters, but junior members of the socialist movement often used it. See Hans-Josef Steinberg, "Revolution und Legalität. Ein

unveröffentlicher Brief Friedrich Engels' an Richard Fischer," *IRSH, 12* (1967), *177-89*. On Engels's posture, see Jörgen Haalck, "Der Besuch Friedrich Engels in Berlin 1893. Nach Akten des Berliner Polizeipräsidiums," *Berliner Heimat* (1958), 30.

[3]*Die Kriegslehre von Friedrich Engels* (Frankfurt a. M.: Europäische Verlagsanstalt, 1969), 19-21. See also Ivanoe Bonomi, "Federico Engels e i problemi della guerra," *Nuova Antologia, 195* (1918), 242-50.

[4]*Friedrich Engels. Eine Biographie* (2nd ed.; The Hague: Nijhoff, 1934), 2 vols. W.O. Henderson's *Life of Friedrich Engels* (London: Frank Cass, 1976) also contains a great deal of material on this aspect of Engels' career, and supersedes both the English abridgment of Mayer (tr. Gilbert and Helen Highet, ed. R.H. S. Crossman, reissued New York: Howard Fertig, 1969) and two lesser biographies: Yelena Stepanova, *Frederick Engels*, tr. John Gibbons (Moscow: Foreign Languages Publishing House, 1958) and Grace Carlton, *Friedrich Engels: The Shadow Prophet* (London: Pall Mall Press, 1965). Military studies in addition to Wallach's include Sigmund Neumann, "Engels and Marx: Military Concepts of the Social Revolutionaries," in *Makers of Modern Strategy*, ed. E. M. Earle (Princeton: Princeton University Press, 1941), 155-71; S. Budkiewitsch, "Engels und das Kriegswesen," in *Friedrich Engels, der Denker. Aufsätze aus der Grossen Sowjet-Enzyklopädie* (Basel: Mundus-Verlag, 1945), 273-304, and "Engels und die Militärwissenschaft," including contributions by Werner Hahlweg, Jehuda L. Wallach, and Claus D. Kernig, in Hans Pelger, ed., *Friedrich Engels 1820-1970. Referate. Diskussionen. Dokumente* (Hannover: Verlag für Literatur und Zeitgeschehen, 1971), 61-96.

[5]Isaac Deutscher, *The Prophet Armed: Trotsky, 1879-1921* (New York: Oxford University Press, 1954), 154. Trotsky's article "Die Rote Armee," in *Die Rote Armee, ein Sammelbuch* (Hamburg: C. Hoym Nachf., 1923), 22-35, explains every turn of policy by reference to the objective necessities of the moment, not to texts. On Engels' links to Lenin, Wallach, 57-68. Cf. Reinhard Brühl, "Lenin und die Militärgeschichte," *ZfMG, 9* (1970), 133-47. Hans Wiesner prefers to stress things that Lenin said that agree with things that Engels said. "Zur Weiterentwicklung des militärischen Ansichten von Marx und Engels durch W.I. Lenin," *ibid.*, 5-18. See also Radek, "Leo Trotzki—der Organisator des Sieges," in *Die Rote Armee*, 47. John Erickson's article "The Origins of the Red Army," in *Revolutionary Russia*, ed. Richard Pipes (Garden City: Doubleday, 1969) 286-325, makes no mention of Engels; and M. Tukhachevski, writing in 1921, referred to militia programs as a superstition, apparently unaware of Engels' qualified approval of militias in certain situations. *Die Rote Armee und die Miliz* (Leipzig: Frankes Verlag).

[6]E.g., G.I. Pokrovsky, *Science and Technology in Contemporary War*, tr. Raymond L. Garthoff (New York: Praeger, 1959), 3, 100.

[7]Gerhard Zirke, *Der General. Friedrich Engels, der erste Militärtheoretiker der Arbeiterklasse* (Leipzig and Jena: Urania-Verlag, 1957), 40-43; another study from a military-history angle is *Friedrich*

Engels. Die Anfänge der proletarische Militärtheorie 1842-52 (Berlin: Deutscher Militarverlag, 1970), by Heinz Helmert, an editor of the *Zeitschrift für Militärgeschichte*.

[8] "Kriegskunst und Kriegswissenschaft bei Friedrich Engels," *Die Glocke*, 2 (1916), 108.

[9] On Engels' life there is an excellent short collection: *Engels: Selected Writings*, ed. W.O. Henderson (Baltimore: Penguin, 1967), and some perceptive comments in Edmund Wilson, *To the Finland Station* (New York: Doubleday, 1953), in addition to the biographies already mentioned.

Notes to Chapter 1

[1] Carlton, p. 3. Most of Carlton's speculations on Engels' youthful infatuation with armies are kept in the subjunctive—wisely, considering the lack of evidence adduced. Engels may have listened to Napoleonic veterans' stories, as Carlton suggests, but he is at least as likely to have absorbed the lively antimilitarist spirit that permeated the Rhineland.

[2] Horst Ullrich, on the other hand, draws quite sweeping conclusions from the *juvenilia*, contending that two poems written at the age of eighteen marked Engels' identification with the cause of the oppressed, and his commitment to revolutionary action. *Der junge Engels. Eine historisch-biographische Studie seiner weltanschaulichen Entwicklung in den Jahren 1834-1845, 1* (Berlin: Deutscher Verlag der Wissenschaften, 1961), 42-44, 48-52.

[3] Engels Senior to Elise Engels, Aug. 27, 1835, *MEGA*, 1, 2, 463; "Eine Seeräubergeschichte," early 1837, *MEW*, Erg. 2, 510-21.

[4] To Marie Engels, Aug. 28-29, 1839, Aug. 20-25, 1840, Erg. 2, 327, 426. On mustaches, cf. letters to Marie, Oct. 29, 1840, Feb. 18, 1841, Mar. 8, 1841, early May, 1841, Erg. 2, 463, 477, 481, 486.

[5] To Marie, Sept. 18-19, 1840; "Schiffahrtsprojekt. Theater. Manöver," Oct. 19, 1840; "Eine Fahrt nach Bremerhafen," Aug. 19, 1841, *MEW*, Erg. 2, 458-59, 103, 84.

[6] To Marie, Mar. 8, 1841, Erg. 2, 481-82.

[7] To Wilhelm Graeber, Nov. 20, 1840, Erg. 2, 465-67 (D. Riazonov pointed out the likely link between the Hanseatic maneuvers and the theological battlepiece in *MEGA*, 1, 2, xxxix); "Die Wahren Sozialisten," written April 1847, *MEW*, 4, 261-62.

[8] (Mannheim: J. Venedey, 1839), esp. pp. 55-72.

[9] To Friedrich Graeber, Oct. 29, 1839, to Wilhelm Graeber, Nov. 13-20, 1839, Erg. 2, 434; "Sankt Helena. Fragment," and "Der Kaiserzug,"

Telegraph für Deutschland, Nov. 1840, Feb. 1841, *MEW,* Erg. 2, 104, 139-40. On the prevalence of Engels' attitude, see Jacques Droz, *Le liberalisme rhenan, 1815-1848* (Paris: Sorlot, 1940), 196-206.

[10]To Marx, Nov. 15, 1857, *29,* 212. On Engels' riding and fencing in Bremen, see his letters to Marie, Dec. 6-9, 1840; to Friedrich Graeber, Feb. 22, 1841; to Marie, Apr. 5, 1841, Erg. 2, 469, 480, 484.

[11]To Marie, Sept. 9, 1841, Erg. 2, 488. Helmert, p. 14, suggests that Engels chose the artillery as a more bourgeois, less aristocratic branch of service than cavalry or infantry, and because there was a *Landwehr* artillery battalion based near Barmen, so that he could later do his reserve duty without undue inconvenience. Ulrich Freye and Helmert contend, without offering evidence, that Engels' family would have liked him rejected on physical grounds, but that Engels himself wished to serve. "Friedrich Engels und die Militärfrage des jungen Proletariats," *ZfMG, 9* (1970), 550.

[12]"The Armies of Europe," *Putnam's, 6* (Aug. 1856), 307; *The Role of Force in History: A Study of Bismarck's Policy of Blood and Iron* (New York: International Publishers, 1968), 50.

[13]Meinecke, "Landwehr und Landsturm seit 1814," *Schmollers Jahrbücher, 40* (1916), 1092. After doing his year, Engels was liable to being called up in the *Landwehr,* and was declared a deserter in 1849, when he failed to answer the call, preferring to fight against the Prussian forces. A fine was levied against his property, but he owned nothing within reach of the Prussian government. Engels to Marx, Jan. 31, 1860, *30,* 16.

[14]As Mayer (*1,* 68-69) laments.

[15]To Marie, Jan. 5-6, Apr. 14-16, Aug. 2-8, 1842, Erg. 2, 490-93, 494-96, 500-04. Carlton's assertion that "no volunteer in the Brigade of Artillery was ever more eager to pick up military knowledge" (p. 10) would seem to demand some evidence, which is not furnished. Zirke (p. 7) and Helmert (p. 15) describe Engels' avoidance of duty as passive resistance against mechanical, dehumanizing drills. Helmert claims, without evidence, that Engels was enthusiastic about real work with the guns.

[16]These works are in *MEW,* Erg. 2, 163-316.

[17]The recommendation is in *MEGA,*1, *2,* 636; Engels to Ruge, June 15, 1842, *27,* 404. The *MEW,* Erg. 2, facing p. 496, includes a picture of Engels in uniform, which would indicate that he was proud enough of his service to have a portrait made; but the picture turns out to represent Friedrich Engels Senior. Klaus Goebel and Helmut Hirsch, "Engels-Forschungsmaterialen im Bergischen Land," *Archiv für Sozialgeschichte, 9* (1969), 430-31.

[18]Feb. 22-26, Mar. 6, 1845, *27,* 20. On the meetings see Mayer, *1,* 210-11; Theodor Zlocisti, *Moses Hess, der Vorkämpfer des Sozialismus und Zionismus, 1812-1875* (2d ed., Berlin: Welt-Verlag, 1921), 187; and Helmut Hirsch, "Carnaps Bericht über die Elberfelder Versammlungen: Ein Dokument zur Geschichte des rheinischen Frühsozialismus," *Bulletin of the International Institute of Social History,* 8 (1953), 104-14. Mayor Carnap's estimate of the attendance at the meetings tallied closely with Engels'.

[19]"Zwei Reden in Elberfeld," *Rheinische Jahrbücher* (1845), *MEW*, 2, 542-43. On the prevalence of similar ideas, see Gerhard Ritter, *Staatskunst und Kriegshandwerk, 1* (Munich: R. Oldenbourg, 1959), 133-38; Reinhard Höhn, *Sozialismus und Heer, 1* (Berlin: Max Gehlen, 1961), 20-30.

[20]"The State of Germany," Nov. 8, 1845; "The Reform Movement in France," Nov. 20, 1847, *MEGA* 1, 4, 488, 6, 356.

[21]Letter to readers, *Sozialdemokrat*, Sept. 27, 1890, *MEW*, 22, 76-77; "Revolution in Paris," *Deutsche-Brüsseler Zeitung*, Feb. 27, 1848, *MEW*, 4, 528-30.

[22]"Der Aufstand in Frankfurt," *NRZ*, Sept. 20, 1848, *MEW*, 5, 410-11.

[23]"Die Niederlage der Piemontesen," Mar. 31-Apr. 4, 1849; "Der Krieg in Italien und Ungarn," Mar. 28, 1849; "Der magyarische Kampf," Jan. 13, 1849; "Ungarn," May 19, 1849, *MEW*, 6, 385-92, 381-84, 165-76, 507-15.

[24]Wilhelm Liebknecht, who had assumed that some Hungarian officer was writing the *NRZ*'s military articles, was astonished to learn that Engels had worked almost exclusively from Austrian victory bulletins. Liebknecht compared Engels' interpretive skill with Roentgen's rays, and to Cuvier's ability to assemble whole creatures from a few scraps of bone. "Friedrich Engels (28. November 1820 bis August 1895)," *Illustrierter neuer Welt-Kalender für das Jahr 1897*, in *Mohr und General*, 421-23. Engels himself thought afterward that he had done well, considering his sources. To Marx, July 6, 1852, 28, 85.

[25]Mayer, 1, 325.

[26]"Die 'Kölnische Zeitung' über die Junierevolution," July 1, 1848; "Die 'Kölnische Zeitung' über den magyarischen Kampf," Feb. 18, 1849, *MEW*, 5, 140; 6, 305.

[27]To Emil Blank, Mar. 26, 1848, 27, 475; cf. Marx to Engels, Mar. 16, 1848, 27, 119; Engels to a group in Vevey, Dec. 25, 1848, 27, 486-88; Marx, Engels, *et al.*, to Cabet, late March, 1848, 5, 6-7. For similar views, with hindsight, see "Zur Geschichte des Bundes der Kommunisten," *MEW*, 8, 587, and Engels' article, "Karl Marx," Brunswick *Volks-Kalender*, 1877, *MEW*, 19, 98, where Engels refers to the legion as a swindle. There seems to be no evidence for Carlton's contention that Engels "longed to join" the legion, but Marx would not let him. Carlton, 69.

[28]Engels was a native of Barmen, where lived the owners of Elberfeld's factories, and had described his neighbors as obsessed with "hatred for the tiny bit of freedom that they have." To Blank, Apr. 15 and May 24, 1848, 27, 483. Barmen stayed neutral during Elberfeld's uprising, subsequently receiving a marble bust of the King of Prussia as reward; the town's principal active response to the events of 1848-49 came when the Barmen *Treubund* sent the king a telegram of thanks for rejecting the Frankfurt constitution. W. Köllmann, *Sozialgeschichte der Stadt Barmen im 19. Jahrhundert* (Tübingen: Mohr, 1960), 228-30.

[29]Happich, 20. Engels described the outbreak in the *NRZ* on May 8: "Die preussische Armee und die revolutionäre Erhebung," *MEW*, 6, 474.

[30]C. H. A. Pagenstecher, *Aus den Lebenserinnerungen von C. H. A. Pagenstecher, 3: Revolutionäre Bewegungen im Rheinlande 1830 bis 1850*

(Leipzig: R. Voigtlander, 1913), 55-62. H. J. A. Körner, *Lebenskämpfe in der alten und neuen Welt. Eine Selbstbiographie* (New York: L. W. Schmidt, 1866), *2*, 87-100, 127-28, contends that Körner, a schoolteacher, directed the erection of barricades; professional revolutionaries came later. For Engels' account, "Die deutsche Reichsverfassungskampagne," *NRZ-Revue*, 1850, *MS, 1*, 59.

[31]Pagenstecher, 62-63; Happich, 22-23; F. Philippi, "Der Elberfelder Aufstand im Mai 1848," *Zeitschrift des Bergischen Geschichtsvereins, 50* (1917), 72-74. Engels says the troops went home the same night ("Reichsverfassungskampagne," *MS, 1*, 60), as do J. P. Becker and C. Esselen, *Geschichte der süddeutschen Mai-Revolution des Jahres 1849* (Geneva: Gottfried Becker, 1849), but neither Becker nor Esselen nor Engels was there at the time.

[32]Körner, *2*, 118.

[33]Happich, 24 (citing records of Mirbach's trial in 1850). Philippi, 75, says that at the outbreak of the rising, Mirbach was working as an engineer on the Berg-Mark railway.

[34] "Elberfeld," *NRZ*, May 17, 1849, *MS, 1*, 41-42; Happich, 25-26; "Reichsverfassungskampagne," *MS, 1*, 61, 68. On the meeting, Mayer, *1*, 339. Mayer's source gives no details of the meeting: Ernst von Eynern, "Friedrich von Eynern. Ein Bergisches Lebensbild. Zugleich ein Beitrag zur Geschichte der Stadt Barmen," *Zeitschrift des Bergischen Geschichtsvereins, 35* (1900-01), 33.

[35]Körner, *1*, 419-26, *2*, 136-37; Pagenstecher, 40, 61-65. Pagenstecher, who organized the *Schützengilde*, advised the group to side neither with the regime nor with the agitators (the text reads *Wähler* but clearly means *Wühler*, which is one of Pagenstecher's favorite words). There was also a democratic *Schutzenverein*, organized by Körner, which seems to have done nothing notable. Neighboring Barmen had not only a *Bürgerwehr*, but a *Turnerwehr* and a volunteer cavalry unit, all devoted to protecting the town from the reds in Elberfeld. Von Eynern, 32.

[36]Körner, *1*, 419-26, *2*, 125-26; "Reichsverfassungskampagne," *MS, 1*, 68; Pagenstecher, 67.

[37] "Der Aufstand im Bergischen," *NRZ*, May 13, 1849, *MS, 1*, 39-40; "Reichsverfassungskampagne," *MS, 1*, 62, 68-69; Körner, *2*, 137-38; Pagenstecher, 66.

[38]Körner, *2*, 137; "Reichsverfassungskampagne," *MS, 1*, 63; Happich, 23, 26.

[39] "Elberfeld," *NRZ*, May 17, 1849, *MS, 1*, 42-43. The *NRZ* added the emphasis when it reprinted the expulsion order (omitting the part about the flags). Happich, 26, has the whole proclamation.

[40]Körner, *2*, 146; Pagenstecher, 68-74; Becker and Esselen, 42. Some of the more determined rebels ended up in Baden, where they made up a company of the Willich *Freikorps* in which Engels served. "Reichsverfassungskampagne," *MS, 1*, 69.

[41]Ludwig Häusser, *Denkwürdigkeiten zur Geschichte der Badischen Revolution* (Heidelberg: E. F. Winter, 1851), is a middle-of-the-road

account; J. B. Bekk, *Die Bewegung in Baden vom Ende des Februar 1848 bis zur Mitte des Mai 1849* (Mannheim: F. Bassermann, 1849) expresses the distress of the liberal minister who was compelled to suppress the Hecker and Struve expeditions, and was overthrown in 1849.

[42]On the problems of Baden's army, see Häusser, 272-94, 453-55, and Bekk, 252, 296-97. Rastatt was a Confederation fort with a mixed garrison, and by one account, Baden infantry had assailed the better-paid Austrian engineers with snowballs in February, 1849. Albert Förderer, *Erinnerungen aus Rastatt 1849* (Lahr in Baden: Chr. Schömperlen, 1899), 3-4, 11-12.

[43]*Bote für Stadt und Land,* June 3, 1849, *MS, 1,* 44-46.

[44]"Reichsverfassungskampagne," *MS, 1,* 92-94, 96. Engels' objections to the caliber of the available talent did not apply to Mieroslawski, who later took over supreme command from Franz Sigel, and whom Engels later called "the most significant of all Polacks." To Marx, July 22, 1852, *28,* 94.

[45] "Reichsverfassungskampagne," *MS, 1,* 85-89, 73. Most observers agreed that the revolution needed a larger base of support than the Palatinate and Baden; Häusser argued (358-61) that the revolution should have limited its goals strictly to the defense of the Frankfurt constitution, in order to attract moderate support; Becker and Esselen (154, 206-7) recommended spreading revolution with the bayonet; Karl Heinzen called for "revolutionary terrorism." *Einige Blicke auf die badischpfälzische Revolution* (Bern: Jenni, 1849), 13-14, 17. The anarchist Abt said that peace should have been maintained at all costs lest war lead to organization; the revolution could be saved only by inspiring revolts in the armies of Baden's neighbors. He did not explain how this was to have been done. *Die Revolution in Baden und die Demokraten* (Herisau: M. Schläpfer, 1849), 145-46.

[46]"Reichsverfassungskampagne," *MS, 1,* 74; Häusser, 453-55. According to Becker and Esselen (149) many of Baden's soldiers collected their pay and went to America. Engels to Jakob Schabelitz, Aug. 24, 1849, *27,* 509.

[47] "Reichsverfassungskampagne," *MS, 1,* 86. Engels' account of this episode is corroborated by Ferdinand Fenner von Fenneberg, commander of the Palatine *Volkswehr: Zur Geschichte des Rheinpfälzischen Aufstandes* (Zurich: E. Kiesling, 1850), 93-100, and by Ludwig Bamberger, *Erlebnisse aus der Pfälzischen Erhebung in Mai und Juni 1849* (Frankfurt: Literarische Anstalt, 1849), 57-60. Charles Dahlinger says that it "reminds one of the brave deeds of the knights of old." *The German Revolution of 1849* (New York: Putnam, 1903). No doubt he has Quixote in mind.

[48]"Reichsverfassungskampagne," *MS, 1,* 100-102.

[49]To Jakob Schabelitz, Aug. 24, 1849, *27,* 509; to Jenny Marx, July 25, 1849, *27,* 501.

[50]Swiss records, compiled when the survivors went into exile at the end of the campaign, confirm Engels' claim that the corps was largely composed of workers. Rolf Dlubek, "Friedrich Engels als publizistischer Anwalt des Willichschen Freikorps," *Beiträge zur Geschichte der deutschen Arbeiterbewegung,* 9 (1964), 237. Willich himself escaped Engels'

criticism until the émigré quarrels arose in London; Mayer (1, 177) suggests that Willich briefly joined the series of masters—Strauss, Börne, Hegel, finally Marx—whom Engels followed.

[51]Mathilde Gieseler-Anneke, "Memoiren einer Frau aus dem Badisch-Pfälzischen Feldzug," *German-American Annals, 16* (1918), 112; "Reichsverfassungskampagne," *MS, 1,* 104-14.

[52]Becker and Esselen (324) consider that Willich's attempt was made "without orders and without reasonable prudence."

[53]"Reichsverfassungskampagne," *MS, 1,* 116-24, 132. Becker and Esselen (396) praise Willich's force in the actions along the Murg.

[54]"Reichsverfassungskampagne," *MS, 1,* 133, 138. The insurgents had about 4000 infantry and 40 guns left, and the artillerymen, at least, were still willing to fight. Becker and Esselen (434-35) confirm Willich's determination, which they consider foolish.

[55]July 25, 1849, 27, 501. According to Marx's daughter Eleanor, all who had seen Engels under fire remarked on his "extraordinary coolness and his total contempt for danger." "Friedrich Engels," *Mohr und General*, 446.

[56]Engels to editor, *AMZ,* Aug. 24, 1860, *30,* 559-60; to Joseph Weydemeyer, June 19, 1851, 27, 553; to Jakob Schabelitz, Aug. 24, 1849, 27, 509. Stepanova (102) attempts to prove that Engels was working hard when he wrote his memoir, contending that it advanced the Marxist theory of insurrection by "showing how the armed uprising should *not* be led." Mayer, *1,* 352, sees the "Reichsverfassungskampagne" as a "masterpiece of German descriptive prose." Mayer is closer to the relaxed spirit of the thing.

Notes to Chapter 2

[1] "Programm der blanquistischen Kommuneflüchtlinge," *Volksstaat,* June 26, 1874, *MEW, 18,* 528.

[2]Fund appeals, etc., 7, 545-60; Marx, *Herr Vogt, MEW, 14,* 394, 440, 443-45; Marx to Engels, Feb. 24, 1851, 27, 198-99.

[3]As Leopold Schwartzschild points out. *Karl Marx: The Red Prussian* (New York: Scribner's, 1947), 217-30, 243-47.

[4]For the Demands, see *MEW, 5,* 3-5; good commentaries on the state of the League and its factions are Shlomo Na'aman, "Zur Geschichte des Bundes der Kommunisten in Deutschland in der zweiten Phase seines Bestehens," *Archiv für Sozialgeschichte, 5* (1965), 5-82, esp. 72-73, and Werner Blumenberg, "Zur Geschichte des Bundes der Kommunisten. Die Aussagen des Peter Gerhardt Röser," *IRSH, 9* (1964), 99, 115-16.

[5]G. A. Techow to A. Schimmelpfennig, Aug.-Sept. 1850, in Carl Vogt,

Mein Prozess gegen die Allgemeine Zeitung (Geneva: the author, 1859), 158; Na'aman, 58.

[6]Marx, *Herr Vogt*, *MEW*, *14*, 668; to Engels, May 6, 1851, *28*, 68; to Engels, Dec. 9, 1851, *27*, 383; "Revue," *NRZ-Revue*, May-Oct. 1850, *MEW*, *7*, 440; to Weydemeyer, Dec. 19, 1849, *27*, 516; Engels to Marx, May 7, 1852, *28*, 68. Engels' business contacts also expected a crash: "Peter Ermen shits his pants whenever he thinks about it, and he's an excellent barometer." Engels to Marx, July 30, 1851, *27*, 290.

[7]Boris Nicolaievsky and Otto Maenchen-Helfen, *Karl Marx, Man and Fighter* (Philadelphia: Lippincott, 1936), 206-18. For the Central Committee's June 1850 statement avowing connections with Blanquist groups, see *MEW*, *7*, 306-12. For the fullest treatment of the Blanquist problem in Marxism, see Richard N. Hunt, *The Political Ideas of Marx and Engels, 1: Marxism and Totalitarian Democracy* (Pittsburgh: University of Pittsburgh Press, 1974), 132-258.

[8]Marx to Engels, Mar. 1, 1869, *32*, 264; to Paul and Laura Lafargue, Feb. 15, 1869, *32*, 592; to Jenny Marx, Aug. 15, 1870, *33*, 137; Engels, "Programm der blanquistischen Kommuneflüchtlinge," *Volksstaat*, June 26, 1874, *MEW*, *18*, 529-30. On Blanqui's popularity on the Marx household, see Werner Blumenberg, "Ein unbekanntes Kapitel aus Marx' Leben," *IRSH*, *1* (1956), 95.

[9]Nicolaievsky and Maenchen-Helfen, 214.

[10]Blanqui sent a toast to a revolutionary banquet which featured an address by Louis Blanc, whom Blanqui considered a traitor. Blanqui's toast was not read, but Marx and Engels published it as a pamphlet. *MEW*, *7*, 568-70. Blanqui's assertion that he who has iron has bread bore a remarkable resemblance to the force theory that Engels later assailed in the *Anti-Dühring*. On this incident see W. I. Fishman, *The Insurrectionists* (London: Methuen, 1970), 71.

[11]Review of works by A. Chenu and L. de la Hodde, *NRZ-Revue*, April 1850, *MEW*, *7*, 267-68, 271-80; Vogt, 153-54.

[12]*The Army, Standing Army or National Army? An Essay* (Cincinnati: A. Frey, 1866) esp. 3, 12-13, 21-23.

[13]Engels to Ernst Dronke, July 9, 1851, *27*, 561; to Marx, Sept. 23, 1851, *27*, 343; Blumenberg, "Röser," 109-110. For other similar schemes, not invented by Willich, see Wolfgang Schieder, "Der Bund der Kommunisten im Sommer 1850. Drei Dokumente aus dem Marx-Engels Nachlass," *IRSH*, *13* (1968), 43-45, 49-50.

[14]Engels to Marx, Mar. 19, 1851, *27*, 223; Marx to Engels, Oct. 28, 1852, *28*, 170; Engels to Marx, Nov. 23, 1853, quoted in Marx, *Der Ritter vom edelmüthigen Bewusstsein*, *MEW*, *9*, 498. Cf. Marx, *Enthüllungen über den Kommunisten-Prozess zu Köln*, *MEW*, *8*, 413.

[15]Engels to Marx, Sept. 23, 1851, *27*, 343; Marx to Engels, July 13, 1851, *27*, 279; Marx, *Enthüllungen*, *MEW*, *8*, 412; Central Committee minutes, Sept. 15, 1860, *MEW*, *8*, 598.

[16]Techow's views were summarized by Marx, to Engels, Sept. 23, 1851, *27*, 347-49. Cf. D. Riazonov, introduction to Engels, "Die Möglichkeiten

und Voraussetzungen eines Krieges der heiligen Allianz gegen Frankreich im Jahre 1852," *Neue Zeit, 33* (1914-15), 266. Engels to Marx, Sept. 26, 1851, 27, 353; to Marx, Mar. 19, 1851, 27, 222. Engels expressed some disillusionment with the Terror (to Marx, Sept. 4, 1870, 33, 53) but later accorded it some value (to Kautsky, Feb. 20, 1889, 37, 155).

[17]To Marx, Feb. 11, 1853, 28, 212-13; Marx to Engels, Feb. 23, 1853, 28, 214-16. Cf. Marx, *Tribune,* Mar. 8, 1853, *MEW, 8,* 527, Engels to Marx, Mar. 9, 1853, 28, 217.

[18]Engels to Marx, Feb. 13, 1851, 28, 190; July 20, 1851, 28, 288-89; Marx to Hermann Becker, Feb. 28, 1851, 28, 546-47; to Weydemeyer, Jan. 23, 1852, 28, 478.

[19]To Marx, Nov. 23, 1853, reprinted by Marx in the *Ritter, MEW, 9,* 500. Engels' "Reichsverfassungskampagne" had painted Willich as almost the only competent officer on the revolutionary side (*MS, 1,* 97), and it was remarked that Engels saw Willich and himself as the only useful people in the campaign. Schieder, 52.

[20]To Weydemeyer, Aug. 7, 1851, 27, 569; on the scandal, wherein Willich was alleged to have been thrown out of Baroness von Brünigk's house after trying to rape his hostess, Marx to Engels, May 22, 1852, 28, 78; Engels to Marx, May 24, 1852, 28, 79; Marx to Engels, July 3, 1852, 28, 81-82; Marx to Adolf Cluss, Oct. 8, 1852, 28, 552-53. Engels said that the affair was surprising, since Willich usually evidenced "more enthusiasm for young blond cobblers'-apprentices than for fair ladies." To Weydemeyer, June 11, 1852, 28, 532.

[21]So translated by Edward Fitzgerald, in Franz Mehring, *Karl Marx: The Story of His Life* (Ann Arbor: University of Michigan, 1962), 223. The title was intended to convey a sense of self-righteousness. Marx asked Engels for material in letters of Apr. 30 and May 6, 1852, 28, 62 and 69.

[22]Engels thought that the £25 offered by Bangya "valent bien un peu de scandale" (May 1, 1852, 28, 64-65), but Bangya never paid. Engels, more worldly than Marx, was first to suspect Bangya. For the booklet, *Die Grossen Männer des Exils,* see *MEW, 8,* 233-335. On Bangya, see R. Rosdolsky, "Karl Marx und der Polizeispitzel Bangya," *IRSH, 2* (1937), 229-45.

[23]To Marx, May 23, 1851, 27, 266; Marx to Engels, Apr. 30, 1852, 28, 61; Engels to Marx, July 15, 1852, 28, 91. Happich, p. 43, considers that this last statement proves that Engels' studies were directed "toward the decisive revolutionary moment," not "merely intended as the basis for journalistic endeavors." It seems not to prove quite that. "Lieutenant" was used as a term of mild derision, owing to the combination of authority and inexperience sometimes present in new officers. See Engels to Marx, Sept. 23, 1852, 28, 138; Engels, "The Armies of Europe," *Putnam's 6* (1855), 309.

[24]To Weydemeyer, June 19, 1851, 27, 553. Engels had asked Marx for Weydemeyer's address on Apr. 3, 1851, 27, 234; Weydemeyer was defending the Marxist position in the United States. On his career, which included service in the Civil War and the posthumous honor of a Liberty

182   ENGELS, ARMIES, AND REVOLUTION

Ship named for him, see Karl Obermann, *Joseph Weydemeyer, Pioneer of American Socialism* (New York: International Publishers, 1947).

[25]To Ruge, July 26, 1842, 27, 408; to Weydemeyer, June 19, 1851, 27, 553-55.

[26]*La petite guerre, ou traité des opérations secondaires de la guerre* (Brussels: Société de librairie belge, 1838). This work went through three editions between 1822 and 1828. Peter Paret, *Yorck and the Era of Prussian Reform, 1807-1815* (Princeton: Princeton University Press, 1966), 176. Engels had used this French edition in Switzerland while writing the *Reichsverfassungskampagne*. To Weydemeyer, Aug. 7, 1851, 27, 568.

[27]Sir William P. Napier, *History of the War in the Peninsula and the South of France, from A.D. 1807 to A.D. 1814* (6 vols., London: Warne, 1850); Engels to Weydemeyer, June 19, 1851, 27, 555. Engels had already praised the Napier work to Marx, and had complained of the difficulty of getting the volumes from his local libraries in proper order. Feb. 26, 1851, 27, 203-04, Mar. 17, 1851, 27, 217. He so admired Napier that when he offered to send some military articles to the London *Daily News* as a sample of his work, he asked that they be judged by Napier rather than any "lesser martinet." To H. J. Lincoln, Mar. 30, 1854, 28, 600.

[28]Apr. 11, 1851, 27, 235-36. Wellington, said Engels, had no spark of genius, but excelled at picking defensive positions and withdrawing from them: *"tel soldat, tel politique"*—the perfect representative of Toryism.

[29]Aug. 27, 1851, 27, 568-69. Weydemeyer was to write to Engels' business address, so that the firm of Ermen and Engels might bear the postage costs of Engels' military education. Cf. similar postal advice, to Weydemeyer, Apr. 16, 1852, 28, 513; to Wilhelm Steffen (who was supposed to send maps), Apr. 15, 1856, 29, 531.

[30]"England," *MEW, 8,* 208-18; to Weydemeyer, Feb. 27, 1852, 28, 500-01. Mayer, 2, 35, points out the showing off in the article.

[31]Jan. 23, 1852, 28, 482-83.

[32]To Weydemeyer, Apr. 16, 1852, 28, 514.

[33]Engels to Marx, July 15, 1852, 28, 91; to Weydemeyer, Apr. 12, 1853, 28, 576.

[34]To Marx, May 7, 1852, 28, 71; to Weydemeyer, April 12, 1853, 28, 576-81. Later Engels could disagree openly with Weydemeyer on a military question. Grant's approach to Richmond from the sea side of the city was not dangerous, as Weydemeyer feared, but proper procedure when one controlled the sea. Engels cited Wellington's campaigns in Spain to prove his case. Mar. 10, 1865, 31, 458-59.

[35]To Marx, Apr. 3, 1851, 27, 231-32. Cf. Marx to Engels, Apr. 2, 1851, 27, 228.

[36]To Marx, May 7, 1852, 28, 72; July 6, 1852, 28, 86; Aug. 16, 1852, 28, 111; June 10, 1854, 28, 365-66; Marx to Engels, Dec. 14, 1854, 28, 315. Engels' library contained a copy of another Hungarian campaign memoir, by Friedrich Heller von Hellwald, carefully annotated and compared with Görgey. Bruno Kaiser, *Ex libris Karl Marx und Friedrich Engels. Schicksal und Verzeichnis einer Bibliothek* (Berlin: Dietz, 1967), 92.

[37]Sept. 30, 1853, *28*, 299. Engels lived in Manchester, Marx in London. Therefore their correspondence.

[38]Marx to Engels, Nov. 2, 1853, *28*, 306; Mar. 10, 1853, *28*, 222. Marx declared that he and Engels had "neglected this subject [international relations] far too long." Nov. 2, 1853, *28*, 307. Marx's curious enthusiasm for the Turcophile "monomaniac" David Urquhart (e.g., Marx to Engels, Feb. 9, 1854, *28*, 324-25) cannot be discussed here. More of Marx's requests for comments on military affairs: Nov. 23, 1853, *28*, 310; Jan. 18, 1854, *28*, 319; Jan. 24, 1854, *28*, 321; Apr. 19, 1854, *28*, 340; June 21, 1854, *28*, 370; July 22, 1854, *28*, 377-79; July 17, 1855, *28*, 453; etc.

[39]Engels to Marx, Mar. 11, 1853, *28*, 226. (A.P.C. was Aurelius Pulszky, a former aide to Kossuth. Engels hoped to demolish him with a display of *Allwissenheit* in Turkish matters, but A.P.C. was durable.) Marx to Engels, Mar. 11, 1854, *28*, 329.

[40]To Engels, Mar. 29, 1854, *28*, 334.

[41]Marx to Engels, Dec. 11, 1853, *28*, 463; *Courier*, Oct. 18, 1853; *Tribune*, Dec. 20, 1853; Marx to Engels, Jan. 5, 1854, *28*, 317.

[42]To Engels, Dec. 2, 1853, *28*, 311; to Engels, Sept. 11, 1855, *28*, 460. Cf. Marx to Engels, Mar. 31, 1851, *27*, 226.

[43]Marx to Engels, Aug. 19, 1852, *28*, 112-13; Engels to Marx, Aug. 24, 1852, *28*, 117; Marx to Engels, June 29, 1855, *28*, 450; July 23, 1855, *28*, 451. Marx's bibliographic assistance to Engels' military efforts are summarized in A. J. Babin, "Die schöpferische Zusammenarbeit von Marx und Engels auf militärgeschichtlichem Gebiet," *ZfMG*, *9* (1970), 420-29.

[44]June 2, 1852, *28*, 252-53; Mar. 29, 1854, *28*, 334; Sept. 7, 1857, *29*, 192-93.

[45]To Engels, Apr. 2, 1851, *27*, 229. There was a falling out with the Baroness, for Engels soon referred to her as a whore (to Marx, Sept. 1, 1851, *27*, 334), and Marx published a notice disavowing all connection with her. *Kölnische Zeitung*, Oct. 9, 1851, *MEW*, *8*, 108. For other Hungarians offered Engels, see Marx to Engels, Apr. 5, 1852, *28*, 49; May 6, 1852, *28*, 68-69; July 13, 1852, *28*, 88; Marx to Szemere, Apr. 4, 1860, *30*, 520; Marx to Engels, Apr. 5, 1852, *28*, 49; May 13, 1852, *28*, 73.

[46]Engels to Weydemeyer, Aug. 7, 1851, *27*, 568; Marx to Engels, May 16, 1855, *28*, 446.

[47]"Quid pro Quo," *Volk*, July 30, 1859, *MEW*, *13*, 450; "Truth Testified," *Tribune*, Aug. 4, 1859, *MEW*, *8*, 440; Maximilien Rubel, "Les cahiers d'étude de Karl Marx, II. 1853-1856," *IRSH*, *5* (1960), 56.

[48]To Engels, Nov. 30, 1854, *28*, 413-14; Dec. 2, 1854, *28*, 416-17; Dec. 15, 1854, *28*, 420-21.

[49]To Engels, Jan. 18, 1854, *28*, 319-20; Jan. 25, 1854, *28*, 321-22. For Engels' view on the fortifications question, "The Movements of the Armies in Turkey," *Tribune*, Nov. 8, 1853, *MEW*, *9*, 438-39; "The Crimean Prospects," *Tribune*, Oct. 1, 1855, *MEW*, *11*, 533; "The Siege of Sevastopol," *Tribune*, Nov. 15, 1854, *MEW*, *10*, 543, repeated in "Rückblicke," *Neue Oder-Zeitung*, Jan. 4, 1855, *MEW*, *10*, 591.

[50]*Inter alia*: Marx to Engels, Mar. 25, 1856, *29*, 32; Apr. 10, 1856, *29*, 38; July 14, 1857, *29*, 155; Aug. 15, 1857, *29*, 160-61; Sept. 17. 1857, *29*, 176 (here

Marx seems to have done some rather technical reading, but he defers to Engels nevertheless); Sept. 23,1857, 29, 188; Nov. 13, 1857, 29, 207; Jan.1, 1858, 29, 246; Feb. 12, 1858, 29, 285; Aug. 8, 1858, 29, 349; Aug. 13, 1858, 29, 352. Marx said that lack of time to master unfamiliar material, rather than any constitutional incapacity, kept him from doing military articles, but they were out of his province anyway. To Engels, Jan. 5, 1858, 29, 247; Aug. 18, 1858, 29, 354.

[51]Engels to Marx, Mar.23, 1854, 28, 331-32; Marx to Lassalle, Apr. 6, 1854, 28, 604-06.

[52]Marx to Engels, Dec. 14, 1853, 28, 316; Engels to H. J. Lincoln, Mar. 30, 1854, 28, 600-03; Engels to Marx, Apr. 3, 1854, 28, 337; Marx to Engels, Apr. 4, 1854, 28, 338.

[53]To Marx, Apr. 20, 1854, 28, 342; Marx to Engels, Apr. 22, 1854, 28, 347.

[54]To Marx, Apr. 21, 1854, 28, 344-45; Apr. 20, 1854, 28, 343; June 10, 1854, 28, 366.

[55]Carlton (161-62) laments the failure to get the job, under the impression that it would have got Engels away from the malevolent influence of Marx. She confuses the positions of war correspondent ("a civilian who goes to the front") and military correspondent ("a soldier who stays at home"). Definitions from The Liddell Hart Memoirs (New York: Putnam, 1965), 1, 80. Engels wanted to move to London, not to Sevastopol. When he and Marx proposed to supply the Tribune with on-the-spot reports, the war correspondent recommended was Otto von Mirbach, Engels' old commander in the Elberfeld revolution. Engels to Marx, Dec. 12, 1855, 28, 464. Engels later preferred to report the Franco-Prussian War from England instead of the battlefield, since England provided more chance for objectivity and more security from the Prussian police. Marx to Engels, July 20, 1870, 33, 6; Engels to Marx, July 22, 1870, 33, 9.

[56]Engels to Lassalle, Mar. 15, 1860, 30, 517 (further correspondence on the anonymity of the pamphlets: Marx to Engels, Feb. 25, 1859, 29, 401; Marx to Lassalle, Feb.25, 1859, 29, 580-81: Engels to Lassalle, March 14, 1859, 29, 582; Marx to Engels, shortly after Jan. 11, 1860, 30, 6; Engels to Marx, Jan. 30, 1860, 30, 14; Engels to Marx, Feb. 4, 1860, 30, 25). Marx's source of military gossip was Countess Hatzfeldt, Lassalle's friend; through her he met General von Pfuel, whom he and Engels had assailed fiercely in 1848-49, and discussed Engels' pamphlet with the General. To Engels, May 7, 1861, 30, 162.

[57]Ernst Drahn, Friedrich Engels als Kriegswissenschaftler (Gautzsch bei Leipzig: Felix Dietrich, 1915), 20. Wolfe's complaint (Marxism, 31-32) that the two strategic pamphlets lack any socialist characteristics misses the point; they were aimed at an audience not noted for socialist sympathies.

[58]The Volunteer Movement was a semiofficial force assembled to repel a possible French invasion, during the war scare that followed the coup of Napoleon III. Engels to editor, AMZ, Sept.8, 1860, 30, 559-60; to Marx, Sept. 15, 1860, 30, 93. The article appeared in AMZ, Sept. 8, 1860, and is in

MEW, *15*, 137-43; English version in *Volunteer Journal*, *1* (Sept. 14, 1860) and is in *EMC*, 1-8.

[59]Marx to Engels, Oct. 2, 1860, *30*, 102; Marx to Lassalle, Oct. 2, 1860, *30*, 568; Engels to Marx, Oct. 5, 1860, *30*, 104; Sept. 15, 1860, *30*, 93.

[60]The pamphlet's component articles are in *EMC*, somewhat rearranged. For the *United Services Gazette* review, see *EMC*, xvi. The pamphlet was said to be "modestly and carefully written," though Engels was "to a considerable extent bitten with that new-fangled admiration for French soldiering which we, after long and intimate knowledge, hold to be an utter delusion." The history of the rifle was particularly praised; later Gordon Craig used it as a handy and accurate summary of the subject. *The Battle of Königgrätz: Prussia's Victory over Austria, 1866* (Philadelphia: Lippincott, 1964), 20.

[61]Gerlach, who had never before seen a socialist, was received with great cordiality and attended one of the drinking parties that Engels held to celebrate election victories by the German Social Democrats. *Von Rechts nach Links* (Zürich: Europa Verlag, 1937), 138. Engels' correspondence with Wachs had begun in 1893, when he noticed Wachs' name in the Military Commission and asked August Bebel to find out whether it was the same Wachs whom Engels had met 25 years before in Manchester. Wachs, a cousin of Engels' friend Eduard Gumpert, had then just joined the Prussian Army, and was depressed to find there the same barrack spirit that he had thought to leave behind in Electoral Hesse. Engels advised him to stick it out. Engels to Bebel, Feb. 9, 1893, *39*, 27-28.

[62]June 19, 1851, *27*, 553.

[63]Nov. 15, 1857, *29*, 212; Dec. 31, 1857, *29*, 245; Feb. 11, 1858, *29*, 278.

[64]Feb. 14, 1858, *29*, 280. Paul Lafargue reports Marx's fear that Engels would kill himself while hunting. "Persönliche Erinnerungen an Friedrich Engels," *Neue Zeit*, *23* (1905), 556. Marx himself could barely ride (Wilhelm Liebknecht, *Karl Marx: Biographical Memoirs* [Chicago: Kerr, 1901], 129); his "horse exercise" probably involved a wooden contraption. Engels to Jenny Marx, May 11, 1858, *29*, 558; Marx to Engels, Sept. 21, 1858, *29*, 355. No doubt Marx also resented Engels' supporting a horse (a Christmas present from his father, 1856) while the Marxes were particularly hungry. Engels to Marx, Jan. 22, 1857, *29*, 100; Aug. 1, 1862, *30*, 261.

[65]Feb. 18, 1858, *29*, 282-83; Engels to Victor Adler, Sept. 25, 1892, *38*, 473. Cf. Mayer, *2*, 173.

[66]Marx to his daughter Jenny, Jan. 11, 1865, *31*, 442; Engels to Marx, Apr. 11, 1859, *29*, 417; to Kugelmann, Nov. 8 and 20, 1867, *31*, 569 (Engels insisted that Kugelmann, a gynecologist, owed some horsemanship to his profession, which concerned "riding and being ridden"); to J. P. Becker, Oct. 15, 1884, *36*, 218; Apr. 2, 1885, *36*, 290; June 15, 1885, *36*, 328.

[67]To Weydemeyer, Apr. 12, 1853, *28*, 581-82, 577; "Betrachtungen und Aussichten eines Krieges der Heiligen Allianz gegen ein revolutionäres Frankreich im Jahre 1852," *MS*, *1*, 220. This essay was first published in *Neue Zeit*, *33* (1914/15) and is in *MEW*, *7*, 468-93, under a somewhat different title. It is cited below as "Holy Alliance vs. France," from the *MS*.

[68]To Marx, Feb. 7, 1856, *29*, 10.

[69]Lafargue to Marx, Apr. 28, 1871, quoted in Celina Bobinska, *Marx und Engels über polnische Probleme* (Berlin: Dietz, 1958), 278.

[70]On Engels' plan, below, pp. 123-24. Delbrück's opinion was expressed to Gustav Mayer, who reports it in his *Erinnerungen: vom Journalisten zum Historiker der deutschen Arbeiterbewegung* (Munich: Verlag der Zwölf, 1949), 357. On Delbrück, see Franz Mehring, "Eine Geschichte der Kriegskunst," *Neue Zeit*, Erg. 4 (Oct. 16, 1908), 1-2; Gordon A. Craig, "Delbruck: The Military Historian," *Makers of Modern Strategy*, 280-83. Delbrück's praise of Engels' military qualities is thus more of an expert judgment than Liebknecht's ("Friedrich Engels," 423).

[71]Lafargue, "Persönliche Erinnerungen," 560-61; Engels to Lafargue, Dec. 30, 1871, *33*, 365-66; to Carlo Terzaghi, Jan. 6, Jan. 14-15, 1872, *33*, 372-75; to Theodor Cuno, Jan. 24, 1872, *33*, 389; "Aus der Internationale," *Volksstaat*, July 2, 1873, *MEW*, *18*, 475; article on authority, *Almonacco Republicano per l'anno 1874*, *MEW*, *18*, 306-07. See also Hans-Jürgen Usczek, "Friedrich Engels zum Volkskrieg in Frankreich," *ZfMG*, *9*(1970), 517-20.

[72]Lafargue, "Persönliche Erinnerungen," 557; Frank Jellinek, *The Paris Commune of 1871* (New York: Grosset & Dunlap, 1965), 241-63.

[73]*Herr Vogt*, *MEW*, *14*, 441; Engels to Weydemeyer, Nov. 24, 1864, *31*, 425; Marx, introduction to a new edition of the *Enthullungen uber den Kommunisten-Prozess zu Köln*, *MEW*, *18*, 569.

[74]*Tribune*, June 22 and Sept. 24, *MEW*, *15*, 60-64, 155-58. Marx did point out that a revolution of sorts was already under way when Garibaldi landed, but he did not attempt to make such developments a precondition for revolutionary invasion. *Tribune*, June 4, Aug. 8, 1860, *MEW*, *15*, 55, 92. Cf. Marx to Hermann Ebner, Dec. 2, 1851, *27*, 597.

[75]To Engels, Sept. 12, 1863, *30*, 372. Marx thought that such a legion would either encourage a German rising, or embarrass the German democrats. According to the prospective leader, Colonel Lapinski, Marx himself suggested the idea. Adam Ciolkosz, "Karl Marx and the Polish Insurrection of 1863," *Polish Review*, *10* (1965), 22-23. Engels apparently made no comment on the project.

[76]He later described his articles, mostly on military topics, for Dana's *New American Cyclopedia* as "strictly business." To Hermann Schlüter, Jan. 29, 1891, *38*, 16.

[77]To Marx, Jan. 7, 1858, *29*, 252. He had previously encountered the historical works of Clausewitz, whom he called "as much a standard author in his line, all over the world, as Jomini" in 1855. *Putnam's*, *6* (Sept. 1855), 309.

[78]*Germany: Revolution and Counterrevolution* (originally articles in *Tribune*, 1851-52), *German Revolutions*, 227-28, 198, 206-207.

[79]"Garibaldi in Sicily," June 14, 1860, *MEW*, *15*, 62.

[80]Happich, 38, 47; the Marx-Engels correspondence contains too many references to suspicion of the mails to enumerate. Wolfe (114) is oddly indignant that Engels and Marx should so suspect the British Government;

as Marx pointed out, violation of the privacy of the mails had been admitted in Parliament. To Engels, Mar. 2, 1852, *28*, 34. Marx said at one point that an Alien Bill would be a good thing, as it would keep the émigrés stirred up, but actual expulsion would have been a great inconvenience. To Engels, Mar. 1, 1851, *27*, 213.

[81]*Grosse Männer, MEW, 8*, 315-16; Engels to Marx, Aug. 16, 1852, *28*, 111; Sept. 24, 1852, *28*, 146. Engels' general assertion that insurrection is an art with (mostly unspecified) rules of its own inspires this tribute from Stepanova (113): "This Marxist teaching on armed insurrection was developed on the basis of the subsequent class struggles of the proletariat and especially of the Moscow rising in December 1905. In the decisive days of October, 1917, the Bolshevik Party gave a classic example of how to prepare and carry out a successful armed revolution."

[82]Engels to Marx, Feb. 11, 1853, *28*, 212-13; Oct. 9, 1857, *29*, 195; "Konflikte zwischen Polizei und Volk," *Neue Oder-Zeitung*, July 9, 1855, *MEW, 11*, 345; Marx to Engels, July 27, 1866, *31*,243.

[83]"The Reform Movement in France," *Northern Star*, Nov. 20, 1847, *MEGA*, 1, *6*, 356; to Kautsky, Nov. 3, 1893, *39*, 161; preface (1895) to Marx's *Klassenkämpfe in Frankreich, MS, 2*, 689-90.

[84]Engels and Marx, "That Bore of a War," *Tribune*, Aug. 17, *MEW, 10*, 380-81; Marx, "Revolution in Spain," *Tribune*, Aug. 18, 1856, *MEW, 12*, 45. The *Werke* attributes this article to Marx, who indeed wrote most of the Spanish pieces, but it seems unlikely that he would have commented upon the tactical aspects of the revolution without consulting Engels.

[85]Debray, *Revolution in the Revolution?* (New York: Grove Press, 1967) is the most forceful advocate of this theory. On the guerrillist school of thought in general, see Theodor Arnold, *Der revolutionäre Krieg* (Pfaffenhofen/Ilm: Ilmgau Verlag, 1967).

[86]Decker, 30; Napier, *1*, iv, also 120-21, 42-43. Napier disapproved of armed peasants and considered regular army support essential to any successful insurrection.

[87] "The Holy War," *Tribune*, Nov. 15, 1853, *MEW, 9*, 156; "England," article sent to Weydemeyer in 1851, *MEW, 8*, 213-14.

[88]Engels and Marx, "Die Lage auf den amerikanischen Kriegsschauplätze," *Presse*, May 30, 1862, *MEW, 15*, 507 (this article follows closely Engels' letter to Marx, May 23, 1862, *30*, 240-41); Engels to Marx, July 30, 1862, *30*, 255; May 23, 1862, *30*, 240; May 29, 1862, *30*, 244; to Hermann Engels, Nov. 2, 1864, *31*, 421; to Weydemer, Nov. 24, 1864, *31*, 424; to Marx, Sept. 4, 1864, *30*, 430; to Rudolf Engels, Jan. 10, 1865, *31*, 440; to Marx, Feb. 7, 1865, *31*, 62.

[89]"The Indian Army," *Tribune*, July 21, 1858, *FIWI*, 175-76; "Garibaldi in Sicily," *Tribune*, June 22, 1860, *MEW, 15*, 62-64. Cf. "Garibaldi in Calabria," *Tribune*, Sept. 24, 1860, *MEW, 15*, 155.

[90]Reinhard Höhn, *Sozialismus und Heer, 1*, 65, suggests that this concentration on real rather than on desirable conditions was somehow derived from Scharnhorst.

[91]"Holy Alliance vs. France," *MS, 1*, 218-21; to Marx, Nov. 15, 1857, *29*, 212.

[92]"Kinglake über die Schlacht an der Alma," ms. probably begun for the *Allgemeine Militär-Zeitung* in 1864, *MEW*, *15*, 589-91; to Marx, Oct. 6, 1857, *29*, 195 (Engels translated for the *Volunteer Journal*, Feb. 9-Mar. 2, 1861, a lecture in which Marshal Bugeaud disapproved of skirmishing, *MEW*, *15*, 248-50); "Taktik der Infanterie aus den materiellen Ursachen abgeleitet, 1700-1870," note intended for the *Anti-Dühring*, *MS*, *2*, 623-24; "Notes on the War, No. IV," *Manchester Guardian*, July 3, 1866, *EMC*, 133-34.

[93]Lafargue, "Persönliche Erinnerungen," 560, reports that Marx accused Engels of studying things just for the fun of it, but these objections probably were aimed at Engels' philological studies; Marx always encouraged the military researches. Heinz Helmert uses Engels' *militaria* as a model for the Marxist military historian, and reasonably; but Engels did not occupy himself with military science in order to inspire future scholars. "Friedrich Engels und die Aufgaben der marxistischen Militärgeschichtsschreibung," *ZfMG*, 5 (1966), 72-84.

Notes to Chapter 3

[1]*Capital* (New York: International Publishers, 1967), *1*, 751.

[2]E.g., Engels' 1886 preface to the English edition of *Capital, ibid.*, 6; Marx, interview in *Woodhull and Claflin's Weekly*, Aug. 12, 1871, *MEW*, *17*, 641, and Engels' 1895 preface to Marx's *Class Struggles in France*, *MS*, *2*, 693. Adam Ulam calls this prophecy an "ingenious prognosis" by which Engels managed to salvage revolutionary rhetoric which had in Ulam's opinion become obsolete. *The Unfinished Revolution: An Essay on the Sources of Influence of Marxism and Communism* (New York: Random House, 1964), 144. It is adopted by the revolutionary pacifist A. J. Muste in his essay "Pacifism and Class War," in *The Essays of A. J. Muste*, ed. Nat Hentoff (Indianapolis: Bobbs-Merrill, 1967), 183.

[3]E.g. Schwartzschild, *passim*. Engels and Marx actually approved peaceful or violent tactics according to the conditions. See Engels, *The Condition of the Working Class in England* (New York: Macmillan, 1958), 291-92; Marx, ". . . Mazzini's Address. . . ," *Tribune*, Dec. 12, 1853, *MEW*, *9*, 521.

[4]Marx, "Die revolutionäre Bewegung," *NRZ*, Jan. 1, 1849, *MEW*, *6*, 148.

[5]Engels, "Progress of the Turkish War," *Tribune*, June 9, 1854, *MEW*, *10*, 243.

[6]As Ludwig von Mises points out; *Nation, Staat und Wirtschaft* (Vienna: Manzsche Verlags- und Universitätsbuchhandlung, 1919), 71.

[7]As von Mises fails to point out.

[8]See Gerhart Niemeyer, "The Second International: 1889-1914," in *The Revolutionary Internationals, 1864-1943* (Stanford: Stanford University Press, 1966), 108-09. The best known text is the *Manifesto, MEW, 4,* 497.

[9]Their opposition to pacifism is discussed by Lotte Kaufmann, *Die Einstellung von Karl Marx und Friedrich Engels zu Krieg und Frieden* (Würzburg: Richard Mayr, 1932), 17-19, 25-32, and Edmund A. Silberner, *The Problem of War in Nineteenth Century Economic Thought* (Princeton: Princeton University Press, 1946), 250-79. Hans Rothfels perceives the incompatibility between Marxism and pacifism, but goes too far in finding "militarism" and "pangermanism" inherent in Marxism. "Marxismus und auswärtige Politik," in *Deutscher Staat und deutsche Parteien* (Munich: R. Oldenbourg, 1922), 320-21. For a collection of antipacifist statements by Marx and Engels see Gerhard Lütkens, "Das Kriegsproblem und die Marxistische Theorie," *Archiv für Sozialwissenschaft und Sozialpolitik, 49* (1922), 475-76. Cf. Oskar Blum, "Jean Jaurès," *Archiv für die Geschichte des Sozialismus und der Arbeiterbewegung, 7* (1916), 22, 53-54, and D. Riazonov, "Die auswärtige Politik der alten Internationale und ihre Stellungnahme zum Krieg," *Neue Zeit, 33* (1915), 463.

[10]Marx, " . . . Mr. Cobden's Pamphlet . . . ," *Tribune,* Feb. 18, 1853, *MEW, 9,* 510.

[11]"Der demokratische Panslawismus," *NRZ,* Feb. 15, 1849, *MEW, 6,* 279. Cf. Marx's interview in the *Chicago Tribune,* Jan. 5, 1879, *MEW, 34,* 515. Kaufmann (29) argues that pacifism implies an acceptance of the status quo, as does the pacifist Albert Goedeckemeyer, who insists that revolutions as well as wars must be eliminated. *Die Idee vom ewigen Frieden* (Leipzig: F. Meiner, 1920), 44-46. Marx and Engels rejected the idea that demonstrations could bring about social changes in a nonviolent way, because they expected that the obsolescent order would resort to force when threatened. Engels considered unarmed demonstrations foolish in some situations. To Marx, Mar. 9, 1848, 27, 115-16. And once violence has broken out, the most a "revolutionary pacifist" can do is to sympathize with the revolutionaries while warning them that violence begets violence. Muste, 180-83.

[12]Werner Heider, *Die Geschichtslehre von Karl Marx* (Stuttgart: Cotta, 1931), 170-71.

[13]Von Mises, 71.

[14]"Marxism and the Southern Slav Question," tr. R. W. Seton-Watson, *Slavonic Review, 2* (1923-24), 290.

[15]Höhn, *Sozialismus und Heer, 1,* xxx; Heinrich Herkner, *Die Arbeiterfrage. Ein Einführung* (Berlin: W. de Gruyter, 1922), 2, 433-37. Max Victor, in contrast, insists that Marxism shares the liberal belief in the superior virtue of defensive wars, basing his argument on his interpretation of Marx's and Engels' stance in 1870-71. "Die Stellung der deutschen Sozialdemokratie zu den Fragen der auswärtigen Politik (1869-1914)," *Archiv für Sozialwissenschaft und Sozialpolitik, 60* (1928), 151. Cf. also Eduard Bernstein, "Karl Marx und Friedrich Engels in der zweiten Phase

des Krieges von 1870/71," *Neue Zeit, 33* (1914), 77-78. Lütkens, 479, says
that Bernstein deviated from Marx's and Engels' views and accorded a
democratic and pacific foreign policy priority over the furtherance of the
class struggle. Cf. G. Zinoviev, *Der Krieg und die Krise des Sozialismus*
(Vienna: Verlag für Literatur und Politik, 1924), 171-76. See also Wallach's
comments in Pelger, 96.

[16]Hermann Oncken finds in Engels a Cobdenite bias against the state.
"Friedrich Engels und die Anfänge des deutschen Kommunismus,"
Historische Zeitschrift, 123 (1920), 258-60. Cf. Friedrich Lenz, "Karl
Marx," *ibid., 124* (1921), 468-73; Hermann Heller, *Sozialismus und Nation*
(Berlin: E. Rowohlt, 1931), 13; Richard Biedrzynski, *Revolution um Karl
Marx* (Leipzig: R. Voigtländer, 1929); and Oswald Spengler, *Preussentum
und Sozialismus* (Munich: Beck, 1934), 4, 10, 69, 75.

[17]Marx to Engels, June 7, 1866, *31*, 222; June 20, 1866, *31*, 229. Engels told
Kautsky that an international movement was possible only between
independent nations. Feb. 7, 1882, *35*, 270.

[18]"What Have the Working Classes to Do with Poland?" *Common-
wealth*, Mar. 31 and May 5, 1866, in *The Russian Menace to Europe*, ed.
Paul W. Blackstock and Bert F. Hoselitz (Glencoe: Free Press, 1952),
97-104. Cf. "Der demokratische Panslawismus," *NRZ*, Feb. 15, 1849,
MEW, 6, 285. The Austro-Marxist Otto Bauer argued that class struggles
were expressed through national forms in the Habsburg Empire, so that
national self-consciousness should be encouraged. *Die Nationalitätenfrage und die Sozialdemokratie* (Marx-Studien, No. 2; Vienna:
Wiener Volksbuchhandlung, 1924), 230, 512-21.

[19]"Kinkel," *NRZ-Revue* (April, 1850), *MEW, 7*, 300.

[20]Frank Zint points out the unsatisfactory character of the 1848
revolutionaries, and the provisional character of Engels' and Marx's
support of them, but errs in ascribing a wholly positive revolutionary role
to various Great Powers. France, he says, was succeeded by England,
then Prussia as Red Hope. *Karl Marx und die grossen europäischen
Mächte. Beitrag zu einer politischen Biographie* (Frankfurt a.M.: A. Beck,
1937), 63-64, 91, 118-19. Kaufmann (33) points out that there is no
satisfactory treatment of Marxist attitudes toward the European powers,
and her own excursion into the area is necessarily sketchy. Karl Kautsky's
Sozialisten und Krieg is more descriptive than analytical, tending to
assume simply that Marx and Engels supported just wars and opposed
unjust ones. Solomon F. Bloom, *The World of Nations: A Study of the
National Implications in the Work of Karl Marx* (New York: Columbia
University Press, 1941), is concerned mostly with national character.

[21]Höhn, *Armee als Erziehungsschule*, 112.

[22]Marx to Engels, Dec. 2, 1856, *29*, 88; Engels to Marx, May 23, 1851, *27*,
266; see Adam Ciolkosz, "Karl Marx and the Polish Insurrection of 1863,"
Polish Review, 10 (1965), 8-51; Bobinska, *passim;* Werner Conze, "Polen,
Preussen und Russland," introd. to Marx, *Manuskripte über die polnische
Frage* (1863-1864), ed. Conze and Dieter Herz-Eichenrode (The Hague:
Mouton, 1961), 91-164; Helmut Krause, *Karl Marx und das zeitgenössische*

Russland (Giessen: W. Schmitz, 1959), 18-37; Malcolm Macdonald, "Marx, Engels, and the Polish National Movement," *Journal of Modern History, 13* (1941), 321-24; V.I. Lenin, "Ergebnisse der Diskussionen über das Selbstbestimmungsrecht," in Lenin and G. Zinoviev, *Gegen den Strom: Aufsätze aus den Jahren 1914-1916* (Hamburg: Verlag der Kommunistischen Internationale, 1921), 383-415; and Riazonov, "Auswärtige Politik," 367-68. On Engels' tendency to ignore minorities within Poland, see Roman Rosdolsky, *Friedrich Engels und die 'geschichtslosen' Völker (Die Nationalitätenfrage in der Revolution 1848-1849 im Lichte der 'Neuen Rheinischen Zeitung')* (Detroit: 1949) (Typed ms. in Ms. Div. of New York Public Library) esp. 71, 100. This article also appears in *Archiv für Sozialgeschichte, 4* (1964), 87-282.

[23]To Marx, Mar. 8, 1860, printed by Marx as an appendix to *Herr Vogt, MEW, 14,* 679. Dana's criticism was of course based upon articles written by Engels as well as by Marx, though Dana did not know it.

[24]Karl Pribram, "Deutscher Nationalismus und deutscher Sozialismus," *Archiv für Sozialwissenschaft und Sozialpolitik, 49* (1922), 298-376; Hans Rothfels, "Marxismus und auswärtige Politik," in *Deutscher Staat und deutsche Parteien. Beiträge zur deutschen Partei- und Ideengeschichte. Friedrich Meinecke zum 60. Geburtstag* (Munich: R. Oldenbourg, 1922), 316-17. Rothfels' article is useful on less abstruse planes. See Spengler for a completely opposite view.

[25]Schwartzschild considers Marx the personification of Prussian authoritarianism. Wolfe's condemnation is similar (though he damns Lenin for unpatriotically advocating his country's defeat).

[26]E.g., Leonard Krieger, intro. to Engels, *German Revolutions,* xxxii. H. Heidegger, *Die deutsche Sozialdemokratie und der nationale Staat. 1870-1920* (Göttingen: Musterschmidt-Verlag, 1956) treats Marx and Engels as antinational, but Engels as less so because of his greater practicality.

[27]*Zukunft* (Berlin), Oct. 30, 1867, *Beobachter* (Stuttgart), Dec. 27, 1867, *MEW, 16,* 207, 226; Marx to Engels, Dec. 7, 1867, *31,* 403.

[28]"Die deutschen Volksbücher," *Telegraph für Deutschland,* Nov. 1839; "Bei Immermanns Tod," *Morgenblatt für gebildete Leser,* Oct. 10, 1840; "Ernst Moritz Arndt," *Telegraph für Deutschland,* Jan. 1841. Engels' review of Immermann's memoirs was also fairly critical. "Immermanns Memorabilien," *Telegraph für Deutschland,* Apr. 1841. *MEW,* Erg. 2, 14, 96-98, 118-31, 141-49.

[29]*Menzel, der Franzosenfresser* (*Gesammelte Schriften, 15;* Paris: Théophil Barrois fils, 1837). For Engels' opinion of this work see his letter to Wilhelm Graeber, Oct. 8, 1839, Erg. 2, 420-21. Hermann Oncken emphasizes the importance of Börne in inoculating Engels against chauvinism. "Friedrich Engels und die Anfänge des deutschen Kommunismus," *Historische Zeitschrift, 123* (1920), 255.

[30]Foreword to Marx, "Kritik des Gothaer Programms," *Neue Zeit, 9* (1890-91), *MEW, 19,* 521. Engels and Marx were not always so closely in touch with German developments as they might have wished to be. See

Roger P. Morgan, *The German Social Democrats and the First International, 1864-1872* (Cambridge: University Press, 1965).

[31] "Der Status Quo in Deutschland," 1847, *MEW*, *4*, 50-51. Cf. Börne, *Menzel*, 50: "I love Germany more than France because it is unfortunate and France is not."

[32] "Von Paris nach Bern," *MEW*, *5*, 463; Weerth to Marx, Apr. 28, 1851, quoted in Engels' memorial article on Weerth in *Der Sozialdemokrat*, June 7, 1863, in Weerth, *Sämtliche Werke*, ed. Bruno Kaiser (Berlin: Aufbau-Verlag, 1956-57), *1*, 14. Weerth, a fellow collaborator on the *NRZ*, also complained of the German climate in this letter. In 1890 Engels regretted the Germans' image as a people that required to be *led*, excellent soldiers but contemptible men. The socialists' electoral victories, he said, would rectify this picture. To Conrad Schmidt, Apr. 12, 1890, 37, 384.

[33] Auguste Cornu, *Karl Marx und Friedrich Engels: Leben und Werke* (Berlin: Aufbau-Verlag, 1954-62), *1*, 17-18; Mayer, *1*, 19; Franz Mehring, "Engels und Marx," *Archiv für die Geschichte des Sozialismus und der Arbeiterbewegung*, *5* (1915), 25. Engels declared, "we Rhinelanders have been made *subjects* and remained *subjects* only through Prussia's power. *We have never been Prussians.*" Prussia's assistance to Russian movements into Hungary, he said, emphasized "*what a disgrace it is to be called a Prussian.*" "Der Dritte im Bunde," *NRZ*, May 4, 1849, *MEW*, *6*, 470. Marx objected to the Prussian Government's charging him with abusing "the hospitality which the brazen intruders, near-Russians (Borussen) extend to *us Rhinelanders* on our own land." "Standrechtliche Beseitigung der 'Neuen Rheinischen Zeitung,'" *NRZ*, May 19, 1849, *MEW*, *6*, 506. See also Marx, *Manuskripte über die Polnische Frage*, 91-164.

[34] See Conze and Groh, 98-99.

[35] Bloom, 185-88, shares this view. Marx said that workers' international cooperation against "M. le Capital" would be more effective than bourgeois pacifist rhetoric in destroying national prejudices. To Engels, Aug. 18, 1869, *32*, 368. It appears, therefore, that he disliked national prejudices, at least in principle; he also condemned Gobineau's racism. To Laura and Paul Lafargue, Mar. 5, 1870, *32*, 655-56.

[36] Zint, 95-96, points out Marx's obsessive concern with Russian machinations. Palmerston was thought a Russian agent. Marx, *Lord Palmerston* (London, 1853), *MEW*, *9*, 353-418. So was Prussia. Conze, "Polen, Preussen und Russland," 40-41. So, in his spare time, was the Bonapartist hireling Karl Vogt. *Heer Vogt*, *MEW*, *14*, 495-510. For an especially elaborate conspiracy, see Marx, "Movement of Mazzini and Kossuth— League with Louis Napoleon—Palmerston," *Tribune*, Oct. 19, 1852, *MEW*, *14*, 364-66. Höhn, *Sozialismus und Heer*, *1*, 62-63, argues that both Engels and Marx contracted Russophobia from reading Dietrich von Bülow, an eccentric military writer of the Napoleonic period, but neither Engels nor Marx seems to have taken Bülow very seriously (Engels to Marx, Apr. 3, 1851, *27*, 233; Marx to Engels, Jan. 18, 1856, *29*, 6) and the Turcophile David Urquhart was certainly a much more significant

influence. Marx's plan to write a biography of Bülow (to Engels, Feb. 22, 1858, 29, 285) referred only to a projected encyclopedia article. Höhn seems to have been led astray by this letter. In any case, Engels and Marx hated Russia before encountering either Bülow or Urquhart; Marx's *Rheinische Zeitung* had been closed down in 1843 on the Tsar's complaints. Nicolaievsky and Maenchen-Helfen, 56-59.

[37]Above, pp. 33-34; "The Real Issue in Turkey," *Tribune*, Apr. 12, 1853, in *MEW*, *9*, 17. Engels and Marx were, of course, not alone in these views. Nesselrode complained in July 1848 that *all* revolutionaries preached against Russia. D. Riazanov, "Karl Marx über den Ursprung der Vorherrschaft Russlands in Europa," tr. A. Stein, *Neue Zeit*, Erg. 5 (March 5, 1909), 1-2.

[38]See Marx to Engels, Apr. 18, 1858, 29, 324, and Oct. 8, 1858, 29, 360. *The Russian Menace to Europe* is a responsible selection which does not concentrate exclusively on the Crimean War statements. J.H. Linkow, "Friedrich Engels und die revolutionäre Bewegung in Russland," in *Friedrich Engels und die internationale Arbeiterbewegung*, 77-105, considers the Russophobe statements a wartime aberration which ended in 1856; Bobinska, 99-100, 186-96, discusses the shift to a less inimical attitude toward Russia without attempting to date it precisely; Krause, 35-36, says the shift had begun by 1867. Benoit P. Hepner, "Marx et la puissance russe," introd. to Marx, *La Russie et l'Europe* (Paris: Gallimard, 1954), 7-90, deals chiefly with the objective accuracy of Marx's statements on Russia.

[39]Wendel, "Marxism and the Southern Slav Question," 290-91.

[40]Though Marx objected that it was "not enough to say, as the French do, that their nation was taken unawares. A nation and a woman are not forgiven the unguarded hour in which the first adventurer that came along could violate them." *The Eighteenth Brumaire of Louis Bonaparte* (New York: International Publishers, 1963), 21. Zint, 64, says that Marx never lost his early Francophilia, despite outbursts at what he considered the pretentiousness of some French revolutionaries. Engels called the French the "chosen people of the revolution" (*NRZ*, May 10, 1849, *MEW*, *6*, 481-82), though he later and more typically said that "the day of chosen peoples [was] gone forever," "Nachwort" to "Soziales aus Russland" in *Internationales aus dem "Volksstaat" (1871-75)* (Berlin: 1894), *MEW*, *18*, 672.

[41]*18th Brumaire*, 18, 121-22, 130. This analysis of the Bonapartist state is discussed in John Plamenatz, *German Marxism and Russian Communism* (New York: Harper, 1965), 144-51. See also Maximilien Rubel, *Karl Marx devant le bonapartisme* ("Société et idéologies. Series 2: Documents et Témoignages, No. 2"; Paris: Mouton, 1960), 47-57.

[42]"Der schweizer Bürgerkrieg," *Deutsche-Brüsseler Zeitung*, Nov. 14, 1847, *MEW*, *4*, 391-98; "Der Nationalrat," *NRZ*, Dec. 10, 1848, *MEW*, *6*, 85-87; Marx and Engels, "Revue," *NRZ-Revue*, Jan.-Feb. 1850, *MEW*, *7*, 223-25; Engels, *Tribune*, May 17, 1853, *MEW*, *9*, 87-94; "The Armies of Europe," *Putnam's*, *6* (Aug. 1855), 567; *Peasant War*, *MEW*, *7*, 344.

[43]To Marx, Dec. 1846, 27, 71-72; "Der dänisch-preussische Waffenstill-stand," *NRZ*, Sept. 10, 1848, *MEW*, 5, 394.

[44]"Der demokratische Panslawismus," *NRZ*, Feb. 15, 1849, *MEW*, 6, 273. The "Saxons" of Siebenbürgen were also supposed to disappear. ("Der magyarische Kampf," *NRZ*, Jan. 13, 1849, *MEW*, 6, 170)—which, as Rosdolsky (104) points out, presents some difficulty to the theory that Engels was simply a German chauvinist. Similarly, the German minorities in Poland were as irrelevant to Germany as the "French colony" in Berlin, or the French population of Montevideo, to France. "Die Polendebatte in Frankfurt," *NRZ*, Aug. 9, 1848, *MEW*, 5, 320-21.

[45]Cf. Bloom's chapter, "Size and Statehood," 33-47.

[46]Weerth's letter to Engels of June 25, 1845, concerns fundraising for a memorial to List. Weerth, *Sämtliche Werke*, 5, 163-64. For List's wish to see neighboring countries annexed to Germany, see his *National System of Political Economy* (Philadelphia: Lippincott, 1856), 265.

[47]Cf. Mayer, *Engels*, 1, 326. William G. Vettes, "The German Social Democrats and the Eastern Question, 1848-1900," *Slavic Review*, 17 (1958), 58, agrees that Hegel's antislav prejudices were less important than his dialectics in influencing Marx's and Engels' attitudes.

[48] "Das Begräbnis von Karl Marx," *Sozialdemokrat*, Mar. 22, 1883, *MEW*, 19, 336.

Notes to Chapter 4

[1]"Die Debatte über den Jacobyschen Antrag," *NRZ*, June 18-25, 1848, *ibid.*, 5, 228. The Vendée had risen against the French revolutionary government in 1793.

[2]"Die auswärtige deutsche Politik und die letzten Ereignisse zu Prag," *NRZ*, July 12, 1848, *ibid.*, 208.

[3]"The Austrian *Soldateska* has drowned in Czech blood all chance of peaceful coexistence between Bohemia and Germany." "Der Prager Aufstand," *NRZ*, June 18, 1848, *ibid.*, 80-82. Cf. Engels, "Neue Politik in Posen," *NRZ*, June 21, 1848, *ibid.*, 94-95, and "Sturz des Ministeriums Camphausen," *NRZ*, June 23, 1848, *ibid.*, 96. There is a good discussion of the prophecy in Rosdolsky, 8-19.

[4]"Der Prager Aufstand," *NRZ*, June 18, 1848, *MEW*, 5, 82. Much of the Germans' disreputable image was Austria's fault—see "Der Anfang des Endes in Österreich," *Deutsche-Brüsseler Zeitung*, Jan. 27, 1848, *ibid.*, 4, 504-10.

[5]Engels, "Auswärtige deutsche Politik," *NRZ*, July 3, 1848, *ibid.*, 5, 154-56; Marx, "Die Bourgeoisie und die Kontrerevolution," *NRZ*, Dec. 10, 1848, *ibid.*, 6, 103.

⁶ "Die Kriegskömodie," *NRZ*, June 5, 1848, *ibid.*, *5*, 34-35; see also Engels, "Berliner Vereinbarungsdebatten," *NRZ*, July 7, 1848, *ibid.*, 180.

⁷ "Der Waffenstillstand mit Dänemark," *NRZ*, July 22, 1848, *ibid.*, 256-59. Engels quoted an official Danish paper's approval of the Malmö armistice in order to embarrass the Camphausen government. He had already published the Danish statement in fuller form. "Das 'Fadreland' über den Waffenstillstand," *NRZ*, July 21, 1848, *ibid.*, 253-55. The Danes' insolence, so useful for showing up the Prussian and Frankfurt leaders, rather charmed Marx. "Eine Neujahrsgratulation," *NRZ*, Jan. 9, 1849, *ibid.*, *6*, 162.

⁸"Der dänisch-preussische Waffenstillstand," *NRZ*, Sept. 10, 1848, *ibid.*, 5, 393-97.

⁹Ritter, *1*, 69-70.

¹⁰Engels, "The State of Germany," *Northern Star*, Nov. 8, 1845, *MEGA*, 1, *4*, 488; to Weydemeyer, June 19, 1851, 27, 555. Most of the Prussian reformers were more interested in what revolution could do for war than in the reverse—Gneisenau hoped to take "weapons from the arsenal of the revolution." Friedrich Meinecke, *Das Zeitalter der deutschen Erhebung* (Göttingen: Vandenhoeck & Rupprecht, 1957), 70.

¹¹Kautsky suggests that not war but *defeat* was the galvanizing factor in 1793; so what France and Germany lacked in 1848 was the clear and present foreign danger (73-78, 96-98).

¹²Marx, *Class Struggles in France*, 120.

¹³ "Der dänisch-preussische Waffenstillstand," *NRZ*, Sept. 10, 1848, *MEW*, *5*, 396.

¹⁴"Die auswärtige deutsche Politik und die letzten Ereignisse zu Prag," July 12, 1848, *ibid.*, 202. The *Werke* does not attribute this article specifically either to Marx or to Engels. Zinoviev, *Krieg und Krise*, 101, alleges that Marx and Engels wished only for a Germany that had conquered its own tyrants to fight Russia; but the attraction of a Russian war was precisely that it would permit simultaneous struggle against the revolution's internal and external enemies, as Bobinska, 98, points out. Much later Marx declared that France could have saved the Republic in 1848 by launching a pro-Polish war against Russia; here the therapeutic value of a Russian war (at least in 1848) was reaffirmed long after Marx and Engels had scrapped the 1793 model. Speech in the General Council of the International, Jan. 17, 1871, *MEW*, *17*, 629-30.

¹⁵ "Der dänisch-preussische Waffenstillstand," *NRZ*, Sept. 10, 1848, *ibid.*, *5*, 397.

¹⁶"Die Ratifikation des Waffenstillstandes," *NRZ*, Sept. 20, 1848, *ibid.*, 408-409.

¹⁷"Die revolutionäre Bewegung," *NRZ*, Jan. 1, 1849, *ibid.*, *6*, 150. Marx had already stressed England's importance; cf. "Die revolutionäre Bewegung in Italien," *NRZ*, Nov. 30, 1848, *ibid.*, 77-78.

¹⁸The resemblance of Marx's offhand prediction to the events of 1917 is a bit vague; Marx did not say *how* war would catapult England to the head of the revolutionary movement, and did not develop the role of

military defeat or stagnation in increasing the war's unpopularity. All that came later, and the 1917 model is discussed in Chapter Five.

[19]"Erste Tat der deutschen Nationalversammlung zu Frankfurt," *NRZ*, June 23, 1848, *MEW, 5,* 99.

[20]"Der Krieg in Italien und Ungarn," *NRZ*, Mar. 28, 1849, *ibid., 6,* 382; "Die Niederlage der Piemontesen," *NRZ*, Mar. 31-Apr. 4, 1849, *ibid.,* 388-91.

[21]*Ibid.,* 386. Engels said later that the French army wanted a war, and would get one. "Ungarn," *NRZ*, May 19, 1849, *ibid.,* 515.

[22] "Der magyarische Kampf," *NRZ*, Jan. 13, 1849, *ibid.,* 173; "Der demokratische Panslawismus," *NRZ*, Feb. 15, 1849, *ibid.,* 275. Cf. *Revolution and Counter-Revolution,* in *German Revolutions,* 178-80.

[23]Rosdolsky, 208.

[24]"Der magyarische Kampf," *NRZ*, Jan. 13, 1849, *MEW, 6,* 170; "Der demokratische Panslawismus," *NRZ*, Feb. 15, 1849, *ibid.,* 278. See Wendel, "Marxism and the Southern Slav Question"; and Erwin Szabo, "Die ungarische Revolution von 1848 (Bemerkungen zu Engels' Artikel über Ungarn in der 'Neuen Rheinischen Zeitung')," *Neue Zeit, 23* (1905), 785-87. Krause, 42, suggests that by the 1850s, Marx and Engels were sufficiently irritated by Hungarian revolutionary exiles to form a more positive, less prejudiced view of the South Slavs. See also Mayer, *Engels, 1,* 326-27.

[25]Thus Lenin, "Ergebnisse der Diskussionen über das Selbstbestimmungsrecht," 399-400. Engels persisted in his belief that the Serbs' "right to cattle-stealing" had to be subordinated to the interests of the European proletariat. To Bernstein, Feb. 22-25, 1882, *35,* 279-81; to Kautsky, Feb. 7, 1882, *ibid.,* 272-73. On the other hand, South Slavs should be supported whenever they opposed Russia. To Bernstein, Oct. 9, 1886, *36,* 546.

[26]"Der magyarische Kampf," *NRZ*, Jan. 13, 1849, *MEW, 6,* 165-66.

[27]"Ungarn," *NRZ*, May 19, 1849, *ibid.,* 512, 515.

[28]"Revue," *NRZ-Revue,* Jan.-Feb., 1850, *ibid., 7,* 215-16. The image of the handless giant recurred early in the Crimean War: Engels, "The European War," *Tribune,* Feb. 2, 1854, *ibid., 10,* 6.

[29]To Marx, Apr. 11, 1851, *27,* 235.

[30] "Holy Alliance vs. France," *MS, 1,* 212. Riazonov, in *Neue Zeit,* suggested that Engels wrote it in response to G. A. Techow's article on a similar theme, and the editors of the *MS* follow Riazonov. The *MEW* editors argue convincingly that Engels took up the subject on his own (7, 621).

[31]"Holy Alliance vs. France," *MS, 1,* 207-11, 226-27.

[32]To Marx, Sept. 26, 1851, *27,* 355.

[33]"Notes on the War, No. III," *Manchester Guardian,* June 28, 1866, *EMC,* 133; "The Revolt in India," *Tribune,* Aug. 4, 1857, *FIWI,* 44. Edmond Laskine uses quotations of this sort to prove to his satisfaction that Engels and Marx really opposed revolution. *L'Internationale et le pangermanisme* (Paris: H. Floury, 1916), 74-78.

[34]"The Fall of Metz," *Pall Mall Gazette,* Oct. 29, 1870, *Notes on the War:*

Sixty Articles reprinted from the "Pall Mall Gazette," 1870-1871, ed. Friedrich Adler (Vienna: Wiener Volksbuchhandlung, 1923), 78-79.

[35]"Notes on the War.—VIII," *Pall Mall Gazette,* Aug. 15, 1870, *Notes on the War,* 21. Cf. Michael Howard, *The Franco-Prussian War: The German Invasion of France, 1870-71* (New York: Macmillan, 1961), 233-49.

[36]"Holy Alliance vs. France," *MS, 1,* 218-22, 211-14.

[37]To Marx, May 19, May 23, 1851, *27,* 260, 266.

Notes to Chapter 5

[1]To Marx, Apr. 21, 1854, May 9, 1854, *28,* 344, 361.

[2] "War—Strikes—Dearth," *Tribune,* Nov. 15, 1853; "The Northern Powers," *ibid.,* Nov. 5, 1853, *MEW, 9,* 447, 434-35.

[3]To Lassalle, Feb. 4, 1859, Mar. 16, 1859, *29,* 577, 585.

[4]Engels to Marx, Apr. 11, 1859; Marx to Engels, Apr. 12, 1859, *29,* 417, 419.

[5]"The War Plans of France and England—The Greek Insurrection—Spain—China," *Tribune,* Mar. 18, 1854, *MEW, 10,* 115.

[6] "Revolutionary Spain, V," *Tribune,* Oct. 30, 1854; "The Spanish Revolution—Greece and Turkey," *ibid.,* Aug. 4, 1854; "Revolution in Spain," *ibid.,* Aug. 18, 1856, *MEW, 10,* 463, 350; *12,* 48.

[7]"Revolutionary Spain, III," *Tribune,* Oct. 20, 1854, *MEW, 10,* 449.

[8]Marx, "Declaration of the Prussian Cabinet—Napoleon Plans—Prussian Politics," *Tribune,* Mar. 9, 1854; Engels, "Deutschland und der Panslawismus," *Neue Oder-Zeitung,* Apr. 21, 1855; "The European War," *Tribune,* Feb. 2, 1854, *MEW, 10,* 77-79, *11,* 193-94, *10,* 4-5.

[9]Marx, "The Imprisonment of Mazzini—Austria—Spain—Wallachia," *Tribune,* Sept. 30, 1854, *MEW, 10,* 497. Cf. Marx's *Tribune* articles of Mar. 29, 1854, May 2, 1854, May 6, 1854, and May 15, 1854, *MEW, 10,* 132-33, 220, 206, 209-10. This was not an anti-Greek bias; in 1850 Marx and Engels had been Hellenophile. "Revue," *NRZ-Revue,* May-Oct., 1850, *MEW, 7,* 441-42.

[10]Marx, "Spree und Mincio," *Volk,* June 25, 1859, *MEW, 13,* 391.

[11]Engels, "Napoleon's War-Plans," *Tribune,* July 2, 1855, *MEW, 11,* 291, 296. Cf. Marx and Engels, "Zur Debatte über Layards Antrag—Der Krieg in der Krim," *Neue Oder-Zeitung,* June 19, 1855, *MEW, 11,* 302.

[12]"The Peace," *Tribune,* July 28, 1859, *MEW, 13,* 431. Solferino was a French victory of sorts, but did not promise a rapid and satisfactory conclusion to the war.

[13]"The Exploits in the Baltic and Black Seas," *Tribune,* June 9, 1854, *MEW, 10,* 245-46.

[14]Praetorians, he said, were throughout history "but indifferent soldiers.

They begin by commanding the civilians, they next proceed to dictating to their generals, and they end by being thoroughly thrashed." "The Attack on Sebastopol," *Tribune*, Oct. 14, 1855, *MEW*, *10*, 511-12.

[15]Marx to Engels, May 18, 1859, *29*, 432.

[16]To Engels, May 6, 1859, *29*, 427.

[17]May 18, 1859, *29*, 605. Stefan Possony, 6, sees this letter as evidence of "revolutionary defeatism," though the clear expectation is that the revolution is to bring about victory and *save* the nation.

[18]As Mayer (*Engels*, *2*, 91) points out, Engels had not yet seen Lassalle's book on the Italian question; Marx summarized it in a letter to Engels written the same day that Engels wrote to Lassalle. (*29*, 431-37.)

[19]This point was made incessantly in the Marx-Engels writings. See Marx, "Affairs in Prussia," *Tribune*, Dec. 27, 1858; Marx and Engels, "The Money Panic in Europe," *ibid.*, Feb. 1, 1859; Marx and Engels, "The War in Europe—Symptoms of Its Approach—Germany Arming," *ibid.*, May 9, 1859; Marx, "Quid pro Quo," *Volk*, July 30, 1859; "Invasion!" *ibid.*, July 30, 1859; "The Treaty of Villafranca," *Tribune*, Aug. 4, 1859; "Truth Testified," *ibid.*, Aug. 12, 1859, *MEW*, *12*, 662, *13*, 174-76, 309-10, 451-54, 444, 446, 423, 449; *Po und Rhein* and *Savoyen, Nizza und der Rhein*, *MS*, *2*, 5, 161; Marx to Lassalle, Feb. 4, 1859, Mar. 16, 1859, Marx to Engels, Apr. 22, 1859, *29*, 576, 584, 426. The same process had driven Napoleon into the Crimean War: Marx, "Parliamentary Debates of February 22—The Dispatch of Pozzo di Borgo—The Policies of the Western Powers," *Tribune*, Mar. 13, 1854, *MEW*, *10*, 101-02. See also Rubel, *Marx devant le bonapartisme*, 67-77.

[20]Lassalle, *Der italienische Krieg und die Aufgabe Preussens* (Berlin: F. Duncker, 1859), esp. 19-25, 49, 56.

[21]To Engels, May 6, 1859, *29*, 428. Marx also said that the party should be so patriotic as to make the rulers appear treasonable and halfhearted by contrast. To Engels, May 18, 1859, *29*, 432. This stance could be either a first step toward a saviors-of-the-nation role, *à la* 1793, or a maneuver for political advantage within states that were expected to last for years. None of it grew out of love for the Habsburg state; see Engels, "Der Anfang des Endes in Österreich, *Deutsche-Brüsseler Zeitung*, Jan. 27, 1848, *MEW*, *4*, 509-10.

[22]Marx brushed off Lassalle's objection that war with Russia would solidify public opinion behind the existing German governments. To Lassalle, Sept. 15, 1860, *30*, 565. See Kautsky, 131-33.

[23]Marx, "Spree und Mincio," *Volk*, June 25, 1859, *MEW*, *13*, 392.

[24] "The Austrian Defeat," *Tribune*, July 8, 1859; "Die Schlacht bei Solferino," *Volk*, July 2, 1859, *MEW*, *13*, 400-01, 404. Engels had already said that 1848 had kindled a patriotic spirit among the Germans (*Tribune*, Mar. 12, 1859, *MEW*, *13*, 194), but had then merely declared them equal to fighting Italians, French, and Russians, without throwing in their own sovereigns.

[25]Below, Chapter 6. Cf. Allan Nevins, *The War for the Union*, *2*: *War Becomes Revolution, 1862-1863* (New York: Scribner's, 1960) and Clinton

Rossiter, *Constitutional Dictatorship: Crisis Government in the Modern Democracies* (New York: Harcourt, 1963), 223-39.

[26] "Why, that is revolution that you're proposing to me," protested Bismarck's King, and Bismarck answered, "But there is no harm in that." And there was *not* much danger in that sort of controlled revolution. Otto Pflanze, *Bismarck and the Development of Germany, 1: The Period of Unification, 1815-1871* (Princeton: Princeton University Press, 1963), 301. On the World War, Rossiter, 104-16, 151-70.

[27] "The Progress of the War," *Tribune*, Jan. 1, 1855; Marx, "Prospects in France and England," *ibid.*, Apr. 27, 1855, *MEW, 10*, 582, *11*, 182-83.

[28] "Rückblicke," *Neue Oder-Zeitung*, Jan. 4, 1855, *MEW, 10*, 591.

[29] Engels, "The Attack on Sebastopol," *Tribune*, Oct. 14, 1854; Marx, "Declaration of the Prussian Cabinet—Napoleon Plans—Prussian Politics," *ibid.*, Mar. 9, 1854; Engels, "Napoleon's Last Dodge," *ibid.*, Apr. 7, 1855; Marx, "The Opening of the Parliament of Labor—The English War Budget," *ibid.*, Mar. 24, 1854, *MEW, 10*, 511-12, 77-79; *11*, 149; *10*, 119.

[30] To Engels, May 6, 1859, *29*, 427.

[31] "Fate of the Great Adventurer," *Tribune*, Apr. 2, 1855, *MEW, 11*, 126-27. A similar line on Austria's vulnerability was taken on May 7, 1855 in the *Tribune*. *MEW*'s editors omit the article, though there is nothing in it that clashes with the views of Engels and Marx, save for praise of the Panslavist Gurowski. It appears in the handy but unreliable collection *The Eastern Question: A Reprint of Letters Written 1853-1856 Dealing with the Events of the Crimean War*, ed. Eleanor Marx Aveling and Edward Aveling (London: S. Sonnenschein, 1897), 550.

[32] *Tribune*, Sept. 5, 1853, "The Imprisonment of Mazzini—Austria—Spain—Wallachia," *ibid.*, Sept. 30, 1854, *MEW, 9*, 291, *10*, 497. Cf. Marx, "Count Orloff's Proposals," *Tribune*, Mar. 9, 1854; "The Secret Diplomatic Correspondence," *ibid.*, Apr. 11, 1854, *MEW, 10*, 77-79, 165.

[33] Marx to Engels, Sept. 26, 1856; Engels to Marx, Sept. 27, 1856; Engels to Marx, Nov. 15, 1857, *29*, 76, 78, 212. By October 7, 1858, Engels had to admit that everything looked "damned optimistic" from the businessman's viewpoint. To Marx, *29*, 357.

[34] "The Question of Italian Unity," *Tribune*, Jan. 24, 1859, *MEW, 13*, 166-67. This article closed with the hope for a "true and just settlement of the Italian question," which was an obstacle to peace and thus to the "progress and prosperity of the whole civilized world"; this "sincere and heartfelt desire" seems a bit out of character, and may be the work of the *Tribune*'s editors, who sometimes doctored the articles sent them by Marx.

[35] E.g., Engels, "Die Russen," *NRZ*, Apr. 22, 1849, *MEW, 6*, 431-33.

[36] To Engels, Dec. 13, 1859, *29*, 525; "Spree und Mincio," *Volk*, June 25, 1859, *MEW, 13*, 392.

[37] *Savoyen, Nizza und der Rhein, MS, 2*, 164-65.

[38] "The European War," *Tribune*, Feb. 2, 1854, *MEW, 10*, 8.

[39] Stressing these differences does not imply an intent to dispute R. R. Palmer's demonstration that the French Revolution did find many echoes

and parallels outside France (*The Age of the Democratic Revolution,* 1 [Princeton: Princeton University Press, 1959]); but however widespread revolutionary sympathies may have been, they did not suffice to erase the existing European governments, as Engels in this extravagant passage expected the next revolution to do.

[40]Marx to Engels, May 18, 1859, *29,* 432.

[41]"The European War," *Tribune,* Feb. 2, 1854, *MEW, 10,* 7.

[42]"The Military Power of Russia," *Tribune,* Aug. 31, 1854; "The Battle of Inkermann," *ibid.,* Dec. 14, 1854, *MEW, 10,* 541, 568.

[43]"The European War," *Tribune,* Feb. 17, 1855; "The War That Looms over Europe," *ibid.,* Mar. 8, 1855, *MEW, 11,* 17, 76.

[44]Marx and Engels, "Rückblicke," *Neue Oder-Zeitung,* Jan. 1, 1855; "Der lokale Krieg," *ibid.,* June 23, 1855; Engels, "The European War," *Tribune,* Feb. 4, 1856, *MEW, 10,* 589-90; *11,* 311, 587.

[45]"The War That Looms over Europe," *Tribune,* Mar. 8, 1855; "The European War," *ibid.,* Feb. 4, 1856, *MEW, 11,* 81, 587.

[46]Oskar Blum's picture of a steadily increasing disillusionment is oversimplified. Blum, 561.

[47]Marx and Engels, "That Bore of a War," *Tribune,* Aug. 17, 1854, *MEW, 10,* 379. *MEW* attributes this article to both Marx and Engels, but it is included in Engels' *MS.*

[48]"The Tsar's Views," *Tribune,* Feb. 11, 1854; "The European War," *ibid.,* Feb. 2, 1854, *MEW, 10,* 42, 7.

[49]Engels to Lassalle, May 18, 1859, *29,* 605.

[50]"A Prussian View of the War," *Tribune,* June 10, 1859, *MEW, 13,* 353-55. Cf. Marx, "Spree und Mincio," *Volk,* June 25, 1859; Engels, "The News from the War," *Tribune,* July 8, 1859, *MEW, 13,* 393, 400-01.

[51]Nevertheless it is wrong to say that Marx and Engels "became convinced that a revolution could occur only as a result of a great war in Europe" (Bloom, 97); revolution might occur without any aid at all from war.

[52]Introduction to S. Borkheim, *Zur Erinnerung für die deutschen Mordspatrioten, 1806-1807, MS,* 2, 632.

Notes to Chapter 6

[1]A. J. P. Taylor contends that in the later nineteenth century Europe's ruling circles discarded the Metternichean assumption that war might mean revolution, and should therefore be avoided. (*Struggle for Mastery,* xxxiii.) Thus Engels and Marx found themselves in agreement with their opponents on this point, if on few others.

[2]To Marx, April 22, 1857, *29*, 127.

[3]To Marx, April 22, 1857, *ibid.*, 454.

[4]*Po und Rhein, MS, 2*, 5-7; Marx to Engels, Mar. 3. 1859, *29*, 406-07. Marx's *Tribune* article, "The War Prospect in Prussia," Mar. 31, 1859, summarized the natural frontiers theory and Engels' attack on it. *MEW, 13*, 283.

[5]*Po und Rhein, MS, 2*, 33-34, 38-39, 42-43, 47. Marx echoed the emphasis on demographic over geographic frontiers in his "Second Address of the General Council on the Franco-Prussian War," Sept. 9, 1870, in *The Civil War in France* (New York: International Publishers, 1940), 31.

[6]*Po und Rhein, MS, 2*, 26-27, 29. On Barbarossa and Radetzky, "Die 'Kölnische Zeitung' über Italien," *NRZ*, Aug. 27, 1848, *MEW, 5*, 370. Engels pointed out that Napoleon had managed to get through the mountain passes, and that mountain artillery had become lighter since Napoleon's day. *Po und Rhein, MS, 2*, 9-12. Cf. "The Conduct of War in the Mountains, at One Time and Now," *Tribune*, Jan. 27, 1857, *MS, 1*, 473-79.

[7]*Po und Rhein, ibid., 2*, 46, 33, 48. For Frederick's characterization of Prussians as gifted in the attack, see "Aus der Instruktion für die Generalmajors von der Cavallerie (14. August 1748)," *Die Werke Friedrichs des Grossen* (Berlin: R. Hobbing, 1913-14), *6*, 310.

[8]Engels to Marx, Jan. 31, 1860, *30*, 14. On the "false solution," See Eduard Bernstein, preface to *Po und Rhein* and *Savoyen, Nizza und der Rhein* (Stuttgart: Dietz, 1915), xii; cf. Engels, "The Austrian Hold on Italy," *Tribune*, Mar. 4, 1859, *MEW, 30*, 14.

[9]*Savoyen, Nizza und der Rhein, MS, 2*, 158-64, 155. Cf. Engels' *Tribune* piece of Feb. 21, 1860, "Savoy and Nice," where he argued that Savoy would eventually become French, but Nice would not. Popular sentiment prevailed over language; it was absurd to call Garibaldi a Frenchman because his compatriots in Nice expressed their Italian patriotism in French. *MEW, 13*, 561.

[10]*Savoyen, Nizza und der Rhein, MS, 2*, 154-55. Cf. *Po und Rhein, ibid.*, 33-39. For comments on Engels' prescience, see Neumann, 165, and Ivanoe Bonomi, "Federico Engels e i problemi della guerra," *Nuova Antologia, 195* (1918), 242-50. Ernst Drahn claimed that since Engels said Belgian neutrality *might* be violated, he *would* have approved of the 1914 invasion. *Engels als Kriegswissenschaftler*, 6.

[11]"Strategy of the War," *Tribune*, June 15, 1859, *MEW, 13*, 363. Marx thought that Cavour had sent Garibaldi into a hopeless corner to be rid of him. To Engels, May 27, 1859, *29*, 444.

[12]"Prospects of the War," *Tribune*, May 12, 1859, *ibid., 13*, 315; "The War," *Tribune*, May 23, 1859, *ibid.*, 328-29, 331. Cf. the *Tribune* articles of Mar. 4, and Mar. 17, 1859, giving a fuller account of the troop dispositions and probable intentions of both sides. *Ibid.*, 195-201, 210-14.

[13]"Der Feldzug in Italien," *Volk*, May 28, 1859; "The Battle of Montebello," *Tribune*, June 10, 1859; "Strategy of the War," *Tribune*, June 15, 1859, *ibid.*, 360, 351-52, 361.

[14] "Progress of the War," *Tribune*, June 17, 1859; "Kriegsereignisse," *Volk*, June 11, 1859; "The Austrian Defeat," *Tribune*, June 22, 1859; "Der Rückzug der Österreicher an den Mincio," *Volk*, June 25, 1859, *ibid.*, 372-73, 376-79, 380-83, 394.

[15] "The Strategy of the War," *Tribune*, June 15, 1859; "The Progress of the War," *Tribune*, June 15, 1859; "Die Schlacht bei Solferino," *Volk*, July 2, 1859; "Der italienische Krieg. Rückschau," *Volk*, July 30, 1859; "Die Schlacht von Solferino," *Volk*, July 9, 1859; "Historic Justice," *Tribune*, July 21, 1859, *ibid.*, 361-64, 372-75, 402-03, 434, 409-10.

[16] "News from the War," *Tribune*, July 8, 1859, *ibid.*, 398-400. Cf. Marx, "The Peace," *Tribune*, July 28, 1859, *ibid.*, 421. Engels had written that Bonapartist corruption would cripple the French in a long war ("Der Feldzug in Italien," *Volk*, May 28, 1859, *ibid.*, 359), but the war ended before such disorganization affected the French efforts.

[17] "The War—No Progress," *Tribune*, May 27, 1859; cf. "Der italienische Krieg. Rückschau," *Volk*, July 23 and 30, Aug. 6, 1859. *Ibid.*, 339, 428-32. Casting about desperately for explanations, Engels suggested that railways had enabled the French to concentrate troops and fend off Austrian attacks. "Der Feldzug in Italien," *Volk*, May 28, 1859, *ibid.*, 358-59.

[18] To Marx, July 23, 1860, Oct. 1, 1860, Oct. 5, 1860, *30*, 79-80, 99, 103. By Oct. 5, Engels' misgivings were over. J. P. Becker wrote from Naples that copies of *Po und Rhein* and *Savoyen, Nizza und der Rhein*, as well as Marx's *Herr Vogt*, had been ordered for Garibaldi. It is not clear whether Garibaldi wanted to read them, or whether Becker wanted him to, but Marx was pleased. Marx to Engels, Dec. 27, 1860, *30*, 136.

[19] "The Sick Man of Austria," *Tribune*, Sept. 1, 1860, *MEW*, *15*, 131.

[20] Engels to Marx, Nov. 15, 1857; Marx to Engels, Sept. 26, 1856, *29*, 212, 76. Marx complained that the cheering prospect came just as he was getting himself settled in new lodgings, and his books moved in. Cf. Engels to Marx, Sept. 27, 1856; Marx to Engels, Mar. 5, 1856, *29*, 78, 28-29.

[21] Engels to Marx, Oct. 7, 1858, *29*, 357. Marx's suggestion (to Engels, Oct. 8, 1858, *29*, 360) that in the face of the world market's expansion, a European revolution might be crushed in "this little corner" was not followed up; Europe remained the center of the world. Cf. Zint, 139-40.

[22] Marx, "The Situation in Europe," *Tribune*, July 27, 1857, and "Political Parties in England—The Situation in Europe," *Tribune*, June 24, 1858, *MEW*, *12*, 234-37, 504-05; Marx to Engels, Jan. 16, 1858, *29*, 259.

[23] "The Indian Revolt," *Tribune*, Sept. 16, 1857. This article also lists British outrages to offset those of the Sepoys. *FIWI*, 91-94.

[24] Engels to Marx, Sept. 21, 1857, *29*, 182 (praising General Havelock); "The Capture of Delhi," *Tribune*, Dec. 5, 1857, "The Fall of Lucknow," *Tribune*, Apr. 30, 1858, *FIWI*, 117-18, 142. At Delhi, the British showed "force of character, judgement and skill," and looked better than they had at Sebastopol; at Lucknow Sir Colin Campbell showed "prudence and vigour." Cf. Engels, "Revolt in the Indian Army," *Tribune*, July 15, 1857; Marx, "Reports from India," *Tribune*, Aug. 14, 1857; Marx, "The Revolt in

India," *Tribune*, Oct. 23, 1857; Marx, "Revolt in India," *Tribune*, Oct. 13, 1857, *FIWI*, 42, 55, 109,100-04; also Engels to Marx, Sept. 24, 1857, *29*, 191.

[25]"The greatest heroism of the Lucknow garrison consists in that they had to face every day the 'coarse beef' cooked by the ladies *entirely unaided.*' Must have been damned badly cooked." Engels to Marx, Jan. 14, 1858, *29*, 257. It takes some diligent stretching to proclaim that Engels' articles on the Mutiny "revealed not so much the 'military expert' as the proletarian revolutionary." (Stepanova, 125.)

[26]Marx, "Revolt in the Indian Army," *Tribune*, July 15, 1857; Engels, "Details of the Attack on Lucknow," *Tribune*, May 25, 1858; "The Indian Army," *Tribune*, July 21, 1858, *FIWI*, 40, 143-45, 175-79. Cf. Engels to Marx, Oct. 21, 1858, *29*, 363.

[27] "Afghanistan," *New American Cyclopedia*, *MEW*, *14*, 80; "Der dänisch-preussische Waffenstillstand," *NRZ*, Sept. 10, 1848, *ibid.*, *5*, 395. In addition to the Indian articles, there is a diatribe by Marx against the opium trade in *Tribune*, June 2, 1857 (omitted from *MEW*). On this whole question, see Horace B. Davis, "Nations, Colonies, and Social Classes: The Position of Marx and Engels," *Science & Society*, *29* (1965), 29-31.

[28]Marx to Engels, Feb. 13, 1863, *30*, 324. See Rubel, *Marx devant le bonapartisme*, 105-13.

[29]Engels to Weydemeyer, Nov. 24, 1864, *31*, 424; preface to first German edition, *Capital*, *1*, 9; Engels to Marx, Nov. 15, 1862, *30*, 299. From Feb. 13 to Mar. 24, 1863, the American Civil War was mentioned only once, at the end of Marx's letter of Feb. 17 (*30*, 324-25).

[30]Marx to Engels, July 6, Mar. 24, 1863, *30*, 361-62,335.

[31]Marx to Weydemeyer, Nov. 29, 1864, *31*, 428.

[32]Marx, "Zur Kritik der Dinge in Amerika," *Presse*, Aug. 9, 1862, *MEW*, *15*, 526; to Engels, Aug. 7, 1862, Sept. 10, 1862, Sept. 7, 1864, *30*, 270, 286-87, 433. "Revolution" is used much as Allan Nevins uses it in *The War for the Union*.

[33]To Marx, June 12, July 3, 1861, May 12, 1862, *30*, 173-74, 181-82, 236.

[34]To Marx, June 4, July 30, Sept. 9, 1862, *ibid.*, 246, 254-56, 284-85.

[35]Marx to Engels, Aug. 7, Sept. 10, Oct. 29, 1862, Marx to Lion Philips, May 6, 1861, *ibid.*, 269-71, 286-87, 290-92, 600. Marx had also defended the Union's war finances, which Engels thought shaky. Engels to Marx, July 30, Marx to Engels, Aug. 7, Engels to Marx, Oct. 16, Marx to Engels, Oct. 29, 1862, *ibid.*, 255, 270, 289, 291.

[36]To Marx, Nov. 5, Dec. 30, 1862, Feb. 17, June 11, 1863, *30*, 294-95, 305, 328, 354. Cf. Engels to Marx, Nov. 15, Marx to Engels, Nov. 17, 1862, Jan. 2, 1863, *ibid.*, 298-99, 300-01, 306-08.

[37]To Marx, Sept. 4, 1864, *ibid.*, 430-31; to Weydemeyer, Nov. 24, 1864, *31*, 424-25. Cf. Engels to Marx, June 9, Sept. 4, Marx to Engels, Sept. 7, 1864, *30*, 410-13, 429-30, 432; Engels to Marx, Dec. 16, 1869, *32*, 420.

[38]"Der amerikanische Bürgerkrieg," *Presse*, Mar. 26 and 27, 1862, *MEW*, *15*, 487-88. Cf. "Lessons of the American War" and "The War in America," *Volunteer Journal*, Dec. 6, 1861, Mar. 14, 1862, *EMC*, 109-17. The main journalistic outlet (and an important source of income) for years, the New

York *Tribune,* ceased running Engels' and Marx's articles in 1862 on the ground that the war diverted the American public from interest in European affairs.

[39]Marx to Engels, Feb. 13, Engels to Marx, Feb. 17, 1863, *30,* 324, 327. Gustav Mayer (*Engels, 2,* 125) points out that the Polish uprising helped to snap Engels out of the depression that followed the death of his mistress, Mary Burns.

[40]To Marx, June 11, 1863, *30,* 354. Mayer (*Engels, 2,* 132) remarks, "This Rhinelander's aversion to everthing Prussian was so deep-rooted that he would not even trust a revolution that originated there."

[41]To Weydemeyer, Nov. 24, 1863, *31,* 424. Marx had also feared a Berlin uprising as a distraction that would enable "Pig-Bonaparte" to gain the Rhine. To Engels, Feb. 21, 1863, *30,* 332.

[42]To Engels, Aug. 15, Sept. 12, 1863, *ibid.,* 370, 372-73. Cf. Marx to Engels, Mar. 24, 1863, *ibid.,* 334-35.

[43]Engels to Marx, June 11, June 24, 1863, *ibid.,* 353, 360; to Weydemeyer, Nov. 24, 1864, *31,* 424.

[44]*MEW, 12,* 662.

[45]Engels to Weydemeyer, Nov. 24, 1864, *31,* 424; to Marx, Apr. 29, 1864, *30,* 393; Nov. 2, 1864, *31,* 6-8; "Die englische Armee," unpublished article probably written in 1864 for the *AMZ;* "Englands Streitmacht Deutschland gegenüber," *AMZ,* July 6, 1854, *MEW, 15,* 605, 583. Engels ridiculed Prussian reactionaries' elation over the costly storming of the Danish forts at Düppel, but was himself impressed. Bismarck had expressly insisted on this operation in order to provide glory and casualties for public relations purposes. See Gordon A. Craig, *The Politics of the Prussian Army: 1640-1945* (rev. ed.; New York: Oxford University Press, 1964), 188-92. Reinhard Höhn correctly points out that Engels' self-congratulation on having long recognized the superiority of Prussian weaponry overlooked several earlier, negative evaluations of the Prussian forces. *Sozialismus und Heer, 1,* 120.

[46]To Marx, Dec. 3, 1863, *30,* 377.

[47]To Marx, June 11, Apr. 2, 1866, *31,* 227, 200-01. Cf. Marx to Engels, Apr. 2, Apr. 6, 1866, *ibid.,* 204, 211. Engels' business partner Gottfried Ermen had talked with a Prussian lieutenant who agreed with Engels' view that Prussia would lose and suffer a revolt in consequence. Engels to Marx, June 11, 1866, *ibid.,* 226.

[48]To Marx, Apr. 10, May 1, May 16, 1866, *ibid.,* 207, 212, 218.

[49]To Marx, May 16, May 25, June 11, 1866, *ibid.,* 217, 220-21, 226-27.

[50]Engels to Marx, May 1, Marx to Kugelmann, Apr. 6, 1866, *ibid.,* 201, 514. This advocacy of Prussian defeat damages Bertram Wolfe's picture (82-101) of Marx and Engels as consistent defensists. The concept of one's "own" country must be applied cautiously in dealing with international revolutionaries, but Engels and Marx certainly had closer connections with Prussia than with Austria.

[51]Engels to Marx, Apr. 2, 1866, *ibid.,* 201; Marx to Engels, Jan. 8, 1868, *32,* 14. Cf. Engels to Marx, Jan. 6, Jan. 16, 1868, *ibid.,* 7, 20.

[52]"Notes on the War, No. I," June 20, 1866, *EMC*, 122-25. For a concise account of how command was really arranged in the two armies, see Heinrich Friedjung, *The Struggle for Supremacy in Germany, 1859-1866* (New York: Russell & Russell, 1966), 141-49.

[53]"Notes on the War, No. IV," *Guardian*, July 3, 1866, *EMC*, 136. Engels' stress on the needle-gun's role was great, but contrary to Craig's representation (Königgrätz, 174), he did not make it the only factor in explaining the course of the war.

[54]To Marx, July 4, 1866, *31*, 230; "Notes on the War, No. IV," "Notes on the War, No. V," *Guardian*, July 3, July 6, 1866, *EMC*, 133-40. Engels stuck to his view of Moltke's strategy; in his preface to the second edition of the *Peasant War* (1870), he maintained that "the astonishingly bad strategy of the Prussians" had triumphed only over "the astonishingly worse strategy of the Austrians." *MEW*, 7, 535. Cf. Georg Eckert's view, in Pelger, 93. His view of Moltke's maneuvers was shared by most military critics of the time (Craig, *Königgrätz*, 176-77) and is consistent with his complaint of American strategic innocence—probably directed against Grant's operations around Vicksburg. To Weydemeyer, Mar. 10, 1865, *31*, 458. In 1870 Engels took Moltke more seriously: "Notes on the War—X," *PMG*, Aug. 19, 1870, *Notes on the War*, 23.

[55]Marx to Engels, July 7, Engels to Marx, July 4, July 9, 1866, *31*, 233, 231, 325.

[56]Engels to Marx, July 25, Marx to Engels, July 7, 1866, *ibid.*, 240-41, 233. Engels, applying the Hegelian irony of history, said that Bismarck's victories would doom *Junker* domination. "Die 'Krisis' in Preussen," *Volksstaat*, Jan. 15, 1873, *MEW*, *18*, 293.

[57]Engels to Marx, Aug. 6, Marx to Engels, July 21, May 17, 1866, *31*, 246, 238, 219. A tide of place-hunters was beginning, led by Ruge and Kinkel; and had Lassalle lived long enough, he would have signed on with Bismarck even before the victory, said Marx.

[58]Engels to Marx, July 25, 1866, Dec. 6, 1867, Marx to Engels, Dec. 17, 1868, *ibid.*, 240-41, 402, 412. Cf. Marx to Kugelmann, Aug. 23, 1866, *ibid.*, 521.

[59]Marx thought that the English oligarchy wanted an intervention in favor of Prussia, but even a war expanded to include England seems to have promised no revolution. To Engels, Aug. 1, 1870, *33*, 20.

[60]Engels to Marx, Sept. 21, Marx to Engels, Sept. 23, Engels to Marx, Oct. 2, Marx to Kugelmann, Oct. 12, 1868, *ibid.*, 159, 160, 172, 567. Cf. Engels to Marx, Sept. 18, Marx to Engels, Sept. 18, 1868, *ibid.*, 153-54, 156. Wolfe (49) incomprehensibly calls Marx's and Engels' reasoning "incomprehensible." It was wrong, but surely not incomprehensible.

[61]First Address, July 23, 1870, *Civil War in France*, 24-27; Engels to Marx, Aug. 15, 1870, *33*, 40. Zint (62) suggests that it shows a misapprehension of the French character to suppose that a beating would cure chauvinism.

[62]Engels to Marx, Aug. 5, Marx to Engels, July 20, 1870, *33*, 30, 5. Cf. Engels to Marx, July 31, 1870, *ibid.*, 15-16.

[63]Red Prussian theorists: Schwartzschild, 364; Wolfe, 50. Engels to Marx, Aug. 15, 1870, 33, 39.

[64]To Paul and Laura Lafargue, July 28, to Engels, July 28, 1870, *ibid.*, 124, 12.

[65]Engels to Marx, Aug. 15, Marx to Engels, Aug. 17, 1870, *ibid.*, 39-40, 43. The relations between Marx and Engels and the two socialist movements in Germany (Liebknecht's *Eisenacher* and Schweitzer's Lassalleans) during the war is much discussed; Mayer (*Engels, 2*, 544) says rightly that most of the World War discussions are worthless polemic. Treatments of some interest are E. Bernstein, "Karl Marx und Friedrich Engels in der zweiten Phase des Krieges von 1870/71," and "Friedrich Engels und die deutsch-französische Frage," *Neue Zeit, 33*, (1914-15), 76-80, 710-17; N. Riazonov, "Zur Stellungnahme von Marx und Engels während des deutsch-französischen Kriegs," *ibid.*, 161-62; Riazonov, "Marx und Engels über den deutsch-französischen Krieg," *Der Kampf, 8* (1915), 129-39.

[66]Engels to Marx, Aug. 15, 1870, 33, 41. (Longuet, 223, uses this letter to prove Engels' lack of real enmity to France, even before the fall of Napoleon III.)

[67]*Civil War in France*, 33; *Daily News*, Jan. 19, 1871, *MEW, 17*, 285; Marx to Adolphe Hubert (in connection with the Versailles government's prosecution of the International), Aug. 10, 1871, *33*, 266.

[68]Engels to Marx, Aug. 10, Aug. 15, 1870, *ibid.*, 34, 41. (Marx had already said that the French were demoralized after two decades of Bonapartism, and could not be counted on for revolutionary heroism. To Engels, Aug. 8, 1870, *ibid.*, 32.) Engels to Marx, Aug. 20,, 1870, *ibid.*, 45; "The Crisis of the War," *PMG*, Aug. 20, 1870, *Notes on the War*, 28.

[69]To Marx, Aug. 20, Sept. 7, 1870, Marx to Cesar de Paepe, Sept. 14, 1870, *33*, 46, 56, 147.

[70]To Marx, Sept. 13, 1870, *ibid.*, 63; "Notes on the War.—XIX," *PMG*, Sept. 27,. 1870, *Notes on the War*, 56. Favre's refusal to surrender Strasbourg was also foolish, since the fort could not be held in any case. "The Story of the Negotiations," *PMG*, Oct. 1, 1870, *ibid.*, 56-57. Cf. also Engels to Marx, Aug. 20, 1870, *33*, 46.

[71]"Saragossa-Paris," *PMG*, Oct. 22, 1870, *Notes on the War*, 73-75. Engels' evaluation of the siege of Saragossa as a bloody waste follows Napier, *1*, 388-90.

[72]Marx to E. S. Beesly, Sept. 12, to Engels Aug. 12 and Sept. 12, 1870, to Paul Lafargue, Feb. 4, 1871, to Kugelmann, Feb 4, 1871; Engels to Marx, Sept. 4, 1870, *33*, 47, 49, 176, 181, 33.

[73]"Notes on the War.—XXI," *PMG*, Oct. 6, 1870, *Notes on the War*, 62. In later years Trochu argued for three-year service instead of five-year. Richard D. Challener, *The French Theory of the Nation in Arms, 1866-1939* (New York: Columbia University Press, 1952), 37.

[74]"Notes on the War.—XXII," *PMG*, Oct. 11, "Notes on the War.—XIV," Aug. 13, "Notes on the War.—XXV," Oct. 27, 1870, *Notes on the War*, 66, 36-37, 75.

[75]Marx to Beesly, Sept. 12, 1870, *33*, 143-45; Engels, "Fortified Capitals,"

PMG, Nov. 21, 1870, *Notes on the War*, 92. Mayer (*Engels, 2*, 207) likens these calls for intervention to the advocacy of expanded wars in 1848; but in 1870, nonrevolutionary powers were invited in without any apparent expectation that their participation in the war would revolutionize anyone. Later Engels decided that a military intervention would come too late and serve no purpose. Outlines for resolutions in the General Council of the International, Jan. 31, 1871, *MEW, 17*, 286.

[76]"Prussian Francs-Tireurs," *PMG*, Dec. 9, "Notes on the War.—XXI," Dec. 17, 1870, *Notes on the War*, 105-8, 109-10. Cf. Marx to Kugelmann, Dec. 13, 1870, *33*, 163. Favre pointed out to Bismarck that the Prussians had risen against the French in 1813, and Bismarck replied that just as Napoleon had hanged the Prussian insurgents, so the Germans of 1870 were hanging the *francs-tireurs*. Howard, 251.

[77]"Notes on the War.—XXII," *PMG*, Oct. 11, 1870, *Notes on the War*, 66; Howard, 300.

[78] "Fortified Capitals," *PMG*, Nov. 21, "The Military Situation in France," Nov. 26, 1870, *Notes on the War*, 91-92, 95-97.

[79]"Notes on the War.—XXXI," *PMG*, Dec. 17, 1870, *Notes on the War*, 110-11. Cf. "Notes on the War.—XXXVIII," *PMG*, Jan. 26, 1871, *ibid.*, 130.

[80]"Notes on the War.—XXXII," *PMG*, Dec. 23, "The German Position in France," Dec. 24, "The Chances of the War," Dec. 8, 1870, *ibid.*, 113-14, 103.

[81]Note on Lissagaray's history of the Commune, 1877, *MEW*, 351-54. Engels at the time had thought the French general d'Aurelle's caution justified, to some extent, by the greenness of his troops. "Notes on the War.—XXVII," *PMG*, Nov. 16, 1870, *Notes on the War*, 88-89. Cf. Howard, 294-95.

[82]Lafargue's commemorative articles on the Commune (*Le Matin*, Nov. 15, 17, 23, 1891) are discussed and quoted in Mayer, *Engels, 2*, 544-45. Engels assured August Bebel, "if something of the sort *did* occur, you were as innocent of it as an unborn baby." Nov 25, 1891, *38*, 220. Cf. Engels to Laura Lafargue, Nov. 27, to Bebel, Dec. 1, to Laura Lafargue, Dec. 1, to Paul Lafargue, Dec. 3, 1891, *ibid.*, 222-223, 225-226, 229, 236. Boris Nicolaievsky discussed the destruction of the papers in 1929 or 1930 with Eduard Bernstein, who remembered little of their contents. Nicolaievsky, "Toward a History of the 'Communist League' 1847-1852," *IRSH, 1* (1956), 239.

[83]Nicolaievsky and Maenchen-Helfen, 319; see Howard, 407-27, on Bourbaki's effort.

[84]Jean Longuet claimed that Engels wrote a plan and Marx dissuaded him from sending it; but Longuet based his claim on a letter in which Marx advised Engels against personally *going* to Paris (which Engels seems never to have intended to do). *La politique internationale du marxisme*, 270. For Marx's alleged warning, see Charles Longuet's preface to Marx, *La guerre civile en France (La commune de Paris)* (Paris: Librairie de l'Humanité, 1925), xv. Edouard Vaillant wrote in 1914 that Engels sent the plan, and offered to serve as military advisor, but got no reply. *Humanité*, Dec. 14, 1914.

[85]"Notes on the War.—XXXVII," *PMG*, Jan. 21, "Notes on the War.—XXXVIII," Jan. 26, "Notes on the War.—XXXIX," Jan. 28, "Notes on the War.—XL," Feb. 2, "The Military Aspect of Affairs in France," Feb. 8, 1871, *Notes on the War*, 128, 129-30, 131, 134-36.

[86]"Notes on the War.—I," *PMG*, July 29, "Notes on the War.—VI," Aug. 11, 1870, *ibid.*, 1, 15; to Marx, Aug. 3, 1870, *33*, 24; Neumann, 166. Ernst Drahn discusses Engels' percipience: Engels was ten miles off in predicting the site of the battle of Sedan. *Engels als Kriegswissenschaftler*, 20-23.

[87]To Marx, July 31, 1870; Marx to Engels, Sept. 2, 1870, *33*, 15, 49. Marx assured Engels that if the war lasted a while, Engels would be acclaimed as the "*first military authority* in London." Aug. 3, 1870, *ibid.*, 27. Cf. also Jenny Marx to Engels, Aug. 10, Marx to Engels, Aug. 30, 1870, *ibid.*, 675, 48.

[88]Engels to Marx, Sept. 12, Marx to Engels, Sept. 6, 1870, Marx to Sigfrid Meyer, Jan. 21, 1871, *ibid.*, 61, 54, 173.

[89]To Kugelmann, Apr. 17, to Liebknecht, Apr. 6, to Kugelmann, Apr. 12, 1871, to Domela Nieuwenhuis, Feb. 22, 1881, *ibid.*, 209, 200, 205-06, 35, 160.

[90]Marx to Kugelmann, April 12, 1871, *33*, 205; Engels to the General Council, *MEW*, *17*, 633-34.

[91]The Commune was a worthy attempt, once concluded. Engels said that the International should take credit, though it had not lifted a finger to set off the rising. To Sorge, Sept. 12-17, 1875, *33*, 642. On the legacy of the Commune, see Jellinek, 419, and Lenin, *State and Revolution* (New York: International Publishers, 1943), *passim*.

[92]Engels to Carl Klein and Friedrich Moll, Mar. 10, 1871, Marx to Kugelmann, Dec. 13, 1870, *33*, 188-89, 163; Marx and Engels to the leaders of the German Social Democratic Party, Aug. 22-30, 1870, *MEW*, *17*, 270.

Notes to Chapter 7

[1]E.g., Marx, "Affairs in Prussia," *Tribune*, Dec. 27, 1858, *MEW*, *12*, 662; to Lion Philips, late March, 1864, in Blumenberg, "Ein unbekanntes Kapitel," *IRSH*, *1*, (1956), 97-99; to Kugelmann, Nov. 29, 1864, Engels to Hermann Engels, Apr. 6, 1866, to Marx, Apr. 27, 1867, Marx to Engels, May 7, 1867, *31*, 430, 512, 295, 299.

[2]Marx and Engels to the German Party, Aug. 22-30, 1870, excerpts in *Manifest der sozial-demokratischen Arbeiterpartei*, Sept. 5, 1870, *MEW*, *17*, 269; Marx to Engels, Sept. 2, 1870, *33*, 49; also Second Address, in *Civil War in France*, 31.

[3]To the German Party, Aug. 22-30, 1870, *MEW*, *17*, 268. Hans Rothfels

notes that Marx and Bismarck agreed on the tension-producing potential of the annexations, but he supposes that Marx—in contrast to Bismarck—welcomed the new wars that were to be expected. "Bismarck und Karl Marx," *Jahresheft der Heidelberger Akademie der Wissenschaften*, 1959/60, 65.

[4]Wars might benefit the original Poland, or Ireland, but such benefits would not make war worthwhile. Marx to Sorge, Sept. 27, 1877, *34*, 297; Engels to Kautsky, Feb. 7, to Bernstein, June 26, to Bebel, Dec. 22, 1882, *35*, 270, 338-39, 416; to Sorge, Jan. 18, 1893, *39*, 9-10.

[5]To Engels, Aug. 8, 1870, *33*, 31-32.

[6]To Sorge, Sept. 1, 1870, Aug. 4, 1874, *ibid.*, 140, 635; cf. Marx to Kugelmann, May 18, 1874, *ibid.*, 628.

[7]To Hepner, Aug. 4, 1872, *35*, 508-09. This expectation of a quick, decisive German victory in the next war was short-lived.

[8]Marx and Engels to the German Party, Aug. 22-30, 1870, *MEW*, *17*, 269. Cf. Engels to J. P. Becker, Sept. 8, 1879, *34*, 391; to Ion Nadejde, Jan. 4, 1888, *37*, 6; to Laura Lafargue, Sept. 13, 1886, *36*, 530.

[9]"The Foreign Policy of Russian Tsardom," *Time* (4th ser.), *1*, (Jan.-June, 1890), 541, 545. This article was also published in *Neue Zeit*, *8* (1890).

[10]To Vera Zasulitsch, Mar. 6, to Bebel, June 6, 1884, to Liebknecht, Dec. 1, 1885, *36*, 120, 158, 397; to Lafargue, Mar. 7, 1890, *37*, 363; excerpts from a letter to Lafargue, in *Le Socialiste*, Sept. 12, 1891, *22*, 241-42; "Der Sozialismus in Deutschland," *Neue Zeit*, *10* (1891-92), *ibid.*, 257-60; interview in *L'Eclair*, Apr. 6, 1892, *ibid.*, 534-36; to Laura Lafargue, Aug. 17, to Danielson, Sept. 2, to Paul Lafargue, Sept. 2, to Bebel, Dec. 1, to Sorge, Aug. 9-11, to Bebel, Oct. 13, 1891, to Bebel, Feb. 2, to Paul Lafargue, July 22, 1892, *38*, 145-46, 148, 151-52, 226, 143, 174-75, 261, 403-04.

[11]"Foreign Policy of Russian Tsardom," 541; interviews in *Figaro*, May 13, *Daily Chronicle*, July 1, 1893, *MEW*, *22*, 541, 546-47. Cf. Engels to Lafargue, Jan. 22, 1895, *39*, 393; to Julie Bebel, Mar. 12, 1887, *36*, 628.

[12]To Bebel, May 1-2, 1891, *38*, 95; "Was nun?" *Der Sozialdemokrat*, Mar. 8, 1890, *MEW*, *22*, 9. Cf. Marx to Engels, Dec. 17, Engels to Marx, Dec. 21, 1866, *31*, 268, 270. Sometimes, on the other hand, it seemed that military preparedness increased the danger of war. To Sorge, Jan. 12, 1889, *37*, 137-38.

[13]To Sorge, Jan. 7, to Liebknecht, Feb. 23, 1888, *37*, 11, 30; to Bebel, Sept. 13-14, 1886, *36*, 525; Feb. 9, 1893, *39*, 27.

[14]To Marx, Aug. 25, July 15, July 19, July 24, July 31, to Liebknecht, July 2, to Bracke, June 25, to Hermann Engels, Oct. 5, 1877, *37*, 73-75, 46-47, 51, 57, 63, 282, 279-80, 299. Both Engels and Marx hoped for a sort of Young Turk revolt to energize the war effort. Engels to Marx, May 27, Marx to Engels, May 31, 1877, *ibid.*, 42, 44. For Engels' early overestimation of the Turks' chances, see Engels to Kugelmann, Oct. 20, to Hermann Engels, Dec. 18, 1876; to Liebknecht, Jan. 9, to Pauli, Mar. 26, to Bracke, Apr. 24, 1877, *ibid.*, 218, 234-35, 239, 260, 274.

[15]To Liebknecht, Jan. 9, to Ferdinand Fleckles, Jan. 21, to Hermann Engels, Oct. 15, 1877, *ibid.*, 239, 244, 298. Cf. Marx to Sorge, Sept. 27, to

Engels, July 18, 1877, *ibid.*, 296, 48; Marx in *Labor Standard*, Mar. 31, 1878, *MEW*, *19*, 136.

[16]Engels to Laura Lafargue, late Sept., to Kautsky, Sept. 23, to Sorge, Nov. 10, 1894, *39*, 298-99, 301, 310.

[17]Marx to Liebknecht, Feb. 4, 1878, *34*, 317; Engels, introduction to Sigismund Borkheim, *Zur Erinnerung für die deutschen Mordspatrioten, 1806-1807* (Höttingen-Zürich, 1888), *MS*, *2*, 632.

[18]To Bebel, Nov. 17, 1885, *36*, 391; cf. Engels to Laura Lafargue, Sept. 13, 1886, *ibid.*, 530.

[19]To J. P. Becker, Dec. 5, Dec. 28, 1885, *ibid.*, 401, 417.

[20]To Sorge, Jan. 7, Jan. 10, 1886, *37*, 10, 14; to Sorge, Jan. 6, 1892, *38*, 245; to Laura Lafargue, Sept. 13, 1886, *36*, 530.

[21]To J. P. Becker, Apr. 12, 1882, June 15, 1885, to Sorge, Sept. 16, 1887, to Bernstein, June 12-13, 1883, to Laura Lafargue, Nov. 12, 1887, to Paul Lafargue, Nov. 16, 1887, *36*, 291, 327, 705, 36-37, 713, 717; to Schlüter, Mar. 17, to Liebknecht, Jan. 10, 1888, *37*, 38, 13.

[22]To Laura Lafargue, Feb. 26, 1890, to Sorge, Feb. 23, 1889, *ibid.*, 359, 161; "Was nun?" *Sozialdemokrat*, Mar. 8, 1890, article in the Newcastle *Daily Chronicle*, Mar. 3, 1890, *MEW*, 22, 9, 5; to Sorge, Jan. 7, 1888, 37, 10.

[23]To Bernstein, June 12-13, 1883, Oct. 22, 1886, *36*, 36, 549; to Victor Adler, July 17, to Paul Lafargue, June 2, 1894, *39*, 270-71, 254; to Laura Lafargue, Dec. 5, 1892, to Paul Lafargue, Jan. 31, 1891, *38*, 545, 20; to Paul Lafargue, June 2, 1894, Feb. 26, 1895, *39*, 254-55, 413.

[24]Engels to Bebel, Feb. 19, 1892, *38*, 282; to Marx, Sept. 9, 1879, *34*, 105. Cf. Engels to Bernstein, Feb. 22-25, 1882, *35*, 282-83.

[25]To Bebel, Dec. 22, 1882, *ibid.*, 416. Cf. Engels to Sorge, Jan. 7, 1888, 37, 11; Marx to Danielson, Sept. 12, 1880, *34*, 464.

[26]To Schlüter, Oct. 3, 1889, to Bebel, Sept. 13-14, 1886, *36*, 632, 536 (cf. Engels to Bebel, Nov. 17, 1885, *ibid.*, 391); to Lafargue, Mar. 25, Oct. 3, 1889, *37*, 171, 279.

[27]To Kautsky, Feb. 7, 1882, *35*, 271-72; to Becker, Nov. 30, 1883, *36*; 73; to Bebel, Dec. 22, to Bernstein, Feb. 22-25, 1882, *35*, 416, 283.

[28]To Lafargue, Oct. 25-26, 1885, *36*, 562; Oct. 3, 1889, Dec. 4, 1888, Mar. 25, 1889, to Laura Lafargue, May 7, 1889, *37*, 280, 123, 171, 199.

[29]To Bebel, Nov. 17, 1885, Sept. 13-14, 1886, *36*, 391, 525-26; Sept. 29-Oct. 1, 1891, *38*, 161.

[30]Published as "Der Sozialismus in Deutschland," *Neue Zeit, 10* (1891-92), *MEW*, *22*, 145-60. Cf. Engels' interview in *L'Eclair*, Apr. 6, 1892, *ibid.*, 537.

[31]To Bebel, Sept. 29-Oct. 1, to Sorge, Oct. 24, 1891, *38*, 161, 176, 184.

[32]To Sorge, Jan. 6, 1892, to Bebel, Oct. 24-26, to Sorge, Oct. 24, 1891, *ibid.*, 245, 189, 184.

[33]To Charles Bonnier, middle Oct., 1892, to Bebel, Sept. 29-Oct. 1, 1891, *ibid.*, 498, 161. The argument against giving up useful military positions on the eve of hostilities recalls *Po und Rhein*.

[34]To Bebel, May 1-2, Sept. 29, 1891, *ibid.*, 95, 162-63; to Lafargue, Feb. 7, 1888, 37, 21; June 27, 1893, *39*, 90; to Bebel, Oct. 13, 1891, *38*, 175. For a

discussion of Bebel's exchanges with Engels on the defense question, see Waldtraut Opitz, "Friedrich Engels und die deutsche Sozialdemokratie in den Jahren 1890/91," *Zeitschrift für Geschichtswissenschaft, 11* (1969), 1403-15.

[35]This is the title of Wolfe's Chapter Four, 72-82.

[36]To Bebel, Oct. 13, to Sorge, Oct. 24, 1891, to Panajionis Argyriades, early July, 1892, *38,* 176, 184, 398.

[37]To Bebel, Oct. 15, 1875, *34,* 163; Sept. 13-14, 1886, *36,* 526. Cf. Engels to Liebknecht, Feb. 23, 1888, to Laura Lafargue, May 7, 1889, *37,* 30, 199, to Bebel, Dec. 22, 1881, *35,* 416; and his preface to *Soziales aus Russland, MEW, 18,* 585.

[38]To Charles Bonnier, Oct. 24, 1892, *38,* 503; to Bebel, Sept. 13-14, 1886, *36,* 525. Even a slowly won victory might have a similar effect. To Sorge, Jan. 7, 1888, *37,* 11.

[39]Perhaps Bismarck's overthrow should be postponed till the start of revolution in Russia, Engels suggested—presumably because the German workers could act more freely if they no longer had to worry about defending their country against the Tsar. To Liebknecht, Feb. 23, 1888, *ibid.,* 29.

[40]To Bebel, Sept. 29, 1891, *38,* 162-63. Under different objective conditions, of course, German and revolutionary interests might cease to coincide, as Karl Radek pointed out. "Marxismus und Kriegsprobleme," *Lichtstrahlen, Monatliches Bildungsorgan für denkende Arbeiter,* 2 (1914), 20-21.

[41]To Bebel, Sept. 29, 1891, *38,* 162; interview in *L'Eclair,* Apr. 6, 1892, *MEW, 22,* 536; to Liebknecht, Feb. 28, Feb. 23, 1888, *37, 37,* 30.

[42]To Sorge, Feb. 22, to Laura Lafargue, Feb. 28, to Paul Lafargue, Feb. 7, to Liebknecht, Feb. 29, Feb. 23, 1888, *ibid.,* 25, 34, 21, 37, 30.

[43]"The Foreign Policy of Russian Tsardom," 356; *L'Eclair,* Apr. 6, 1892, *MEW, 22,* 537; Engels to Lafargue, Mar. 19, 1888, 37, 40; to Bebel, Sept. 29-Oct. 1, 1891, *38,* 161-62.

[44]"Foreign Policy of Russian Tsardom," 537; *Kann Europa abrüsten? MS, 2,* 674; to Bebel, Sept. 13-14, 1886, *36,* 525; to Laura Lafargue, May 7, 1889, to Sorge, Feb. 22, 1888, *37,* 199, 25; to Bebel, Sept. 29, to Laura Lafargue, Oct. 31, 1891, *38,* 162, 202. If the war was fought out with no revolutions, Europe's exhaustion would result in the general triumph of American industry. To Sorge, Jan. 7, 1888, *37,* 11.

[45]To Sorge, Jan. 7, Feb. 22, 1888, *ibid.,* 11, 25.

[46] "Kann Europa abrüsten?" *Vorwärts,* Mar. 1893 (reprinted as a pamphlet, 1893), *MS, 2,* 650-75.

[47]Marx to Engels, Sept. 16, 1868, *32,* 150-51; Engels to Bonnier, Oct. 24, 1892, *38,* 503; to Kautsky, Nov. 3, 1893, *39,* 161-63.

[48]Convenient discussions of Bebel's position in the general strike dispute are James Joll, *The Second International, 1889-1914* (New York: Harper & Row, 1966), 126-57, and Carl E. Schorske, *German Social Democracy, 1905-1917: The Development of the Great Schism* (Cambridge: Harvard University Press, 1955), 73-75, 80-84. Adler quoted from Joll, 154.

[49]On the effect of the SPD's vote for war credits, see Julius Braunthal, *History of the International*, tr. Henry Collins and Kenneth Mitchell (New York: Frederick A. Praeger, 1967), 2, 1-35.

[50]To Bebel, Sept. 29-Oct. 1, Oct. 13, 1891, *38*, 161, 175.

Notes to Chapter 8

[1]*The Origin of the Family, Private Property and the State: In the Light of the Researches of Lewis R. Morgan* (New York: International Publishers, 1942), 82-83, 93-97, 103, 116-18, 130-31, 138-39, 149-50, 87. For elaboration on Engels' effort to connect military and social systems, see Helmert, "Friedrich Engels und die Aufgaben der marxistischen Militärgeschichtsschreibung." Engels was more systematic than, say, Kipling, who shared his respect for the valor of the "Fuzzy-Wuzzy."

[2]"Army" and "Infantry," *New American Cyclopedia, MEW, 14*, 11-12, 342.

[3]*Ibid.*, 347-48; "Zur Urgeschichte der Deutschen," "Frankische Zeit," unpublished mss. written 1881-82, *ibid., 19*, 447, 491-94. Cf. *Capital, 3*, 588-89.

[4]To Engels, Sept. 25, 1857, *29*, 192-93. Cf. Marx to Engels, July 7, 1866, *31*, 234.

[5]Tr. Emile Burns (New York: International Publishers, 1939), 184-92. A further note on infantry tactics was omitted from the published work. *MS, 2*, 618-24.

[6]To Marx, July 9, 1866, *31*, 235. Cf. Marx to Engels, July 7, Engels to Marx, July 12, 1866, *ibid.*, 234, 237.

[7]To Marx, Mar. 10, 1868, *32*, 40; above, 128-29.

[8]*Anti-Dühring*, 188, 185. Cf. "Holy Alliance vs. France," *MS, 1*, 221.

[9]Ernst Huber observes that Prussian army reformers of the early nineteenth century used the same slogans, contrasting "national" militias and "standing" armies, which were later directed against armies incorporating the reformers' universal service system. *Heer und Staat in der deutschen Geschichte* (Hamburg: Hanseatische Verlagsanstalt, 1938), 128-29.

[10]Isegrim (Max Schippel), "War Friedrich Engels milizgläubisch?" *Sozialistische Monatshefte, 2* (1898), 495-98; Karl Kautsky, "Friedrich Engels und das Milizsystem," *Neue Zeit, 17* (1898-99), 335-42; Schippel, "Friedrich Engels und das Milizsystem," *ibid.*, 580-88, 613-17; Kautsky, "Schippel und der Militarismus," *ibid.*, 618-26, 644-54, 686-91; Schippel, "Siehe da: Das stehende Milizheer!" *ibid.*, 780-86; Kautsky, "Siegfried der Harmlose," *ibid.*, 787-91.

[11] "Miliz und stehendes Heer," *ibid.*, *31* (1912-13), 850.

[12] Venedey had relied upon "the *spirit* that inspires the people and its fighters," which could never be defeated. *Preussen und das Preussenthum*, 57. Carl Bleibtreu likewise maintained that battles were won by numbers and spirit, leaving aside the occasional strategic genius, whom no system could produce on demand. "Die zukünftige Ueberlegenheit des Milizsystems," *Sozialistische Monatshefte*, *3* (1899), 518. Cf. Höhn, *Armee als Erziehungsschule*, 36-43.

[13] See Ritter, *1*, 133-38; Höhn, *Sozialismus und Heer*, *1*, 20-30. An excellent survey of works on the militia idea is Günter Nickolaus, *Die Milizfrage in Deutschland von 1848 bis 1933* (Berlin: Junker und Dünnhaupt, 1933).

[14] "Zwei Reden in Elberfeld," *Rheinische Jahrbücher für gesellschaftliche Reform*, *1* (1845), *MEW*, *2*, 543-44.

[15] "Now that we are not writing an *NRZ*," Engels said in 1851, "we have no need for illusions"—so he could give the reactionary Austrian general Radetzky the praise he deserved. "Holy Alliance vs. France," *MS*, *1*, 212.

[16] "Forderungen der Kommunistischen Partei Deutschlands," *MEW*, *5*, 3; *8*, 586; tax refusal resolutions signed by Marx and Schapper, *NRZ*, Nov. 19, 1848, *ibid.*, *6*, 33; Central Committee's address to Bund, March, 1850, *ibid.*, *7*, 250; Höhn, *Sozialismus und Heer*, *1*, 36-40.

[17] Above, 82-84.

[18] "The Armies of Europe," *Putnam's*, *6* (1855), 567, 306.

[19] Chaloner and Henderson, introduction, *EMC*, xix. The Volunteers were themselves a middle-class institution, as noted in Engels' article, "The British Volunteer Troops," *Tribune*, July 11, 1860, *MEW*, *15*, 70.

[20] "Volunteer Generals," "A Review of English Volunteer Riflemen," "Aldershot and the Volunteers," "Volunteer Officers," *Volunteer Journal*, Mar. 16, 1861, Sept. 14, 1860, May 11, 1861, Nov. 22, 1861, *EMC*, 24-25, 28, 7-8, 36, 39-43; "Eine englische Freiwilligen-Inspektion," *Allgemeine Militär-Zeitung*, Nov. 8, 1862, *MEW*, *15*, 539.

[21] "Lessons of the American War," "Volunteer Generals," *Volunteer Journal*, Dec. 6, Mar. 16, 1861, *EMC*, 109-13, 24; "Could the French Take London?" "The British Volunteer Troops," *Tribune*, Aug. 11, July 11, 1860, *MEW*, *15*, 107, 71. His most negative assessments were those written for the *Tribune* before he became a contributor to the *Volunteer Journal*.

[22] To Kautsky, Apr. 30, 1891, *38*, 88; to Marx, Jan. 16, 1868, *32*, 20-21.

[23] *Die Preussische Militärfrage und die deutsche Arbeiterpartei* (Hamburg, 1865), *MS*, *2*, 319, 315.

[24] *Ibid.*, 309; "Die englische Armee," ms. probably written for the *Allgemeine Militär-Zeitung* in 1864, *MEW*, *15*, 611, 616, 619; Marx and Engels, "Züchtigung der Soldaten," *Neue Oder-Zeitung*, Aug. 31, 1855, *ibid.*, *11*, 509-11; "The Armies of Europe," *Putnam's*, *6* (1855), 201-02.

[25] *Preussische Militärfrage*, *MS*, *2*, 309, 315-16.

[26] "The Armies of Europe," *Putnam's*, *6* (1855), 308. The reference to the English opinion on training time is from Napier, *2*, 366. Cf. *Preussische Militärfrage*, *MS*, *2*, 317.

[27]"The German Resources for War," *Tribune*, Mar. 12, 1859, *MEW, 13*, 192; "Military Reform in Germany," *Tribune*, Feb. 20, 1860, *ibid., 15*, 18.

[28]"Kinglake über die Schlacht an der Alma," unfinished ms. probably begun for the *Allgemeine Militär-Zeitung* in 1864, *ibid.*, 597.

[29]Above, 124-25.

[30]"The Armies of Europe," *Putnam's, 6* (1855), 197, 306; *Preussische Militärfrage, MS, 2*, 316, 309.

[31]"How to Fight the Prussians," "The Rationale of the Prussian Army System," *PMG*, Sept. 17, Oct. 8, 1870, *Notes on the War*, 53-54, 64.

[32]Engels to Hermann Engels, Jan. 9, 1877, *34*, 240-41; to Liebknecht, Jan. 9, 1877, *ibid.*, 239; to Bebel, Sept. 13-14, 1886, *36*, 524-25; to Sorge, Apr. 6, 1887, *ibid.*, 636; to Lafargue, Mar. 7, 1890, *37*, 363; *Kann Europa abrüsten? MS, 2*, 664-66; "The Foreign Policy of Russian Tsardom," *Time*, 4th ser., *1* (1890), 356. Austria was similarly handicapped. Engels to Salo Faerber, Oct. 22, 1885, *36*, 374-75.

[33]"The Rationale of the Prussian Army System," *PMG*, Oct. 8, 1870, *Notes on the War*, 62. On this concept see Höhn, *Armee als Erziehungsschule*, 30-33.

[34] "The Armies of Europe," *Putnam's, 6* (1855), 308; *Preussische Militärfrage, MS, 2*, 315. Jean Jaurès likewise described the Prussian system as a bastard arrangement because of its excessive emphasis on the active, "standing" part of the army. *L'organisation socialiste de la France: l'armée nouvelle* (Paris: l'Humanité, 1915), 16.

[35]Vagts, *A History of Militarism: Civilian and Military* (New York: Meridian, 1959), 13-17.

[36]*Preussische Militärfrage, MS, 2*, 331, 317; for an echo of Engels' view, see the anonymous note, "Ein und dreijährig," *Neue Zeit, 2* (1884), 239. Though Engels never took the Lassallean line of siding with the *Junkers* and Bismarck against the bourgeoisie, he seems to have relished the army organization fight as a demonstration of the confusion and spinelessness of Prussian liberalism. "Die 'Krisis' in Preussen," *Volksstaat*, Jan. 15, 1873, *MEW, 18*, 291-92. For the official view on the need for three years' service, see Craig, 146, 157.

[37]*Preussische Militärfrage, MS, 2*, 319, 318; "The Armies of Europe," *Putnam's, 6* (1855), 308. In his army reorganization scheme of 1893 Engels contended that cavalry training could be speeded up by more efficient planning, but he admitted that some long-term volunteers would be needed. *Kann Europa abrüsten? MS, 2*, 656.

[38] "Brief an das Organisationskomitee des internationalen Festes in Paris," Feb. 13, 1887, *Sozialdemokrat*, Mar. 11, 1887, *MEW, 21*, 344-45.

[39]*Anti-Dühring*, 188-92. Cf. Engels' article in *La Plebe*, Jan. 22, 1878, *MEW, 19*, 114.

[40]*Kann Europa abrüsten? MS, 2*, 650-51. Boys would take naturally to hiking and elementary drill, and retired noncommissioned officers could find employment as instructors. *Ibid.*, 659-61. Engels does not seem to have envisioned anything so extensive as Kipling's "Army of a Dream" (*Traffics and Discoveries* [New York: Doubleday, 1904], 223-78), in

which the male population would spend all its free time in war games; Engels' emphasis was on physical fitness. For echoes of Engels' line see Bebel, *Nicht stehendes Heer, sondern Volkswehr!* (Stuttgart: Dietz, 1898), 50-53; Jaurès, 215-19, 480, 550; G. Moch, *L'armée d'une démocratie* (Paris: Revue Blanche, 1900).

[41]*Preussische Militärfrage*, MS, 2, 319. Cf. Marx's instructions to the Central Committee of the International, Feb. 20, 1867, advocating gymnastics and military practice as part of the youth program. *MEW, 16,* 195.

[42]*Kann Europa abrüsten?* MS, 2, 659-69. Cf. Engels to Lafargue, Jan. 3, 1894, to Kautsky, Mar. 25, 1895, 39, 190-92, 446. Bebel considered Engels' proposal as to how to introduce the militia impractical. To Engels, Feb. 28, Mar. 12, 1893, *Briefwechsel*, 670-73.

[43]In 1859 he wrote that although the Prussian mass army was inferior to the Austrians at the beginning of a war, it was correspondingly superior in defense, once it survived the initial clashes. "The German Resources for War," *Tribune*, Mar. 12, 1859, *MEW, 13,* 192.

[44]*Preussische Militärfrage*, MS, 2, 316, 308; "Varia über Deutschland," 1873-74, *MEW, 18,* 594.

[45]In 1888, as earlier in 1866, Engels hoped that the *Landwehr* would balk at an unpopular war. "With 5,000,000 Germans under arms, ordered to fight for things in which they have no interest, Bismarck [would] no longer be master of the situation." To Lafargue, Feb. 7, 1888, 37, 20-21. The idea that the *nation armée* would perforce be the *nation juste* was followed up by Jaurès, 48. For earlier exponents of this view, see Nickolaus, 28-34.

Notes to Chapter 9

[1]The view that Engels' analyses of military organization were essentially tactical studies, intended to help bring about the revolution, is shared by Heinz Helmert and Ernst Roloff, who do not, however, concur in this chapter's arguments as to where Engels' tactical studies led him. "Die militärtheoretische Tätigkeit von Friedrich Engels in der Periode nach der Pariser Kommune," *ZfMG, 9* (1970), 645-58.

[2]Speech to the General Council of the International on the League for Peace and Freedom, Aug. 13, 1867, *MEW, 16,* 530; "Revolution in Spain," *Tribune*, Aug. 8, 1856, *ibid., 12,* 42; *The Belgian Butchery* (London, 1869), *ibid., 16,* 352.

[3]"Die Bewegungen von 1847," *Deutsche-Brüsseler Zeitung*, Jan. 23, 1848, "Details über den 23. Juni," *NRZ*, June 26, 1848 (Extrabeilage), *ibid.,*

4, 497, *5*, 113-14; Marx, "Camphausen," *NRZ*, Feb. 4, 1849, "Political Consequences of the Commercial Excitement," *Tribune*, Nov. 2, 1852, *ibid.*, *6*, 219, *8*, 376-78; Engels to Kautsky, Apr. 30, 1891, *38*, 88.

[4]Engels observed to Marx that Ireland served the British as a pretext for maintaining a *Soldateska* (Oct. 24, 1869, *32*, 379) and Marx wrote similarly to others. Message of the General Council of the International to the Federal Council of French-speaking Switzerland, Jan. 1, 1870; confidential report, Mar. 28, 1870, *MEW*, *16*, 388, 417.

[5]"Die englische Armee," 1864, *ibid.*, *15*, 618; to Kautsky, Apr. 30, 1891, *38*, 88.

[6]*Civil War in France*, 57.

[7]To Kautsky, Nov. 3, 1893, *39*, 161-63.

[8]To Bebel, Dec. 11-12, 1884; to Sorge, June 3, 1885, *36*, 253, 325; to Lafargue, Nov. 3, 1892, *38*, 505. Cf. Lenin's comments on innovations in urban tactics, "Lessons of the Moscow Uprising," *Collected Works* (Moscow: Foreign Languages Publishing House, 1962), *11*, 176-77.

[9]*MS*, *2*, 689-90. Cf. Engels to Marx, Nov. 20, 1868, *32*, 209.

[10]To Laura Lafargue, Feb. 26, to Paul Lafargue, Mar. 7, 1890, *37*, 359, 362. J. C. G. Röhl agrees with Engels' view that plans for a massacre were in the air; the prospect of a coup, he says, dominated German politics from Bismarck's fall in 1890 till the Navy Bill of 1898. *Germany without Bismarck: The Crisis of Government in the Second Reich* (Berkeley: University of California Press, 1967), 277, 50-55, 111-15, 217-22. Cf. Craig, 241-42.

[11]Marx, interview in *Chicago Tribune*, Jan. 5, 1879, *MEW*, *34*, 516; Engels, article in *Newcastle Daily Chronicle*, Mar. 3, "Was nun?" *Sozialdemokrat*, Mar. 8, 1890, *ibid.*, *22*, 6, 9; to Liebknecht, Mar. 9, 1890, *37*, 365.

[12]Farewell to readers, *Sozialdemokrat*, Sept. 27, "Was nun?" Mar. 8, 1890, *MEW*, *22*, 79, 10. Cf. article in *Newcastle Daily Chronicle*, Mar. 3, 1890, and interview in *ibid.*, July 1, 1893, *MEW*, *22*, 6, 546; Engels to Lafargue, middle Dec., 1884, *36*, 255. On the army's intended role see Höhn, *Armee als Erziehungsschule*, 140-455.

[13]To Lafargue, Feb. 16, 1886, late Oct., 1887, *36*, 449, 712; to Liebknecht, Jan. 10, 1888, *37*, 14; to Lafargue, Feb. 26, 1895, *39*, 413.

[14]"Der Sozialismus in Deutschland," *Neue Zeit*, *10* (1891-92), *MEW*, *22*, 251. Engels' words recalled the battle of Fontenoy in 1745, where Marshal Saxe's French were said to have been invited to fire first, but instead waited until their volley would be absolutely devastating. Here Engels discussed the German bourgeoisie, but there is no indication that he expected a peaceful transition to socialism anywhere else either.

[15]Noted by Wilson, 335-39.

[16]Note on *Anti-Dühring*, *MEW*, *20*, 586-87; to Natalie Liebknecht, Dec. 1, 1893, *39*, 170-71. On the other hand, he told Domela Nieuwenhuis that there was nothing in principle wrong with purchasing his son's exemption from service in the Dutch army; such a step depended on local conditions with which Engels was not familiar. Dec. 3, 1890, *37*, 509-10.

[17]*Le Socialiste*, Mar. 26, 1892, *MEW*, 22, 285. Cf. Lenin's vigorous emphasis on using capitalist armies as free military academies for the workers, "Über die Lösung der 'Abrüstung,'" *Gegen den Strom*, 505-06.

[18]To Lafargue, Nov. 3, 1892, 38, 505; to Bebel, Nov. 18, 1884, 36, 240.

[19]Engels to Schmidt, June 12, 1889, 37, 236; *Ein Complott gegen die Internationalen Arbeiter-Association* (Leipzig: Bracke, 1874), *MEW*, 18, 432-38.

[20]Marx, "The Rule of the Pretorian," *Tribune*, Mar. 12, Engels, "The Prosecution of Montalembert," *ibid.*, Nov. 24, 1858, *MEW*, 12, 400, 630. Cf. David B. Ralston, who contends that the French Army was generally apolitical, and that Louis Napoleon had some trouble finding officers to support his coup. *The Army of the Republic: The Place of the Military in the Political Evolution of France, 1871-1914* (Cambridge, Mass.: M.I.T. Press, 1967), 17.

[21]Marx to Engels, Mar. 29, 1858, 29, 310; "The Rule of the Pretorian," *Tribune*, Mar. 12, 1858, *MEW*, 12, 400-01; Engels to Marx, Dec. 10, 1851, 27, 385-86, Jan. 4, 1866, 30, 324; Marx to Engels, Nov. 2, 1867, 31, 275; Engels to Marx, Nov. 5, 1867, 31, 378; to Kugelmann, Nov. 8 and 20, 1867, 31, 568; Marx to Engels, July 22, 1869, 32, 345.

[22]Engels to Marx, Mar. 17, 1858, 29, 305. Cf. Marx, "Bonaparte's Present Position," *Tribune*, Apr. 1, 1858, *MEW*, 12, 413-14. The Foreign Legion does not seem to have been considered a major prop of Bonapartism, contrary to Höhn's assertion (*Sozialismus und Heer, 1,* 77); Höhn's citation refers to St. Arnaud and his fellow Bonapartist officers as a "foreign legion." Marx, " . . . Saint Arnaud," *Tribune*, June 24, 1854, *MEW*, 10, 272.

[23]To Marx, Mar. 17, 1858, 29, 303-04. Sometimes student demonstrations seemed apt to provoke repercussions in the army. Engels to Marx, Feb. 7, 1856, 29, 8-9, Marx to Engels, Dec. 26, 1865, 31, 163. And in 1870, Marx commented hopefully on the soldiers who had voted no on Napoleon's plebiscite. To Engels, May 10, 1870, 32, 504.

[24]To Marx, Dec. 21, 1866, 31, 270. The peasantry would be particularly enraged, since all other classes would still be able to hire substitutes. Engels was commenting on Napoleon's army reform proposal, published in the *Moniteur* of Dec. 12. See Challener, 19, and Gordon Wright, "Public Opinion and Conscription in France, 1866-1870," *Journal of Modern History, 14* (1942), 29-33.

[25]To Marx, Nov. 20, 1868, 32, 209. Cf. Marx to Engels, Nov. 14, 1868, 32, 203. The *garde mobile* in fact remained "still nothing but a list of names" in 1870. Wright, 44.

[26]To Bebel, Sept. 29-Oct. 1, Oct. 13, 1891, 38, 161, 175. Bebel had made similar suggestions to Engels on Sept. 12. Bebel-Engels *Briefwechsel*, 431.

[27]*Preussische Militärfrage, MS, 2,* 331; *Anti-Dühring*, 189.

[28]Article in *La Plebe*, Jan. 22, "The Workingmen of Europe in 1877," *Labor Standard*, Mar. 24, 1878, *MEW, 19,* 114, 131. Cf. Marx to Engels, July 23, 1877, Engels to J. P. Becker, Jan. 11, 1878, 34, 53, 316.

[29]To Lafargue, Nov. 16, 1887, 36, 718; Vagts, 217-18.

[30]To Lafargue, Nov. 16, 1887, 36, 717; May 11, 1889, 37, 204. Cf. Engels to Laura Lafargue, Nov. 24, 1888, *ibid.*, 120-21.

[31]To Laura Lafargue, Nov. 24, 1888, Feb. 4, 1889, *37*, 120-21, 148.

[32]To Laura Lafargue, July 15, 1887, Engels-Lafargue *Correspondence*, 2, 50.

[33]To Paul Lafargue, May 19, 1891, *38*, 104-05; Dec. 5, 1887, *36*, 728. Guy Chapman suggests that in fact neither army nor people had much to do with the maneuvering that gave the presidency to Carnot. *The Third Republic of France: The First Phase. 1871-1914* (London: St. Martin's Press, 1962), 277-79.

[34]Dec. 22, 1892, *38*, 555.

[35]Critique of the Erfurt Program (1891), *MEW*, *22*, 233-34.

[36]*Preussische Militärfrage, MS*, *2*, 327; "The State of Germany," *Northern Star*, Nov. 8, 1845, *MEGA*, 1, *4*, 488.

[37]*Preussische Militärfrage, MS*, *2*, 331. Bebel's Reichstag speech of Oct. 17, 1867, made an interesting play on this connection, claiming that Prussia had corrupted universal service just as Napoleon III had corrupted universal suffrage to despotic ends. *Diesem System keinen Mann und keinen Groschen* (Berlin: Dietz, 1961), 17.

[38]To Carlo Bignami, *La Plebe*, Feb. 26, 1877, *MEW*, *19*, 89-90.

[39]Interview in *Le Figaro*, May 13, 1893, *ibid.*, *22*, 542; to Lafargue, Nov. 12, 1892, *38*, 513-14.

[40]To Lafargue, mid-December, 1884, *36*, 355; cf. Engels to Bebel, Dec. 11-12, 1884, *ibid.*, 253.

[41]"Der Sozialismus in Deutschland," *Neue Zeit*, *10* (1891-92), *MEW*, *22*, 251.

[42]"The Foreign Policy of Russian Tsardom," *Time*, 4th ser., *1* (1890), 544; to Lafargue, Mar. 7, 1890, *37*, 362.

[43]To Liebknecht, Mar. 9, to Laura Lafargue, Mar. 14, 1890, *37*, 365, 368; to Laura Lafargue, Aug. 17, 1891, *38*, 146-47; "Die Bauernfrage in Frankreich und Deutschland," *Neue Zeit*, *13* (1894-95), *MEW*, *22*, 504-505.

[44]To Bignami, *La Plebe*, Feb. 26, 1877, *ibid.*, *19*, 90; to Sorge, Apr. 12, 1890, *37*, 381. Engels emphasized this passage in the letter to Sorge with a double vertical line in the margin.

[45]To Liebknecht, Mar. 9, to Laura Lafargue, Mar. 14, to Paul Lafargue, Mar. 7, 1890, *37*, 365, 368, 362.

[46]*Reminiscences and Reflexions of a Mid and Late Victorian* (London: Unwin, 1918), 48-49.

[47]To Kautsky, Nov. 3, 1893, *39*, 161; to Lafargue, mid-December, to Bebel, Dec. 11-12, 1884, *36*, 255, 253.

[48]To J. P. Becker, Apr. 2, to Bernstein, Oct. 8, 1885, *36*, 290, 365-66; to Bebel, Mar. 8, 1892, *38*, 292.

[49]Note (c. 1878) on the *Anti-Dühring*, *MEW*, *20*, 586-87.

[50]*Ibid.;* to Bebel, Nov. 18, Dec. 11-12, 1884, *36*, 240, 253.

[51]"The Foreign Policy of Russian Tsardom," *Time*, 4th ser., *1* (1890), 544.

[52]Article on the twentieth anniversary of the Commune, *Le Socialiste*, Mar. 25, 1891, *MEW*, *22*, 186-87. The reference to shooting relations referred to a characteristically offensive remark of Wilhelm II, addressed

to a group of recruits the previous November. Wilhelm spoke similarly, to greater publicity, in November of 1891. See J. Alden Nichols, *Germany after Bismarck: The Caprivi Era, 1890-1894* (New York: Norton, 1968), 108, 130. On Caprivi's fears of a disintegrating army and the attempt to provide re-enlistment bonuses for noncommissioned officers, see Höhn, *Armee als Erziehungsschule*, 161-62.

[53]*Anti-Dühring*, 189; interview in *Le Figaro*, May 13, 1893, *MEW*, 22, 542.

[54]Valentine Chirol, *Fifty Years in a Changing World* (London: Jonathan Cape, 1927), 274.

[55]As the spokesman for an increasingly significant party, Bebel commanded considerable attention; his pamphlet, *Nicht stehendes Heer, sondern Volkswehr!* inspired a military counterattack. Albert von Boguslawski, *Volksheer nicht "Volkswehr." Ein Wort über Heereseinrichtungen für weitere Volkskreise* (Berlin: Schall & Grund, 1898).

[56]For a typical example see his Reichstag speech of June 25, 1890, on suicides in the army. *Diesem System*, 34-36.

[57]*Nicht stehendes Heer*, 44-53. See also Günter Hennig, *August Bebel, Todfeind des preussisch-deutschen Militärstaats, 1891-1899* (Berlin: Dietz, 1963), 159-289, and Schorske, 76-78.

[58]Arthur Dix, *Sozialdemokratie, Militärismus und Kolonialpolitik, auf den Sozialisten-Kongressen 1907* (Berlin: Verlag der Nationalliberalen Partei, 1907), 14-15.

[59]*Nicht stehendes Heer*, 75-78.

[60]Heinz Erich Fick, *Der deutsche Militärismus der Vorkriegszeit. Ein Beitrag zur Soziologie des Militärismus* (Ohlau i. Schles.: H. Eschenhagen, 1930), 44, 52-59, discusses Bebel's practicality in military questions as the antithesis of militarism, much in the manner of Alfred Vagts.

[61]Horst Bartel, et al., *August Bebel. Eine Biographie* (Berlin: Dietz, 1963), 201-202, 220-21. There is also a good discussion of Bebel's opposition to war in Hennig, 39-46.

[62]Hennig's work on Bebel has some quotations on the revolutionary importance of the dissolving army, but Hennig finds it necessary to get them from Engels, not Bebel. 251-52, 258-59.

[63]*L'armée nouvelle*, 8-14. On Jaurès' army plans, see Milorad M. Drachkovitch, *Les socialismes français et allemand et le probleme de la guerre, 1870-1914* (Geneva: E. Droz, 1953), 114-21.

[64]*L'armée nouvelle*, 215, 221-23.

[65]Belfort Bax declared in 1918 that "Engels would certainly not have recognized the Socialism (?) of Scheidemann, Südekum, Noske, and the rest of the present 'Revisionist' crew constituting the majority of the party representation in the Reichstag as anything else than reaction in its worst ɔorm." (49) As yet the SPD had only supported the national war effort, as had most other socialist parties; the worst was yet to come.

[66]"Lessons of the Moscow Uprising," *Collected Works*, 11, 174. Lenin protested the "extremely biased view" that "there is no possibility of fighting modern troops," that "the troops must become revolutionary." The troops, he said, would have to be won to revolution.

Bibliography

SOURCES: COLLECTIONS AND EDITIONS CITED

Engels, Friedrich. "The Armies of Europe," *Putnam's Monthly, 6* (1855), 193-206, 306-17, 561-71.

———. *Ausgewählte militärische Schriften.* 2 vols. Berlin: Verlag des Ministeriums für nationale Verteidigung, 1958-64.

———. *Correspondence* with Paul and Laura Lafargue. Tr. Yvonne Kapp. 2 vols. Moscow: Foreign Languages Publishing House, 1959-60.

———. *Engels as Military Critic: Articles by Friedrich Engels Reprinted from the Volunteer Journal and the Manchester Guardian of the 1860s.* Ed. W. H. Chaloner and W. O. Henderson. Manchester: Manchester University Press, 1959.

———. "The Foreign Policy of Russian Tsardom," *Time: A Monthly Magazine,* 4th ser., *1* (1890), 353-69, 525-45.

———. *The German Revolutions: The Peasant War in Germany and Germany: Revolution and Counter-Revolution.* Ed. Leonard Krieger. Chicago: University of Chicago Press, 1967.

———. *Herr Eugen Dühring's Revolution in Science (Anti-Dühring).* Tr. Emile Burns. New York: International Publishers, 1939.

———. *Notes on the War: Sixty Articles Reprinted from the "Pall Mall Gazette," 1870-1871.* Ed. Friedrich Adler. Vienna: Wiener Volksbuchhandlung, 1923.

———. *The Origin of the Family, Private Property and the State: In the Light of the Researches of Lewis H. Morgan.* New York: International Publishers, 1942.

——. *The Role of Force in History: A Study of Bismarck's Policy of Blood and Iron.* Tr. Jack Cohen, ed. Ernest Wangermann. New York: International Publishers, 1968.

Marx, Karl. *Capital: A Critique of Political Economy.* Tr. Samuel Moore and Edward Aveling. 3 vols. New York: International Publishers, 1967.

——. *The Civil War in France.* New York: International Publishers, 1940.

——. *The Eighteenth Brumaire of Louis Bonaparte.* New York: International Publishers, 1963.

Engels, Friedrich, and Karl Marx. *The Civil War in the United States.* 3d ed. New York: International Publishers, 1961.

——. *The Eastern Question: A Reprint of Letters Written 1853-1856 Dealing with the Events of the Crimean War.* Ed. Eleanor Marx Aveling and Edward Aveling. London: S. Sonnenschein, 1897.

——. *The First Indian War of Independence.* Moscow: Foreign Languages Publishing House, 1960.

——. *The German Ideology.* New York: International Publishers, 1947.

——. *Historisch-kritische Gesamtausgabe.* Ed. D. Riazonov. Series 1 (Works), 7 vols. Moscow: Marx-Engels-Lenin Institut, 1927-35. Cited as *MEGA*, 1.

——. *The Russian Menace to Europe.* Ed. Paul W. Blackstock and Bert F. Hoselitz. Glencoe: The Free Press, 1952.

——. *Werke.* 41 vols. and two supplementary vols. Berlin: Dietz, 1960-74.

OTHER WORKS CITED

Abt. *Die Revolution in Baden und die Demokraten. Vom revolutionären Standpunkt aus beleuchtet.* Herisau: M. Schläpfer, 1849.

Arnold, Theodor. *Der revolutionäre Krieg.* Pfaffenhofen/Ilm: Ilmgau-Verlag, 1961.

Babin, I. A. "Die schöpferische Zusammenarbeit von Marx und Engels auf militärgeschichtlichem Gebiet," *ZfMG*, 9 (1970), 420-29.

Balfour, Michael. *The Kaiser and His Times*. Boston: Houghton Mifflin, 1964.

Bamberger, Ludwig. *Erlebnisse aus der Pfälzischen Erhebung im Mai und Juni 1849*. Frankfurt a. M.: Literarische Anstalt, 1849.

Bartel, Horst, et al. *August Bebel. Eine Biographie*. Berlin: Dietz, 1963.

Bauer, Otto. *Die Nationalitätenfrage und die Sozialdemokratie*. 2d ed.; Marx-Studien, No. 2; Vienna: Wiener Volksbuchhandlung, 1924.

Bax, Ernest Belfort. *Reminiscences and Reflexions of a Mid and Late Victorian*. London: Allen & Unwin, 1918.

Bebel, August. *August Bebels Briefwechsel mit Friedrich Engels*. Ed. Werner Blumenberg; Quellen und Untersuchungen zur Geschichte der deutschen und österreichischen Arbeiterbewegung, No. 6; The Hague: Mouton, 1965.

————. *Diesem System keinen Mann und keinen Groschen: Aus Reden und Schriften*. Ed. Heinrich Gemkow. Berlin: Dietz, 1961.

————. *Nicht stehendes Heer, sondern Volkswehr!* Stuttgart: Dietz, 1898.

Becker, Johann Philipp, and Christian Esselen. *Geschichte der süddeutschen Mairevolution des Jahres 1849*. Geneva: Gottfried Becker, 1849.

Bekk, J. B. *Die Bewegung in Baden vom Ende des Februar 1848 bis zur Mitte des Mai 1849*. Mannheim: F. Bassermann, 1850.

Bernstein, Eduard. "Friedrich Engels und die deutschfranzösische Frage," *Neue Zeit*, 33 (1914-15), 710-17.

————. "Karl Marx und Friedrich Engels in der zweiten Phase des Krieges von 1870/71," *ibid.*, 76-80.

————. Intro. to Engels, *Po und Rhein* and *Savoyen, Nizza und der Rhein*. Stuttgart: Dietz, 1915.

Biedrzynski, Richard. *Revolution um Karl Marx*. Leipzig: R. Voigtländer, 1929.

Birdseye, Clarence F. *American Democracy versus Prussian Marxism: A Study in the Nature and Results of Purposive or Beneficial Government*. Chicago: Fleming H. Revell, 1920.

Bleibtreu, Carl. "Die Zukünftige Ueberlegenheit des Milizsystems," *Sozialistische Monatshefte*, 3 (1899), 510-18.

Bloom, Solomon F. *The World of Nations: A Study of the National Implications in the Work of Karl Marx.* New York: Columbia University Press, 1941.

Blum, Oskar. "Jean Jaurès," *Archiv für die Geschichte des Sozialismus und der Arbeiterbewegung,* 7 (1916), 18-59.

_____. "Die weltpolitischen Lehrjahre von Marx und Engels," *Archiv für Sozialwissenschaft und Sozialpolitik, 44* (1918), 530-66.

Blumenberg, Werner. "Ein unbekanntes Kapitel aus Marx' Leben," *IRSH, 1* (1956), 54-111.

_____. "Zur Geschichte des Bundes der Kommunisten. Die Aussagen des Peter Gerhardt Röser," *ibid.,* 9 (1964), 81-122.

Bobinska, Celina. *Marx und Engels über polnische Probleme.* Tr. Rudolf Pabel. Berlin: Dietz, 1958.

Boguslawski, Albert C. F. W. *Volksheer nicht "Volkswehr." Ein Wort über Heereseinrichtungen für weitere Volkskreise.* Berlin: Schall & Grund, 1898.

Bonomi, Ivanoe. "Federico Engels e i problemi della guerra," *Nuova antologia, 195* (1918), 242-50.

Börne, Ludwig. *Menzel der Franzosenfresser. Gesammelte Schriften, 15.* Paris: Théophile Barrois fils, 1837.

Bracke, Wilhelm. *Der Braunschweiger Ausschuss der Sozialdemokratischen Arbeiter-Partei in Lötzen und vor dem Gericht.* Brunswick: Graff & Müller, 1872.

Braunthal, Julius. *History of the International.* Tr. Henry Collins and Kenneth Mitchell. 2 vols.; New York: Praeger, 1967.

Brühl, Reinhard. "Lenin und die Militärgeschichte," *ZfMG,* 9 (1970), 133-47.

Budkiewitsch, S. "Engels und das Kriegswesen," *Friedrich Engels, der Denker. Aufsätze aus der Grossen Sowjetenzyklopädie.* Basel: Mundus-Verlag, 1945, 273-304.

Carlton, Grace. *Friedrich Engels: The Shadow Prophet.* London: Pall Mall Press, 1965.

Challener, Richard D. *The French Theory of the Nation in Arms, 1866-1939.* New York: Columbia University Press, 1952.

Chapman, Guy. *The Third Republic of France: The First Phase, 1871-1914.* London: St. Martin's, 1962.

Chirol, Valentine. *Fifty Years in a Changing World.* London: Jonathan Cape, 1927.

Ciolkosz, Adam. "Karl Marx and the Polish Insurrection of 1863," *Polish Review, 10* (1965), 8-51.

Conze, Werner. Intro. to Marx, *Manuskripte über die polnische Frage (1863-1864)*. Ed. Conze and Dieter Hertz-Eichenrode. The Hague: Mouton, 1961, 7-41.

Cornu, Auguste. *Karl Marx und Friedrich Engels. Leben und Werke*. 2 vols. Berlin: Aufbau-Verlag, 1954-62.

Craig, Gordon A. *The Battle of Königgrätz: Prussia's Victory over Austria, 1866*. Philadelphia: Lippincott, 1964.

_____. *The Politics of the Prussian Army, 1640-1945*. New York: Oxford University Press, 1964.

Dahlinger, Charles W. *The German Revolution of 1849, Being an Account of the Final Struggle, in Baden, for the Maintenance of Germany's First National Representative Government*. New York: Putnam's, 1903.

Davis, Horace B. "Nations, Colonies and Social Classes: The Position of Marx and Engels," *Science & Society, 29* (1965), 26-43.

Debray, Regis. *Revolution in the Revolution? Armed Struggle and Political Struggle in Latin America*. Tr. Bobbye Ortiz. New York: Grove Press, 1967.

Decker, Carl. *La petite guerre, ou traité des opérations secondaires de la guerre*. Tr. Ravichio de Peretsdorf. Brussels: Société de librairie Belge, 1838.

Deutscher, Isaac. *The Prophet Armed: Trotsky, 1879-1921*. New York: Oxford University Press, 1954.

Dix, Arthur. *Sozialdemokratie, Militarismus und Kolonialpolitik, auf den Sozialisten-Kongressen 1907*. Berlin: Nationalliberalen Partei, 1907.

Dlubek, Rolf. "Friedrich Engels als publizistischer Anwalt des Willichschen Freikorps," *Beiträge zur Geschichte der deutschen Arbeiterbewegung, 9* (1964), 235-44.

Drachkovitch, Milorad M., ed. *The Revolutionary Internationals, 1864-1943*. Hoover Institution Publications. Stanford: Stanford University Press, 1966.

_____. *Les socialismes français et allemand et le problème de la guerre, 1870-1914*. Etudes d'histoire économique, politique et sociale, No. 3. Geneva: E. Droz, 1953.

Drahn, Ernst. *Friedrich Engels als Kriegswissenschaftler.* Kultur und Fortschritt, no. 524/25. Gautzsch bei Leipzig: Felix Dietrich, 1915.

————. "Kriegskunst und Kriegswissenschaft bei Friedrich Engels," *Die Glocke, 2* (1916), 107-12.

Droz, Jacques. *Le liberalisme rhénan, 1815-1848; contribution à l'histoire du libéralisme allemand.* Paris: Sorlot, 1940.

"Ein- und dreijährig," *Neue Zeit, 2* (1884), 239.

Erickson, John. "Origins of the Red Army," in *Revolutionary Russia,* ed. Richard Pipes. Garden City: Doubleday, 1969.

von Eynern, Ernst. "Friedrich von Eynern. Ein Bergisches Lebensbild. Zugleich ein Beitrag zur Geschichte der Stadt Barmen," *Zeitschrift des Bergischen Geschichtsverein, 35* (1900-01), 1-103.

Fenner von Fenneberg, Ferdinand. *Zur Geschichte der Rheinpfälzischen Revolution und des Badischen Aufstandes.* Zürich: E. Kiesling, 1850.

Fick, Heinz Erich. *der Deutsche Militarismus der Vorkriegszeit. Ein Beitrag zur Soziologie des Militarismus.* Ohlau i. Schleswig: H. Eschenhagen, 1930.

Fishman, William I. *The Insurrectionists.* London: Methuen, 1970.

Forder, Herwig. *Marx und Engels am Vorabend der Revolution. Die Ausarbeitung der politischen Rechtlinien für die deutschen Kommunisten (1846-1848).* Schriften des Instituts für Geschichte, ser. 1, Allgemeine und deutsche Geschichte, no. 7. Berlin: Akademie-Verlag, 1960.

Förderer, Albert. *Erinnerungen aus Rastatt 1849.* Lahr in Baden: Chr. Schömperlen, 1899.

Freye, Ulrich, and Heinz Helmert. "Friedrich Engels und die Militärfrage des jungen Proletariats," *ZfMG, 9* (1970), 547-54.

Friedjung, Heinrich. *The Struggle for Supremacy in Germany, 1859-1866.* Tr. A. J. P. Taylor and W. L. McElwee. New York: Russell & Russell, 1966.

Friedrich II of Prussia. *Die Werke Friedrichs den Grossen.* 10 vols. Berlin: R. Hobbing, 1913-14.

von Gerlach, Hellmut. *Von Rechts nach Links.* Zürich: Europa-Verlag, 1937.

Giesler-Anneke, Mathilde Franziska. "Memoiren einer Frau aus dem Badisch-Pfälzischen Feldzug," introd. A. B. Faust, *German American Annals, 16* (1918), 73-140.

Goebel, Klaus, and Helmut Hirsch. "Engels-Forschungsmaterialen im Bergischen Land," *Archiv für Sozialgeschichte, 9* (1969), 429-50.

Goedeckemeyer, Albert. *Die Idee vom ewigen Frieden.* Leipzig: F. Meiner, 1920.

Guillaume, James. *Karl Marx, pangermaniste, et l'association internationale des travailleurs de 1864 à 1870.* Paris: A. Colin, 1915.

Haalck, Jörgen. "Der Besuch Friedrich Engels' in Berlin 1893. Nach Akten des Berliner Polizeipräsidiums," *Berliner Heimat,* 1958, 28-30.

Happich, August. *Friedrich Engels als Soldat der Revolution.* Hessische Beiträge zur Staats- und Wirtschaftskunde, no. 6. Borna-Leipzig: R. Noske, 1931.

Häusser, Ludwig. *Denkwürdigkeiten zur Geschichte der Badischen Revolution.* Heidelberg: E. F. Winter, 1851.

Heidegger, H. *Die deutsche Sozialdemokratie und der nationale Staat, 1870-1920.* Göttingen: Musterschmidt-Verlag, 1956.

Heider, Werner. *Die Geschichtslehre von Karl Marx.* Stuttgart: Cotta, 1931.

Heinzen, Karl. *Einige Blicke auf die badisch-pfälzische Revolution.* Bern: Jenni, Sohn, 1849.

Heller, Hermann. *Sozialismus und Nation.* Berlin: E. Rowohlt, 1931.

Helmert, Heinz. *Friedrich Engels. Die Anfänge der proletarische Militärtheorie (1842-1852).* Berlin: Deutscher Militärverlag, 1970.

_____."Friedrich Engels und die Aufgaben der marxistischen Militärgeschichtsschreibung," *ZfMG, 5* (1966), 72-84.

_____,and Ernst Roloff. "Die militärtheoretische Tätigkeit von Friedrich Engels in der Periode nach der Pariser Kommune," *ibid., 9* (1970), 645-58.

Henderson, W.O. *Life of Friedrich Engels.* 2 vols.; London: Frank Cass, 1976.

Hennig, Günter. *August Bebel, Todfeind des preussischdeutschen Militärstaats, 1891-1899.* Berlin: Dietz, 1963.

Hepner, Benôit P. "Marx et la puissance russe," intro. to Marx, *La Russie et l'Europe (Revelations on the Diplomatic History of the Eighteenth Century)*. Paris: Gallimard, 1954, 7-90.

Herkner, Heinrich. *Die Arbeiterfrage. Eine Einführung*. Berlin: Vereinigung Wissenschaftlicher Verleger, 1922.

Hirsch, Helmut. "Carnaps Bericht über die Elberfelder Versammlungen. Ein Dokument zur Geschichte des rheinischen Frühsozialismus," *Bulletin of the International Institute of Social History*, 8 (1953), 104-14.

Höhn, Reinhard. *Die Armee als Erziehungsschule der Nation. Das Ende einer Idee*. Bad Harzburg: Verlag für Wissenschaft, Wirtschaft und Technik, 1953.

_____. *Sozialismus und Heer*. 2 vols. to date. Berlin: Verlag Max Gehlen, 1959-.

Howard, Michael. *The Franco-Prussian War: The German Invasion of France, 1870-1871*. New York: Macmillan, 1961.

Huber, Ernst Rudolf. *Heer und Staat in der deutschen Geschichte*. Hamburg: Hanseatische Verlagsanstalt, 1938.

Hunt, Richard N. *The Political Ideas of Marx and Engels, I: Marxism and Totalitarian Democracy, 1818-1850*. Pittsburgh: University of Pittsburgh, 1974.

Jaurès, Jean. *L'Organisation socialiste de la France: l'armée nouvelle*. Paris: L'Humanité, 1915.

Jellinek, Frank. *The Paris Commune of 1871*. New York: Grosset & Dunlap, 1965.

Joll, James. *The Second International, 1889-1914*. New York: Harper, 1966.

Kaiser, Bruno, ed. *Ex libris Karl Marx und Friedrich Engels. Schicksal und Verzeichnis einer Bibliothek*. Berlin: Dietz, 1967.

Kaufmann, Lotte. *Die Einstellung von Karl Marx und Friedrich Engels zu Krieg und Frieden*. Würzburg: Mayr, 1932.

Kautsky, Karl. "Friedrich Engels und das Milizsystem," *Neue Zeit*, 17 (1898-99), 335-42.

_____. "Schippel und der Militarismus," *ibid.*, 618-26, 644-54, 686-91.

_____. "Siegfried der Harmlose," *ibid.*, 787-91.

_____. *Sozialisten und Krieg. Ein Beitrag zur Ideengeschichte des Sozialismus von den Hussiten bis zum Völkerbund*. Prague: Orbis-Verlag, 1937.

Kipling, Rudyard. *Traffics and Discoveries*. New York: Doubleday, 1904.

Köllmann, Wolfgang. *Sozialgeschichte der Stadt Barmen im 19. Jahrhundert*. Tübingen: J. C. B. Mohr, 1960.

Körner, H. J. A. *Lebenskämpfe in der alten und neuen Welt. Eine Selbstbiographie*. 2 vols. New York: L. W. Schmidt, 1865-66.

Krause, Helmut. *Karl Marx und das zeitgenössische Russland*. Giessen: W. Schmitz, 1959.

Lafargue, Paul. "Persönliche Erinnerungen an Friedrich Engels," *Neue Zeit, 23* (1905), 556-61.

Laskine, Edmond. *L'Internationale et le pangermanisme*. Paris: H. Floury, 1916.

_____. *Les socialistes du Kaiser: La fin d'un mensonge*. Paris: H. Floury, 1915.

Lassalle, Ferdinand. *Der italienische Krieg und die Aufgabe Preussens*. Berlin: F. Duncker, 1859.

Lenin, V. I. *Collected Works, 11*. Moscow: Foreign Languages Publishing House, 1962.

_____, and G. Zinoviev. *Gegen den Strom: Aufsätze aus den Jahren 1914-1916*. Hamburg: Verlag der Kommunistische Internationale, 1921.

Lensch, Paul. "Sozialismus und Annexionen in der Vergangenheit," *Die Glocke*, Jan. 1916, 493-500.

Lenz, Friedrich. "Karl Marx," *Historische Zeitschrift, 124* (1921), 466-74.

Lichtheim, George. *Marxism: An Historical and Critical Study*. New York: Praeger, 1961.

Liebknecht, Wilhelm. *Karl Marx: Biographical Memoirs*. Tr. Ernest Untermann. Chicago: Kerr, 1901.

Longuet, Charles. Preface to Marx, *La guerre civile en France (La commune de Paris)*. Paris: L'Humanité, 1925.

Longuet, Jean. *La politique internationale de marxisme; Karl Marx et la France*. Paris: F. Alcan, 1918.

Lütkens, Gerhard. "Das Kriegsproblem und die marxistische Theorie," *Archiv für Sozialwissenschaft und Sozialpolitik, 49* (1922), 467-517.

MacDonald, H. Malcolm. "Marx, Engels, and the Polish National Movement," *Journal of Modern History, 13* (1941), 321-34.

————. "Karl Marx, Friedrich Engels, and South Slavic Problem in 1848-9," *University of Toronto Quarterly*, 8 (1939), 452-60.

Mayer, Gustav. *Erinnerungen. Vom Journalisten zum Historiker der deutschen Arbeiterbewegung.* Munich: Verlag der Zwölf, 1949.

————. *Friedrich Engels. Eine Biographie.* 2 vols. The Hague: Nijhoff, 1934.

Mehring, Franz. Intro. to Engels, *Der deutsche Bauernkrieg.* Berlin: Vorwärts, 1920.

————. "Engels und Marx," *Archiv für die Geschichte des Sozialismus und der Arbeiterbewegung*, 5 (1915), 1-38.

————. "Eine Geschichte der Kriegskunst," *Neue Zeit*, Erg. *4* (Oct. 16, 1908).

————. "Miliz und stehendes Heer," *Neue Zeit*, *31* (1912-13), 553-58, 673-79, 705-12, 850-57, 909-14.

Meinecke, Friedrich. "Landwehr und Landsturm seit 1814," *Schmollers Jahrbücher*, *40* (1916), 1087-1112.

————. *Das Zeitalter der deutschen Erhebung.* Göttingen: Vandenhoeck & Rupprecht, 1957.

Michels, Robert. *Political Parties: A Sociological Study of the Oligarchical Tendencies of Modern Democracy.* Tr. Eden and Cedar Paul. New York: Dover, 1959.

Minz, I. *The Red Army.* New York: International Publishers, 1943.

von Mises, Ludwig. *Nation, Staat und Wirtschaft.* Vienna: Manzsche Verlags-und Universitätsbuchhandlung, 1919.

Moch, G. *L'Armée d'une démocratie.* Paris: Revue Blanche, 1900.

Mohr und General. Erinnerungen an Marx und Engels. Berlin: Dietz, 1964.

Morgan, Roger P. *The German Social Democrats and the First International, 1864-1872.* Cambridge: University Press, 1965.

Muste, A. J. *The Essays of A. J. Muste.* Ed. Nat Hentoff. Indianapolis: Bobbs-Merrill, 1967.

Na'aman, Shlomo. "Zur Geschichte des Bundes der Kommunisten in Deutschland in der zweiten Phase seines Bestehens," *Archiv für Sozialgeschichte*, 5 (1965), 5-82.

Napier, W. P. *History of the War in the Peninsula and in the South of France, from A. D. 1807 to A. D. 1814.* 6 vols. London; Warne, 1850.

Nettlau, Max. "Londoner deutsche kommunistische Diskussionen, 1845," *Archiv für die Geschichte des Sozialismus und der Arbeiterbewegung, 10* (1922), 362-91.

Neumann, Sigmund. "Engels and Marx: Military Concepts of the Social Revolutionaries," in *Makers of Modern Strategy: Military Thought from Machiavelli to Hitler*, Ed. E. M. Earle. Princeton: Princeton University Press, 1941, 155-71.

Nevins, Allan. *The War for the Union, 2: War Becomes Revolution, 1862-63.* New York: Scribner's, 1960.

Nichols, J. Alden. *Germany after Bismarck: The Caprivi Era, 1890-1894.* New York: Norton, 1968.

Nickolaus, Günter. *Die Milizfrage in Deutschland von 1848 bis 1933.* Berlin: Junker und Dünnhaupt, 1933.

Nicolaievsky, Boris, and Otto Maenchen-Helfen. *Karl Marx, Man and Fighter.* Tr. Gwenda David and Eric Mosbacher. Philadelphia: Lippincott, 1936.

Nicolaievsky, Boris. "Toward a History of the 'Communist League' 1847-1852," *IRSH, 1* (1956), 234-52.

Obermann, Karl, ed. *Friedrich Engels und die internationale Arbeiterbewegung.* Berlin: Akademie-Verlag, 1962.

————.*Joseph Weydemeyer, Pioneer of American Socialism.* New York: International Publishers, 1947.

Oncken, Hermann. "Friedrich Engels und die Anfänge des deutschen Kommunismus," *Historische Zeitschrift, 123* (1920), 239-66.

————."Marx und Engels," *Preussische Jahrbücher, 155* (1914), 209-56.

Opitz, Waldtraut. "Friedrich Engels und die deutsche Sozialdemokratie in den Jahren 1890/91," *Zeitschrift für Geschichtswissenschaft, 11* (1969), 1403-15.

Pagenstecher, Carl H. A. *Revolutionäre Bewegungen im Rheinlande 1830 bis 1850.* Leipzig: R. Voigtländer, 1913.

Paret, Peter. *Yorck and the Era of Prussian Reform, 1807-1815.* Princeton: Princeton University Press, 1966.

Pelger, Hans, ed. *Friedrich Engels 1820-1970. Referate—Diskussionen—Dokumente.* Schriftenreihe des Forschungsinstituts der Friedrich-Ebert Stiftung, *85;* Hannover: Verlag für Literatur und Zeitgeschehen, 1971.

Pflanze, Otto. *Bismarck and the Development of Germany: The Period of Unification, 1815-1871.* Princeton: Princeton University Press, 1963.

Philippi, F. "Der Elberfelder Aufstand im Mai 1849," *Zeitschrift des Bergischen Geschichtsvereins, 50* (1917), 66-80.

Plamenatz, John. *German Marxism and Russian Communism.* New York: Harper, 1965.

Pokrovsky, G. I. *Science and Technology in Contemporary War.* Tr. Raymond L. Garthoff. New York: Praeger, 1959.

Pomeroy, William J., ed. *Guerrilla Warfare and Marxism: A Collection of Writings from Karl Marx to the Present on Armed Struggles for Liberation and for Socialism.* New York: International Publishers, 1968.

Pribram, Karl. "Deutscher Nationalismus und deutscher Sozialismus," *Archiv für Sozialwissenschaft und Sozialpolitik, 49* (1922), 298-376.

Radek, Karl ("Parabellum"). "Marxismus und Kriegsprobleme," *Lichtstrahlen, monatliches Bildungsorgan für denkende Arbeiter, 2* (1914), 19-23, 42-45, 59-62.

Ralston, David B. *The Army of the Republic: The Place of the Military in the Political Evolution of France, 1871-1914.* Cambridge: M.I.T. Press, 1967.

Randall, J. G., and David Donald. *The Civil War and Reconstruction.* Boston: Heath, 1961.

Riazonov, D. "Die auswärtige Politik der alten Internationale und der Krieg," *Neue Zeit, 33* (1914-15), 329-34, 360-69, 438-43, 463-69, 509-19.

———."Karl Marx über den Ursprung der Vorherrschaft Russlands über Europa. Kritische Untersuchungen," tr. A. Stein, *ibid.,* Erg. 5 (March 5, 1909).

———."Karl Marx und Friedrich Engels über die Polenfrage," *Archiv für die Geschichte des Sozialismus und der Arbeiterbewegung, 6* (1915), 175-221.

———."Marx und Engels über den deutsch-französischen Krieg," *Der Kampf, 8* (1915), 129-39.

———."Zur Stellungnahme von Marx und Engels während des deutsch-französischen Kriegs," *Neue Zeit, 33* (1914-15), 161-71.

Ritter, Gerhard. *Staatskunst und Kriegshandwerk: Das Problem des "Militarismus" in Deutschland, 1.* Munich: R. Oldenbourg, 1959.

Röhl, J. C. G. *Germany without Bismarck: The Crisis of Government in the Second Reich.* Berkeley: University of California Press, 1967.

Rosdolsky, Roman. "Friedrich Engels und das Problem der 'geschichtlosen' Völker (Die Nationalitätenfrage in der Revolution 1848-1849 im Lichte der 'Neuen Rheineschen Zeitung')." Typed ms, in Ms. Division of New York Public Library. Detroit, 1949. Also in *Archiv für Sozialgeschichte*, 4 (1964), 87-282; cited from ms.

_____."Karl Marx und der Polizeispitzel Bangya," *International Review for Social History*, 2 (1937), 229-45.

Rossiter, Clinton. *Constitutional Dictatorship: Crisis Government in the Modern Democracies.* New York: Harcourt, Brace & World, 1963.

Die Rote Armee, ein Sammelbuch. Hamburg: C. Hoym, 1923.

Rothfels, Hans. "Bismarck und Karl Marx," *Jahresheft der Heidelberger Akademie der Wissenschaften,* 1959/60, 51-67.

_____."Marxismus und auswärtige Politik," in *Deutscher Staat und deutsche Parteien. Beiträge zur deutschen Partei-und Ideengeschichte. Friedrich Meinecke zum 60. Geburtstag.* Munich: R. Oldenbourg, 1922, 308-41.

Rubel, Maximilien. "Les cahiers d'étude de Karl Marx, II. 1853-1856," *IRSH*, 5 (1960), 38-78.

_____.*Karl Marx devant le bonapartisme.* Société et idéologies. Ser. 2: Documents et témoignages, no. 2. Paris: Mouton, 1960.

Schieder, Wolfgang. "Der Bund der Kommunisten in Sommer 1850: Drei Dokumente aus dem Marx-Engels Nachlass," *IRSH, 13* (1968), 29-57.

Schippel, Max. "Friedrich Engels und das Milizsystem," *Neue Zeit, 17* (1898-99), 580-88, 613-17.

_____."Siehe da: Das stehende Milizheer!" *ibid.,* 780-86.

_____."War Friedrich Engels milizgläubisch?" *Sozialistische Monatshefte, 2* (1898), 495-98.

Schorske, Carl E. *German Social Democracy, 1905-1917: The Development of the Great Schism.* Cambridge: Harvard University Press, 1955.

Schwartzschild, Leopold. *Karl Marx: The Red Prussian.* Tr. Margaret Wing. New York: Scribner's, 1947.

Silberner, Edmund. *The Problem of War in Nineteenth Century Economic Thought.* Tr. Alexander H. Krappe. Princeton: Princeton University Press, 1946.

Spengler, Oswald. *Preussentum und Sozialismus.* Munich: Beck, 1934.

Staroste. *Tagebuch über die Ereignisse in der Pfalz und Baden im Jahre 1849. Ein Erinnerungsbuch für die Zeitgenossen und fur Alle, welche Theil nahmen an der Unterdrückung jenes Aufstandes.* 2 vols. in one. Potsdam: Riegel, 1852-53.

Steinberg, Hans-Josef. "Revolution und Legalität: Ein unveröffentlicher Brief Friedrich Engels' an Richard Fischer," *IRSH, 12* (1967), 177-89.

Stepanova, Yelena. *Frederick Engels.* Tr. John Gibbons, Moscow: Foreign Languages Publishing House, 1958.

Szabo, Erwin. Review of Guillaume, *Karl Marx pangermaniste, Archiv für die Geschichte des Sozialismus und der Arbeiterbewegung, 7* (1916), 462-68.

————. "Die ungarische Revolution von 1848 (Bemerkungen zu Engels Artikel über Ungarn in der 'Neuen Rheinischen Zeitung')," *Neue Zeit, 23* (1905), 782-87, 811-18.

Taylor, A. J. P. *The Struggle for Mastery in Europe, 1848-1918.* Oxford: the Clarendon Press, 1954.

Tukhachevski, M. *Die Rote Armee und die Miliz.* Kleine Bibliothek der Russischen Korrespondenz, no. 29-30. Leipzig: Frankes Verlag, 1921.

Ulam, Adam B. *The Unfinished Revolution: An Essay on the Sources of Infuence of Marxism and Communism.* New York: Random House, 1960.

Ullrich, Horst. *Der junge Engels. Eine historisch-biographische Studie seiner weltanschaulichen Entwicklung in den Jahren 1834-1845.* 2 vols. Berlin: Deutscher Verlag der Wissenschaften 1961-66.

Usczek, Hansjürgen. "Friedrich Engels zum Volkskrieg in Frankreich," *ZfMG, 9* (1970), 517-31.

Vagts, Alfred. *A History of Militarism: Civilian and Military*. New York: Meridian, 1959.

Vaillant, Edouard. "Á propos de Karl Marx," *L'Humanité*, Dec. 14, 1914.

Venedey, Jakob. *Preussen und das Preussenthum*. Mannheim: J. Venedey, 1839.

Vettes, William G. "The German Social Democrats and the Eastern Question, 1848-1900," *Slavic Review, 17* (1958), 86-100.

Victor, Max. "Die Stellung der deutschen Sozialdemokratie zu den Fragen der auswartigen Politik (1869-1914)," *Archiv für Sozialwissenschaft und Sozialpolitik, 60* (1928), 147-79.

Vogt, Carl. *Mein Prozess gegen die Allgemeine Zeitung*. Geneva: the author, 1859.

Wallach, Jehuda L. *Die Kriegslehre von Friedrich Engels*. Hamburger Studien zur neuren Geschichte, *10*.Frankfurt a. M.: Europäische Verlagsanstalt, 1968.

Weerth, Georg. *Sämtliche Werke*. 5 vols. Ed. Bruno Kaiser. Berlin: Aufbau-Verlag, 1956-57.

Wendel, Hermann. "Marxism and the Southern Slav Question," tr. R. W. Seton-Watson, *Slavonic Review, 2* (1923-24), 289-307.

Wiesner, Hans. "Zur Weiterentwicklung der militärischen Ansichten von Marx und Engels durch W. I. Lenin," *ZfMG, 9* (1970), 5-18.

Willich, August. *The Army, Standing Army or National Army? An Essay*. Cincinnati: A. Frey, 1866.

Wilson, Edmund. *To the Finland Station: A Study in the Writing and Acting of History*. Garden City: Doubleday, 1953.

Wolfe, Bertram D. *Marxism: One Hundred Years in the Life of a Doctrine*. New York: Dell, 1967.

Wright, Gordon. "Public Opinion and Conscription in France, 1866-70," *Journal of Modern History, 14* (1942), 26-45.

Wuppertal, eine interessante Stadt. Ed. Kurt Hackenberg. Wuppertal: Hans Putty, 1960.

Zinoviev, G. *Der Krieg und die Krise des Sozialismus*. Vienna: Verlag für Literatur und Politik, 1924.

Zint, Frank. *Karl Marx und die grossen europäischen Mächte. Beitrag zu einer politischen Biographie*. Frankfurt a. M.: A. Beck, 1937.

Zirke, Gerhard. *Der General. Friedrich Engels, der erste Militärtheoretiker der Arbeiterklasse*. Berlin and Jena: Urania-Verlag, 1957.
Zlocisti, Theodor. *Moses Hess, der Vorkämpfer des Sozialismus und Zionismus, 1812-1875*. Berlin: Welt-Verlag, 1921.

Index